'I LOVE ME COUNTY'
Waterford
Sporting Stories

'I LOVE ME COUNTY'
Waterford Sporting Stories

Cian Manning

First published 2024

The History Press
97 St George's Place, Cheltenham,
Gloucestershire, GL50 3QB
www.thehistorypress.co.uk

© Cian Manning, 2024

The right of Cian Manning to be identified as the Author
of this work has been asserted in accordance with the
Copyright, Designs and Patents Act 1988.

All rights reserved. No part of this book may be reprinted
or reproduced or utilised in any form or by any electronic,
mechanical or other means, now known or hereafter invented,
including photocopying and recording, or in any information
storage or retrieval system, without the permission in writing
from the Publishers.

British Library Cataloguing in Publication Data.
A catalogue record for this book is available from the British Library.

ISBN 978 1 803 99255 6

Typesetting and origination by The History Press
Printed and bound in Great Britain by TJ Books Limited, Padstow, Cornwall.

Trees for Life

Contents

Introduction   8

1   'Savage Manners and Inhuman Barbarity': Bull-Baiting at Ballybricken, 1714–1826   11
2   'The Hub of Hikers': Waterford and Rambling, 1775–1930   16
3   Johnny Ryan (1826–1907): Portlaw's Pre-Eminent Sportsman   20
4   Hugh Collender: Cappoquin Sports Manufacturer and Rebel   23
5   Patrick Hearne: 'The Gambler'   25
6   The Irish Giant 'Who Gained Notoriety, if Not Fame, as a Pugilist': Lismore's Ned O'Baldwin (1840–75)   27
7   Vere Thomas St Leger Goold (1853–1909): Waterford Tennis Player and Monte Carlo Murderer   32
8   'Died of Inanition': County Waterford Archery Club, 1860–65   34
9   Thomas Joseph Dart Kelly: Waterford Man and Aussie Cricketer   40
10   Joe Tracy: America's Greatest Race Car Driver   42
11   Waterford's First Hurling Revival, 1884–1934   45
12   Patrick Street, Pugilism and Preaching: Stories of Arthur Clampett   53
13   Dungarvan was his Hometown: Shaw Desmond (Author and Spiritualist)   56
14   To the Waterford Coast and Along it: Arthur Ignatius Conan Doyle (1859–1930)   60
15   'The Palm of Superiority': Handball in Waterford, 1887–1911   65
16   Heavyweight Boxing: Champion of the World Visits Waterford, December 1887   70
17   Jack Mitchell: 'The Man with the Plate in his Head'   71

18	*Urbs Intacta* was Supposed to be at Stake': Oxford and the Waterford City Regatta, 15 July 1890	73
19	'A Cycling Carnival': Ireland vs England, People's Park, Waterford, 11 August 1891	78
20	T.O. Jameson: The Captain at Cappoquin	82
21	Dan Cooney (1892–1940): 'Our Dan' from Near Dungarvan	85
22	The Wild Man from Borneo: Grand National Winner 1895	89
23	'The First Waterford Men to Win All-Ireland Medals': Jack Dwan and Larry Tobin, Tipperary Footballers	90
24	'Battling Brannigan': The Story of Gerald Hurley	94
25	An American Millionaire at Waterford Harbour	98
26	'Aesthetic Appeal': The Many Lives of Edward Augustine McGuire (1901–92)	102
27	'I Fail to See Why we Cannot Play Polo': Waterford Polo Club, 1904–06	111
28	Patrick Joseph Mahon: Forgotten World No. 1 Golfer?	118
29	'Old Men and Novices': Roller Hockey in Waterford, 1910–85	125
30	Danny Morgan: Cheltenham Gold Cup-Winning Jockey and Trainer	131
31	Camogie in County Waterford, 1913–17	136
32	Matt O'Mahoney: Kilkenny Soccer Pioneer	140
33	'Sleeping Draught': Michael Lacey, the Forgotten Contender	142
34	Check Mate: Austin Bourke, Chess and the Irish Weather	148
35	Dungarvan's Denis Kelleher: An 'Unpredictable Irishman'	152
36	'"Non-Political" Bosh …': Gaelic Games Abandoned at the Sportsfield, 21 October 1923	155
37	A Portrait of my Grandfather as a Young Man	157
38	Waterford Hockey Players Tour America, 1925	160
39	Waterford City: Munster Junior Cup Winners, 1928	163
40	A Tale of Two Millionaires: Donaghy and Capelli, 1937–38	166
41	Josie McNamara: Waterford's 'Queen of Sport'	168
42	'Ideally Suited to the Irish Temperament': Waterford Fencing Club, 1948–73	172
43	Colonel James Flynn: Irish Olympic Basketballer	179
44	Waterford FC in Iceland, May–June 1953	183

Contents

45	Mutiny on a Boundary: The Blyth Affair, Waterford, 1954	187
46	Waterford and District Table Soccer League, 1957–60	192
47	Suirsiders, Sliotars and the Silver Screen: Hollywood and the 1957 All-Ireland Hurling Final	194
48	Sea Lions and Walruses: Baseball in Tramore and Waterford City, 1958–66	198
49	The Brown Bomber at the Arch in Tallow	202
50	Waterford Ladies' Soccer League, 1967–70	204
51	'Sell A Dummy': Louis Fulloné, Failed Waterford Trialist, and Diego Maradona	208
52	Poles Apart: Piotr Suski, Włodzimierz Lubański and the League of Ireland	212
53	Celtic Squash Club: A 'Great Waterford Nursery'	216
54	Alma Delahunty: Ruánmhór Rúnaí (1981–85)	220
55	Samba in the South-East: A Brazilian in the League of Ireland	225
56	Jason Phelan (BMX Rider): Déise Daredevil	229
57	Grace Doyle: 'The Stoke and Love of Surfing'	232
58	Evan Power: The Future of Irish Polo	235

Epilogue   237
Acknowledgements   239

Introduction

The motto for Waterford city is the Latin, *Urbs Intacta Manet Waterfordia* – literally translating as 'Waterford remains the untaken city'. The County Waterford motto reads as *Déisi oc Declán co Bráth*, with the Old Irish corresponding in English as 'May the Déise remain with Declan forever'. Both are reflective of the eras in which they were given. The Latin motto dates to the fifteenth century, bestowed by King Henry VII after Ireland's oldest city repelled two pretenders to the English throne. The county motto is taken from a ninth-century text on the life of Saint Declan, who founded the renowned monastic settlement at Ardmore. It was adopted as the motto on the county coat of arms on 9 June 1997. They illustrate the differences that are often displayed and felt in the histories of the city and county.

However, both have been usurped in the modern local lexicon by the phrase 'I love me county'. On 27 June 2004, Waterford defeated Cork in the Munster Senior Hurling Championship final for the first time since 1959. Prior to the game (which would subsequently be considered one of the greatest provincial finals of all time) the Rebel County had beaten Na Déise 8–3 in head-to-heads in the Munster decider. Although the neighbours had met in the 2003 final, the previous times they faced each other in the Munster showpiece (in 1982 and 1983), the Leesiders had run out winners on both occasions, by a combined total of 50 points. To conclude that these were chastening defeats fails to convey adequately the sheer devastation, which wasn't just disappointment but later evolved into apathy that lasted nearly a decade.

The dawn of a new millennium had been ushered in with a stirring in Waterford hurling, but also a renewed confidence in the city and county itself. The impact of the Celtic Tiger had generated social and economic progress in an area that had been in continual stagnation since the 1950s. The recession of the 1980s cast a 'greyness' over Waterford, which witnessed the generational wave of emigration that decimated Irish society, both socially and spiritually. As the Celtic Tiger roared, the area known as *Cuan-na-Greinne* (Harbour of the Sun) saw a city and county emboldened by membership of the European Union, looking out into the world, with a sense of pride in its cultural heritage and economic lot. This would be reflected in the county's hurling team, as they displayed the character and colour of its people.

The star of the Waterford side from the defeat in the 2003 Munster final was De La Salle's John Mullane. His 3–1 couldn't propel Waterford to victory, as they lost by 4 points. The following year witnessed a see-saw match, which appeared to be turned on its head by the sending off of Mullane for an off-the-ball incident. As he made his way to the sideline, head bowed in a mixture of disappointment and self-disgust, it looked like his county's chances had evaporated. However, his teammates had other ideas, and despite being a player down, they won the game by a solitary point. Mount Sion's Ken McGrath lifted the trophy, becoming the second Waterford man in the twenty-first century to captain the county to provincial success.

A day of iconic moments was encapsulated by Mullane's post-match interview on the field. Heartbroken amidst the triumph, the man who would go on to win five All-Star Awards uttered the phrase 'I love me county.' It was unvarnished, raw and from the heart. The words came from a place of bittersweetness. It was a reflection of the depth of affection that many inhabitants of the Gentle County feel for the area. They weren't prose or poetry from a playwright or patriot, it wasn't an earth-shattering historical event like a revolution or plague, but the result of an impulse due to sporting endeavours. It came from an ordinary working man, who on the field with his caman was transformed into a warrior, a hero. Not only did the phrase encapsulate the people of Waterford, but it also demonstrated what sport does to people, and why it is so influential. To paraphrase Jürgen Klopp, sport is the most important of the least important things in life.

The reason why sport is so important in Waterford, city and county, from Tourin to Tramore, along the rivers Blackwater and Suir, be it quaint villages like Lismore to housing estates like Lisduggan, is because it represents community. Sport can form the background of social calendars, be it christenings, weddings or even funerals. It is evocative and emotive, can lead to tears of joy or despair. Though John Mullane never did win an All-Ireland medal that he so richly deserved, he left a legacy far greater. In those few minutes in Semple Stadium, surrounded by Waterford supporters, he held up a mirror to the people of the Gentle County, and showed them themselves. All of us can relate to 'I love me county', Mullane gave words to what many felt.

This collection of stories is not the entire history of Waterford sport. It hopes to provide a flavour of the social, cultural, political and economic history of an area and its people through leisure pursuits and competitive endeavours. It is to acknowledge some of those figures whose stature have faded in time. We cast an eye over several neglected stories of Waterford sportswomen who pioneered various sports, and would take great pride in the healthy state and promotion of women's sports today. The aim is to cast a different light on sports and trends that were once popular, and played frequently, which are now probably stuttering in their existence, while also looking at a couple of neglected stories in popular sports. Often times, with the proximity of events, we can turn away from the past, and forget about those who came before us. This is a tapestry of Waterford sport, from the niche to the underappreciated. Like John Mullane, a lot of these figures had a strong connection to the city and county. Hopefully, their stories will convey as much.

These stories are not about untaken cities or saints, but about the people of Waterford, and what it means to love one's county.

1

'Savage Manners and Inhuman Barbarity': Bull-Baiting at Ballybricken, 1714–1826

> Bull-baiting, prize-fighting, and the cockpit were 'pleasures' then much patronised by the bucks as well as the lower orders of society. The great prevalence of bull-baiting in Ireland has been ascribed to the old-time close connection of the country with Spain, and the consequent adoption of many Spanish usages and sports, as also to the fact that the Midland counties formed one great bullock walk entirely given up to the grazing of cattle to be deported from Cork, Waterford or Dublin.
>
> Ballybricken, outside Waterford, was a favourite resort for bullbaiters, and was surrounded by houses from which spectators looked on as at a Spanish bull-fight. The centre for bull-baiting in Dublin was in the Corn Market. But these brutal exhibitions very often gave rise to much riot and bloodshed, and in 1798 were prohibited by law, and the 'sport' discontinued.
>
> Nora Tynan O'Mahony, *Freeman's Journal*, Thursday, 6 February 1913

The custom of bull-baiting in Waterford, staged at Ballybricken, where the Bull Post serves as one of the area's most recognisable landmarks, saw the old Waterford Corporation 'Ordered that a bull rope be provided at charge of the city revenue' in October 1714, at the start of the slaughtering season. In the preceding centuries, Spanish merchants trading wine and fruit regularly traversed the Suir estuary. So extensive was their business that many of these families settled in the port city. Over time, they introduced their customs and pastimes to Ireland's oldest city. Ballybricken came to be recognised as the perfect arena for bull-baiting, one twentieth-century commentator noting that it was 'then an open space outside the city walls, but now surrounded by well-built residential and business houses, and also the venue of an important monthly cattle fair'.

In addition to the rope provided by the city for bull-baiting, dogs were required and easily procured. These canines were specially trained by locals, with one contemporary account detailing how 'to enhance and render perfect the sport, a peculiar breed of dogs was cherished, the purity of whose blood was marked by small stature, with enormous disproportionate heads and jaws, the upper short and snub, and the under projecting beyond it'. It appears that the two breeds popular for bull-baiting were the bulldog and the Staffordshire bull terrier.

Ballybricken Gaol.

The custom then, come slaughtering season, was that every bull intended for butchery in the city could be commandeered by the crowd and baited before being killed. The historian Jack O'Neill suggests that the 'justification for the barbarism of bull baiting, it was claimed that the baiting caused the heart to pump the blood at a faster than normal rate and this, it was contended, tenderized the meat'. The days surrounding baiting were big business, as people bet on dogs in the action, drank, etc.

Another right claimed by bull-baiters was that upon the election of a mayor, the civic official had to supply a brand new rope. This rope was given to the 'Grand Council of the Bull Ring' and placed in the city jail, where it was kept by the head gaoler until needed. This 'Grand Council' was selected by the citizens, and the leader known as the 'Mayor of the Ring' was appointed by the High Constable of Waterford city. The position was one of the most envied in the area, surpassing the role of the Corporation's official 'butter taster' or 'nightwatchman'. The latter in the nineteenth century was given a grappling hook to aid their effort in helping individuals from the river.

One newly elected mayor refused to supply the rope, leading to a bull being driven into his hallway, while a mob prepared to ransack and loot his residence. The mayor quickly granted the rope before his house was destroyed. 'Rambler' wryly remarked in the *Cork Examiner* that, 'One has often heard of a bull in a china shop, but never of a bull in a Mayoral chamber.' Another mayor refused to grant a rope, leading to authorities quelling a riot in Waterford. The 'Mayor of the Ring' had to arrange bull-baits on two feast days each year: Michaelmas and New Year's Day. These were great civic occasions with much pageantry, as the Lord Mayor and Waterford Council walked to the hill through St Patrick's Gate in their robes, while the first citizen carried a staff with a copper bull figure on top.

Otherwise, Jack O'Neill suggests that the season for bull-baiting lasted from October to 1 April. On the occasions of the mayor's attendance, up to ten animals could be baited in one day. Another custom on the day when the council attended was for newly wed brides to kiss the mayor as another of his duties was to guard bachelors and approve of their subsequent choice of partner. At the conclusion of the bait, the grooms were expected to entertain the mayor and council.

The exercise of bull-baiting saw a bull tied to a rope, about 2in in diameter with a leather collar and buckle, with the rope being passed through a ring in the ground. Once the bull was secured, the dogs were let loose, and the poor animal was baited until it was exhausted. Of the dogs, John P. Pender wrote (in 1929):

> The savage ferocity and tenacity of these small animals was quite extraordinary. We are told that a single one, unsupported, would seize a fierce bull by the lip or nose, and pin to the ground the comparatively gigantic animal as if he had been fixed with a stake of iron. Even after the fracture of their limbs, the dogs never relaxed their hold, and it was often necessary at the conclusion of a day's sport to cut off broken legs, and even in that mutilated state they were seen on three legs, running at the bull.

The citizens of Waterford formed a circle around the scene, while other spectators viewed from windows in nearby houses. Certainly in the seventeenth century, many of these dwellings had been built by Cromwellian settlers, transforming Ballybricken into a new suburb of the city. In the centre of the green, where the bull was tied, was a pole bearing a large copper bull on its top. This was removed near the end of the eighteenth century, replaced by a concrete structure mounted by a lamp. Referred to as the Bull Post, it would witness the speeches of Daniel O'Connell, Charles Stewart Parnell and John Redmond in the subsequent centuries. The steps of the Bull Post were to aid dogs in their attack on the animal. However, it appeared that this edifice was on the verge of being removed in 1929, with Pender noting that, 'Now this again is threatened to be replaced by a ferro-concrete tower in connection with the Shannon Scheme. Progress!'

Fifty years later, Waterford Corporation approved the erection of a concrete statue of a bull to be placed on Ballybricken Hill, to symbolise the city's association with the cattle trade in the nineteenth century, and as a traditional site of bull-baiting when the hill was considered 'the Irishtown of Waterford'. It was hoped that the statue would be similar to monuments in Munich. This monument never came to pass.

In December 1988, Jack O'Neill said of the Bull Post, 'Nowadays, it's a place where people gather to sit and chat in the summer sun, where old men speak of the days of the fairs and of days when this city was not an unemployment black spot. You can be at peace on Ballybricken Hill.'

An Act of George III in 1779 forbade the practice of bull-baiting, but was rarely enforced. After the 1798 Rebellion, the 'sport' was prohibited, although it continued to be staged in Waterford for another five years. However, the *Waterford Mirror* on 28 September 1808 reported:

> The shameful practice of Bull-baiting has commenced in the city and neighbourhood, with all its usual symptoms of savage manners and inhuman barbarity. It may be useless to tell those who indulge themselves in this horrid amusement that it is utterly at variance with moral feelings and with the sacred obligations of religion.
>
> In the pursuit of this immoral, irreligious and criminal sport, they violate the laws of society, and subject themselves to the full penalties of their transgressions. They trespass upon the property of their neighbours, and put the lives of their fellow citizens in the most hazardous jeopardy. Let them not imagine that they can do this with impunity.
>
> We have only to add, that the Mayor and Recorder, with their unusual attention to the interests and peace of the city have resolved to punish every offender with the utmost severity, in order to secure the total suppression of a practice so injurious to morals, and so hostile to civilisation.

The effort to end the pastime was enhanced by a celebrated Quaker missionary visiting the city the same year. They formed a deputation to visit the Protestant bishop at his country seat at Dunmore East. Accompanied by Thomas Jacob and John Strangman,

Irish politician and leader of the Irish Parliamentary Party John Redmond, c.1909. Michael Laffan noted of the Waterford City MP's legacy that, 'Nonetheless he was a worthy and noble representative of the Irish political tradition, he proved that patience, negotiation and compromise could bring about important reforms, he helped to embed parliamentary procedures in the habits and instincts of Irish nationalists, and he played a significant role in transforming Ireland in the decades before the First World War. The miscalculations and failures of his later years have obscured his many achievements.'

'Savage Manners and Inhuman Barbarity': Bull-Baiting at Ballybricken, 1714–1826

they made their way to Dunmore, where the lordship assured them he 'would make a special effort to stop the practice, which was shortly afterwards discontinued'. Yet in 1826, bull-baiting was being revived in Ballybricken, with increased outrage over the now illegal sport being pursued on the Sabbath. Eventually, the practice died out and there were talks in 1884 to knock down the Bull Post. It was concluded by Alderman Smith that it was 'a relic of barbarism and bull-baiting had now gone out of fashion'.

From a former Attorney General for Ireland, John Edward Walsh (whose father was from Waterford) we have a lively description of bull-baiting in Ballybricken. His memoir, *Ireland Sixty Years Ago* (published in 1847), details:

> The south of Ireland, connected by several ties with Spain, adopted many Spanish usages and sports, among the rest, bull fighting, which degenerated into bull-baiting …
>
> The place for baiting was an open space outside the city gate, called Ballybricken. It was surrounded with houses, from which spectators looked on, as at a Spanish bull fight. In the centre of the ring through which the rope was passed …
>
> In 1798, when bull baits were prohibited, this apparatus was removed, and the sport discontinued; But prior to that it was followed with the greatest enthusiasm, and it was not unusual to see eighteen or twenty of these animals baited during the season.

Although the Bull Post remains, when reflecting on this practice of cruelty, it brings to mind the phrase of the past being a foreign country. As times change, and what is accepted as sport today can be completely different to prior decades, let alone centuries, it's worth acknowledging what was considered entertainment all those years ago. It is better to recognise these troublesome aspects of our history, rather than ignore them. We do a disservice to the past and future generations if we don't explore our history, even to the darkest recesses.

The Bull Post, Ballybricken, 1890s. John Edward Walsh detailed in his memoirs, 'The place for baiting was an open space outside the city gate, called Ballybricken. It was surrounded with houses, from which spectators looked on, as at a Spanish bull fight. In the centre of the ring through which the rope was passed …'

2

'The Hub of Hikers': Waterford and Rambling, 1775–1930

As the pursuit of hiking became an increasingly popular pastime in the early 1930s, the *Waterford News* noted that 'Waterford walkers in the past went on their travels with a less sense of its being "the thing." They experienced, perhaps, more of the thrill of adventure.' The same periodical believed that County Waterford could develop into a 'hikers' paradise', such as a central point of Kilmacthomas, where 'every road radiates towards fair region'. Furthermore, one could appreciate 'the beauty of the mountains, the lure of the woodlands, the charm of waterscape (lake, sea and river) – all are at call'.

One author suggested that Melleray was selected as a monastic settlement for such reasons, 'as the place for these pilgrimages of good pleasure and good health – health of soul and body'. Prior to the monks in Melleray, the summit of the Knockmealdown was the birthplace of Henry Eeles, who published numerous papers on electricity.

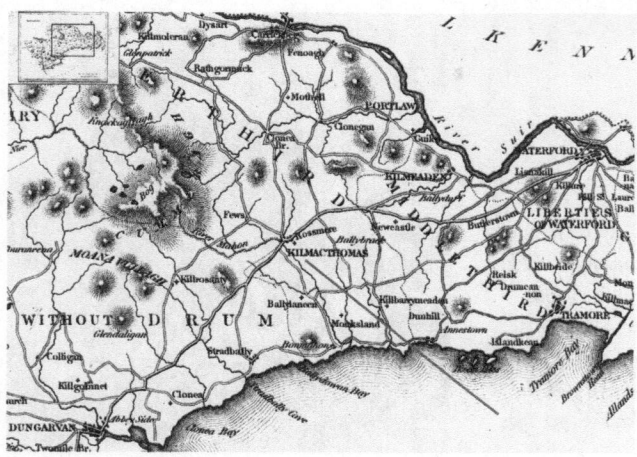

The Waterford News believed that County Waterford could develop into a 'hikers' paradise', such as a central point of Kilmacthomas, where 'every road radiates towards fair region'.

'The Hub of Hikers': Waterford and Rambling, 1775–1930

Britannica notes that 'Lismore, Irish Lios Mor, market town, County Waterford, Ireland. It lies in the Blackwater valley, at the southern foot of the Knockmealdown Mountains. A monastery was founded in Lismore by St Cartagh about 633. In the ninth and tenth centuries the Norsemen plundered it.'

He was known as Major Eeles, and worked as an agent to the Duke of Devonshire and watched over the erection of the bridge that spanned the River Blackwater in 1775. Additionally, in 1758, Eeles invented and exhibited his 'flying coach' at the grounds of Lismore Castle, which was later seen as a precursor to the glider. Retrospectively described as a primitive aeroplane, the 'coach' worked by a sail, with masts 11½ft high. The historian R.H. Ryland noted that Eeles' work 'appeared in the form of Letters from Lismore, and was printed in Dublin in 1771, he claimed credit of discovering the identity of electricity and lighting'.

Eeles' final wish was to be buried on the highest part of the Knockmealdown (which stands at 2,609ft) with his horse and dog. At one time, Eeles was 'disputed with Benjamin Franklin [for] the right to be hailed as the discoverer of the fact that lightning and electricity were identical'. Dr Grattan Flood questioned the location of the burial of Eeles. He wrote:

> Ryland, the historian of Waterford, is more or less responsible for the legend. The real fact is that Henry Eeles, popularly known as Major Eeles, died at Lismore on October 7th, 1781, and by the terms of his will, was buried on the summit of Knockmealdown, so as to be nearer the home of his beloved lightning. He was the first to discover the identity of lightning with electricity, and his famous Letters from Lismore were communicated to the Royal Society, London, in 1755 and 1756 – his experiments, however, dating from 1745. One who had been present at the internment of Eeles in 1781 gave a graphic description of the burial, and he adds that the Major was not buried with his horse, dog, and gun, as chronicled on hearsay testimony by Ryland, for the simple reason that he had given up hunting in 1777, and at the time of his death had neither horse, dog, nor gun.

Portrait of Benjamin Franklin by Joseph Duplessis, 1778. At one time, Lismore's Eeles was 'disputed with Benjamin Franklin [for] the right to be hailed as the discoverer of the fact that lightning and electricity were identical'.

Some believed that Mackey's book *Porcelain* was written as a guide to Waterford hikers, with the *Waterford News* commenting of the publication that it was the 'first of the first in this hiking business'. During the author's own journey, he was accompanied by an ass that drew a chariot for him.

There have been generations of Waterfordians who extolled the virtues and pleasures of walking; figures like Paddy Walsh, who would walk from the city to Dunhill and back, and Thomas Newenham Harvey, who believed that it was 'an unwritten law that Waterfordmen must walk' and detailed his marches in his diaries, which were later serialised by the *Waterford News*. Harvey lived at Cove Cottage, and became a member of Waterford Corporation in 1901. His business dealings included large printing works, which the *Waterford Standard* noted in November 1901 was 'one of the leading firms of its kind in the south of Ireland, and finds not a little employment to-day both for male and female labour in the city'. Harvey was a much-respected stockbroker, and was only 65 years old when he died. He was buried at the Friends' Burial Ground at Lower Newtown. Harvey's legacy was assured when he left a substantial bequest, originally directed towards the freeing of the Waterford toll bridge, and if this wasn't needed, that the funds would pass to the Corporation to be used for the extension of the free library, or towards establishing a technical school.

Others included John Ernest Grubb of Seskin, near Carrick-on-Suir, who was devoted to 'hitting the road'; there was Mr Beckett, a member of the staff at Hearne & Co., who used to spend his weekends hiking to places such as Carrick; Ronayne Jennings and Johnny Walker, who would walk from 'Elysium' to Dungarvan. In his youth, Willie Fanning would make his way to Tory Hill at any opportunity, while Dr Storer, an organist at Waterford Cathedral, 'rambled far and wide over the Waterford terrain'.

Furthermore, the burial places of General Blakeney and the electricity pioneer Eeles on different summits of the Comeragh and Knockmealdown Mountains illustrated the joy derived from hiking to such vantage points in the mountains and soaking in the views and tranquillity. James J. Healy wrote that Blakeney 'was an eccentric being, who loved not man or woman either, and who after a period of some years in the gaieties of the world, and while still in the prime of life, constructed a dwelling on one of the hills, and with a single male attendant retired to live there in solitude'. He was later described by the *Munster Express* as the 'Crusoe of the Comeraghs'.

The *Waterford News* from Friday, 12 June 1931 would conclude of hiking in County Waterford that:

> One could go on indefinitely giving instances of walking as the chief inspiration of health and pleasure seekers in Urbs Intacta. There is no shadow of a doubt that Waterford could substantiate a claim to be the abiding place of pioneers in the latest development of athletics. One of our Dublin dailies has declared that hiking has 'come to stay' in Ireland. Waterford ought to stake its claim to being the hub of hikers.

However, not everyone was enamoured with this trendy hobby. Leesider in the *Cork Examiner* remarked:

> It may be, as you say, a very healthy hobby, but it is to my mind being very much overdone. Clerks and typists who have to work all the week would do much better service to their health by having a good rest during the week-end instead of walking fifteen or twenty miles, which is far too much. The only advantage I can see in it is that it has made courtship a good deal easier on the man's part. He hasn't to be hiring cars and paying train fares and bus fares, as he had to do a few years ago before the craze began. What do you think of it?

Nearly two decades later, in February 1949 the An Óige organisation's first outing for the season was a hike from Waterford to the Minaun at Cheekpoint. Thirty members set out at 1.30 p.m. and covered the distance at a brisk pace in two hours. The weather was so good that the group remarked that they could see the Saltee Islands from the top of the Minaun.

In the 1970s, a Comeragh Mountaineering Club was formed in Waterford for those interested in the mountains and all things concerning hillwalking, rambling, hiking, orienteering and the great outdoors. The club's membership stood at sixty people, with nearly thirty participating in treks every Sunday. They would gather at the Hypermarket at 10.30 a.m. before starting their journey for the day.

Since the Covid-19 pandemic there has been an upsurge in people taking up hiking again, and perhaps when on their travels they can note the paths beaten by figures like Eeles and Blakeney before them. Even the *Cork Examiner* recognised that hiking was courtship, so could be the start of a totally different journey – romantically speaking.

3

Johnny Ryan (1826–1907): Portlaw's Pre-Eminent Sportsman

On Wednesday, 30 October 1907, Portlaw bade a final farewell to Johnny Ryan. For over fifty years, Ryan served the family of the Marquess of Waterford, working for the third, fourth, fifth and sixth Marquesses before his death at the advanced age of 81 years old. The *Waterford Standard* noted that Ryan was 'respected and beloved by all, but by none more genuinely than by the noble family whose predecessors he served as faithfully and well'. In addition to his connections with the de la Poer Beresford family, Ryan had at one time been a professional jockey, and had the distinction of one of the most impressive winning records in the history of horse racing, be it amateur or professional, on the flat or steeplechasing.

Ryan was born in Mountjoy Forest in Omagh, Co. Tyrone, in June 1826. His father was gardener to Sir Charles J. Gardner. At that time, Gardner kept a racing stable, and when Johnny was 11 years old, he hid under a barrow to avoid going to school. Ryan hoped to talk to Sir Charles to allow him to ride a horse. A deal was made that if young Johnny could ride a certain 'wicked mare' over hurdles, he would be allowed to visit the stables. This was achieved by Johnny, and it was the start of a seven-year apprenticeship to Sir Charles. From there, Ryan went to Captain Henrick of Johnstown, Co. Kildare, where he rode Black Dwarf. He competed at the Ballybar (Co. Carlow) races on the same animal and came to the attention of Lord Waterford. The horse was purchased by Waterford, and Ryan would say of that transaction that, 'I believe [he] bought me too'. Ryan would remain at Curraghmore from 1834 until his death in the early years of the twentieth century.

Ryan's prowess as a jockey found the perfect patrons in the form of the Curraghmore estate, for the 3rd Marquess, known as Henry Waterford, came fourth in the 1840 Grand National on his own horse, The Sea. Nearly thirty years later, in

1866, the National Hunt Steeplechase was run in Scotland for the first time. There at the Bogside meeting, the race was won by Lord Marcus Beresford aboard G. Ballard's Burford. Marcus along with his brothers raced each other in a three-horse sweepstake run over the Williamstown Course as part of the annual steeplechase meeting at the Curraghmore Hunt. The three siblings rode in Beresford blue colours with distinctive caps. When Marcus finished riding in public, he was appointed starter to the Jockey Club. He resigned this position in 1890 to become the Master of the Horse to the future King Edward.

By 1844, Lord Waterford (Henry) had sixteen horses in training, which provided Johnny Ryan with ample time to train and practise. The Tyrone native was made second horseman, with the pack established at Curraghmore under the title of Lord Waterford's Foxhounds. Ryan would carry the 'Waterford blue' during the racing season on horses such as Blue Skin, Redwing, Ballysax, Firefly, Lord George and The Sea, to name a few of the animals who would become celebrated across County Waterford. The writer Harry R. Sargent believed that Ryan's record stood at 130 races rode for Lord Waterford, with no fewer than 112 victories. He finished second five times, and in third place on three occasions. This trio of bronze finishes all came at the Liverpool Grand National.

It was noted in *Bailey's Magazine* (1904) that:

This extraordinary record was chiefly accomplished in Ireland, where there were many steeplechase fixtures during the forties and early fifties that have been long since abandoned; but many of his most brilliant victories were won in England, notably the Grand Autumn Free Handicap Steeplechase of four miles at Liverpool in 1849, which Johnny won on Sir John by two lengths from Vain Hope. The Doctor steered by Lord Strathmore, and Preceed, with Jem Mason in the saddle, were among the seventeen competitors in this great race.

Ryan and Sir John (carrying 11st 8lb) were the favourites for the 1850 Grand National, but were unlucky to place third in a field of thirty-two competitors. Even without claiming the 'greatest race', Johnny Ryan believed that Sir John was the best horse he ever rode over fences. His style of horsemanship was noted as 'never flurried or excited, [Ryan] never lost a chance or took an ounce out of his horse unnecessarily, while his finish was most resolute and artistic'.

The autumn of the following year Ryan, with the mount of Lord George, won the Great Metropolitan Steeplechase at Epsom, the same year as winning the Epsom Hurdle Race. The death of Lord Waterford in 1859 was the end of Ryan's career as a jockey. He then was tasked with looking after animals for hunting and hounds. The year before the lord's demise, Ryan had swept the boards in Ireland, as they looked to finally win a Grand National, which the pair eagerly chased. An overview by Sargent in *Thoughts Upon Sport* on Ryan detailed:

> He came from a racing stable at the Curragh, entered the service of Lord Waterford in 1842, and continued as first steeplechase and flat-race jockey, also as second horseman, until his lordship's death in 1859. During these seventeen years Ryan distinguished himself on that flat and between flags in the 'light blue and black cap' to quite an unparalleled degree ... Thus showing a record which I should say was never approached by any other jockey, professional or otherwise, in the annals of racing or steeplechasing.

His later years were in service as stud groom to Lord Waterford, where his horses were continually admired for their conditioning as hunts and hounds. Nevertheless, the man always known as Johnny in Portlaw would be affectionately known on the lands of Curraghmore as 'the Jock'.

Curraghmore near Portlaw, County Waterford, is a historic house and estate and the seat of the Marquess of Waterford. The estate was part of the grant of land made to Sir Roger le Puher (la Poer) by Henry II in 1177 after the Anglo-Norman invasion of Ireland.

4

Hugh Collender: Cappoquin Sports Manufacturer and Rebel

Hugh Collender was born in Cappoquin, Co. Waterford, in December 1828. Hugh grew up in a small farm just outside the town. Collender was a fervent nationalist and was involved in an ill-fated attack on a police barracks, which led him to flee to America in 1849. While in the United States, Collender became an acquaintance of Kilkenny man Michael Phelan, who was considered the 'father of billiards' in America. Collender became Phelan's protégé.

In 1853, Collender was Thomas Francis Meagher's manager for his lecture tour of the southern states. Meagher became the godfather to Collender and Julia Phelan's (daughter of Michael Phelan) first child. In 1855, Michael Phelan and Collender set up a joint venture named Phelan and Collender. They co-published *The Rise and Progress of the Game of Billiards* in 1860. Collender had a keen interest in chemistry and technology, which led him to develop the 'combination cushion' for billiards. The success of their business led them to donate much of their money to the cause of the Fenians.

In 1871, after Phelan's death, the company was renamed the H.W. Collender Company. Two years later, Collender built a substantial factory in Connecticut for the manufacture of billiards tables. It would go on to employ 200 people, and subsequently become the market leader in billiards tables. The factory was destroyed and rebuilt after a fire in 1883, and a year later merged with a couple of other companies to become the Brunswick Bake Collender Company, with Collender as president. It has continued in existence since 1960 as the Brunswick Corporation. Collender died of kidney failure in New York in 1890.

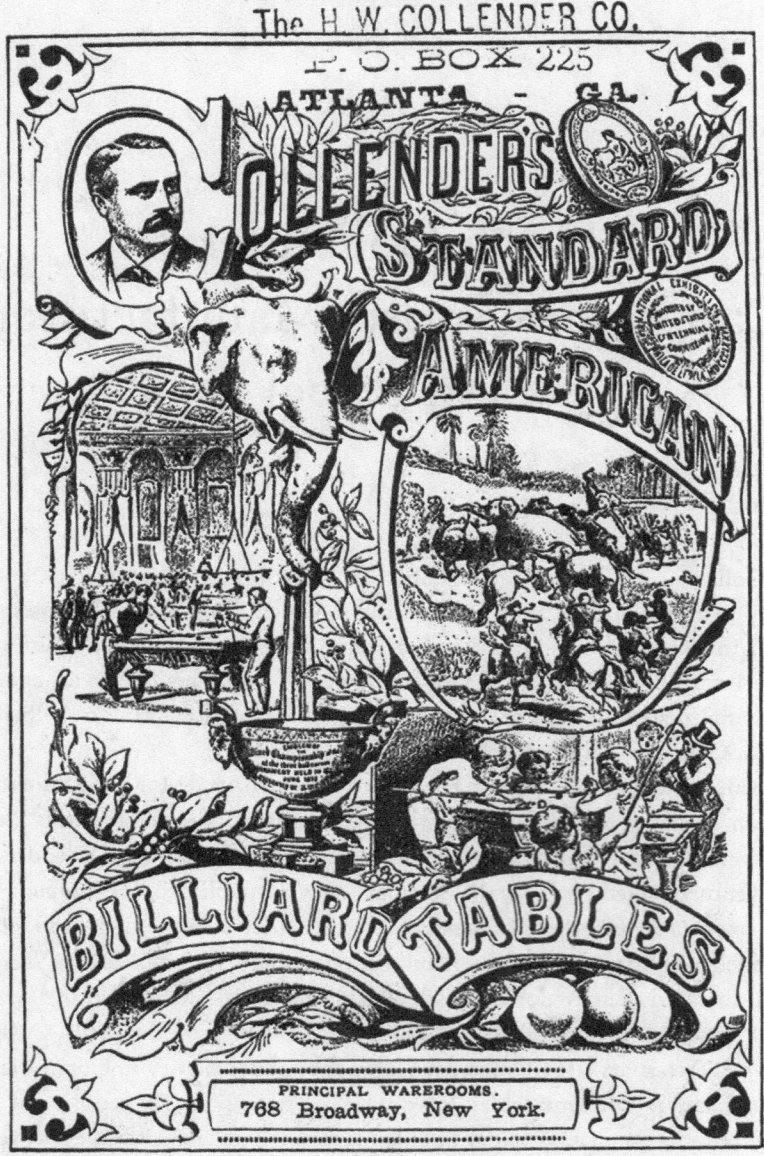

H.W. Collender Catalogue (1879).

5

Patrick Hearne: 'The Gambler'

Patrick Hearne was born in Waterford. One of four siblings, Patrick was the son of a solicitor. He and one of his brothers would follow in their father's footsteps, practising law in North America. Hearne received a BA from Dublin University (more commonly referred to today as Trinity College Dublin). He travelled to Canada in the early 1830s, but limited opportunity for employment led him to venture south to New York.

Such is the spread of the Irish diaspora: by chance, Hearne met an old friend from Dublin while walking down Broadway on his first day in the Big Apple. From there, he travelled to New Orleans, which was termed the 'El Dorado' of the nineteenth-century USA. The journey itself was owed to the kindness of the ship's captain, who allowed the Waterford man to travel without paying the fare on the basis it would be paid when financial circumstances could permit.

The southern city became the third most populous in the States, with substantial numbers of German and Irish immigrants such as Hearne inhabiting it. There he found employment at a local law firm and the tidy sum of $1,800 a year, but his services were then severed due to the illness of his employer. The chance to become an accountant for a local gambling house, though not deemed a respectable job, certainly alleviated his financial difficulties.

With increased prosperity, a strong reputation in the casinos of New Orleans and good connections within gambling circles, Hearne returned to New York, eventually residing at 187 Broadway in the latter half of the 1830s. This move was precipitated by the tightening of restrictions on illegal gambling within New Orleans. His premises in New York was patronised by senators, socialites and wealthy businessmen of the day. Bearing his name, this gambling house (one of the first casinos in the city) opposite the well-known Metropolitan Hotel took considerable sums each night. Some of Hearne's most renowned frequenters included prize fighters such as Yankee Sullivan and the popular minstrel Dan Bryant. Hearne's gambling house was popular for 'skins games' such as bowling.

One of his gambling operation's notable debtors was John James (an uncle of the novelist Henry James), who owed over $2,000 to Hearne. A campaign against the Irishman would see the term 'social vermin' aligned to his name in the local papers. The only case to be taken for 'faro' in New York was against Hearne; however, he was fined $100 with no term of imprisonment given. One writer quibbled, 'What is a fine of $100, to Pat Hearne? He wins at an average, ten times the amount every night.' Hearne was represented by the lawyer Daniel Edgar Sickles, who was later acquitted of the murder of his wife's lover on the grounds of 'temporary insanity', which was also the first instance of its use in legal defence in the United States. It appears Hearne's own trial impacted his enterprise on Broadway, which closed in 1856.

Yet, his wealth saw him buy the mansion of John Jacob Astor (a multimillionaire whose wealth derived from the fur trade) before selling it to be developed into an opera house. Of course, now Broadway is synonymous with theatre.

Upon his death in 1859, his obituary in the *New York Times* noted:

> Mr Hearne was in his private relations so much of a gentleman, was so generous in his charities and so genial and kindly in his nature as to almost make us desire to forget that his profession was one which neither the laws of God or society could regard without condemnation.

His charitable nature would see little left for his grieving wife and two adopted daughters. From his 'respectable' origins in Waterford to becoming a pioneer in the gambling industry in New York, Hearne became one of the most well-known sportsmen before the outbreak of the American Civil War, but is largely forgotten in his adopted home and his native Ireland.

6

The Irish Giant 'Who Gained Notoriety, if Not Fame, as a Pugilist': Lismore's Ned O'Baldwin (1840–75)

Along the 169km River Blackwater is the small town of Lismore, founded by St Carthage, which is dwarfed by the imposing Gothic-styled Lismore Castle. Among the near 3,000 population of this historic town in the 1840s was a child who would go on to be described as the greatest bareknuckle boxer prior to the great John L. Sullivan, but would meet a bloody end in a saloon in New York. Such was his pugilistic ability, C.J. Gannon described the Waterford boxer as 'the Primo Carnera of his day'. Quite the claim by Gannon as the 'Ambling Alp' Carnera, who was the same height as the Irishman, has the record of more fights won by knockout than any other Heavyweight Champion.

Ned O'Baldwin was born in Lismore, Co. Waterford, in 1840. From that small town, O'Baldwin would grow to 6ft 6½in and weigh 200lb, with such a physical presence leading to him being dubbed 'The Irish Giant'. *The Sporting Life* wrote that O'Baldwin 'was brought up in the "land of prates [sic]" at Waterford, where many of the natives are vegetarians, and it is more than probable that Edward O'Baldwin was of that "persuasion".'

O'Baldwin moved to London to spar at Langham's but was outboxed by many of his opponents, who knocked him all over the shop.

NED O'BALDWIN. (Irish Giant,)

Captain Francis O'Neill in the Chicago Citizen was far more ruthless in his summation that Ned O'Baldwin 'gained notoriety, if not fame as a pugilist. Although but little short of seven feet in height and well-proportioned, his performance in the prize ring fell far short of his pretensions.'

'Just Like That…': The Schooling of a Fighter by Tommy Cooper

By his early 20s, O'Baldwin had amassed a series of impressive performances in his early forays in the fistic arts, such as an admirable defeat to Andrew Marsden (1863) followed by a victory over George Iles (February 1866, for £50 a side). He would avenge his loss to Marsden by vanquishing him in a rematch in eleven rounds in the autumn of 1866. The change in fortunes was noted by *The Sporting Life*: 'of three years ago … [O'Baldwin] was then only a mere tyro in the sparring school, but was also wanting in strength and stamina … [he] was a giant of the beanstalk kind – thin, easily shaken, and apt to break away at the slightest touch'. A large part of his progress was due to the tutelage of Tommy Cooper of Birmingham, with *Sporting Life* recording of the second duel with Marsden:

> The result has proved Marsden to have been clearly overmatched, and O'Baldwin has come out of the fray with his reputation considerably enhanced as a dangerous

man to tackle in the 24ft ring. Marsden used his great strength by lunging out tremendous blows on O'Baldwin's body and head, and at the end of the third round a swinging right-hander on the back of the neck was of such a stunning nature as to make Ned stagger, and a dish of cold water was thrown over his head to bring him to. This rendered Ned's 'headpiece' rather shaky, and it was not till the sixth round that he recovered his true form, and then he dabbed on Marsden's face and dropped his right on the ribs without any effectual returns. He gained a knock-down blow with a right cross-counter, and it was all up with Marsden after that; Andrew was bleeding profusely from two wide gashes on the nose and upper lip, and he was nearly choked with the blood running into his mouth ... O'Baldwin soon found out that he had nothing to do but bide his time and let out his left, and it was sure to land on the dial somewhere. Had not the ropes and stakes been pulled up, we are of opinion that Marsden could not have stood up more than ten minutes, and we must confirm the referee's decision in favour of O'Baldwin.

Of this run of noteworthy bouts, the *Cork Examiner* was more forgiving and positive of the Lismore man's earlier forays in the ring, and added an air of mystique by proclaiming:

He has risen, meteor-like, to the zenith of gladiatorial fame. We have no record of his enduring the chrysalis state of the pugilistic pot-boy, and so far as we are aware, his great spirit has never been trammelled in laborious and degrading industry. When first heard of he was already the feared of doughty chiefs – vanquisher of Chickens, the exterminator of Pets, a dreaded antagonist of Bantams.

Aside from inflicting suffering on the animal kingdom (perhaps that's why he was a vegetarian), O'Baldwin had placed himself with the opportunity to become champion with a bout against Jem Mace, which was scheduled for Tuesday, 15 October 1867 in London. However, before even a punch was thrown, the fight was cancelled when the police arrested Mace when he was asleep in his bed in an attempt to clamp down on boxing and the vices that surrounded its staging.

The Irish Giant in America

This left the pair with the decision to leave for the United States to explore fighting opportunities there, as it was becoming increasingly difficult in England. However, O'Baldwin got on the wrong side of the law across the Atlantic, when he was committed to Tombs in New York for defaulting on a $1,000 bail in 1868. This was followed by a sentence of eighteen months' hard labour at the House of Corrections, due to his involvement in an arranged fight with Joe Wormald at Lynnville, Massachusetts. His opponent escaped the same fate by absconding and giving 'straw bail'. In one last attempt for O'Baldwin to salvage his petering pugilistic career, a fight was arranged between him and Mace again for 1872. O'Baldwin entered into a training regime in West Philadelphia, but was arrested and placed under a $5,000 bail not to leave Pennsylvania for the purpose of prize fighting. The *New York Clipper* suggested that this was 'a put-up job' by the backers of the 'Irish Giant', with their opinion being that 'they were determined not to [let O'Baldwin] fight under any circumstances, as … [he] was not well, and they did not wish to lose their money'.

However, the truth appears to be that the Lismore man had a dispute with his backers when he received only $45 out of the $1,000 he was promised, leading him to strike a supporter named Mart Killacky. Some believed that if O'Baldwin had got his hands on a weapon, there would have been a fatality. Killacky owned a hotel in Atlantic City, New Jersey, where O'Baldwin stayed when preparing to fight Mace. Previously, *Bell's Life* had reported that O'Baldwin had been 'hard at work for some time past, and looks in prime order now'. Concluding of the whole episode, the *Clipper* decided that:

> After all the expenditure and loss of time involved in the endeavour to bring about a consummation of the match between Jim Mace and Ned O'Baldwin within the orthodox enclosure, it has, as many have predicted would be the case, ended in a most unsatisfactory manner.

If anything, this summed up not only the repeated attempts of a championship fight between the pair, but was an apt way to look at the career of O'Baldwin, which after such great promise (after the second Marsden fight) was faltering.

Last-Chance Saloon: Slaying the Giant

Clearly, boxing wasn't paying the County Waterford native, so he entered into a liquor store enterprise with Mike Finnell. It was located on West Street in New York in 1875. However, only a month into the endeavour, O'Baldwin was looking to call it quits as the business was not profitable, and to give one last attempt at making it in prize fighting in America. He had already started issuing challenges 'to fight any man in the world'. This rather erratic behaviour enraged Finnell so much that on 27 September 1875 he entered the saloon and shot O'Baldwin twice. One bullet entered his abdomen and the second into his chest. O'Baldwin battled his wounds like he was in a prize fight, but eventually succumbed to his injuries two days later. Only in his mid-30s, O'Baldwin's remains were buried at Holyhood Cemetery at

Brookline, Massachusetts. Some in the New York press felt that O'Baldwin's murder by Finnell had done a service to wider society, with the *New York Herald* claiming his demise may have been to the 'public benefit'. Thus, with such sentiment, Finnell was found not guilty of 'first-degree murder', claiming he shot in self-defence.

Legacy

The Sporting Life believed that O'Baldwin's untimely end 'prevented the Irish giant's true calibre from being ascertained', while a Captain Francis O'Neill in the *Chicago Citizen* was far more ruthless in his summation of Ned O'Baldwin, 'who gained notoriety, if not fame, as a pugilist. Although but little short of 7ft in height and well-proportioned, his performance in the prize ring fell far short of his pretensions.' Some likened O'Baldwin to Jim Jefferies due to his size, but the Irishman was deemed slower compared to the Ohio-born 'Boilermaker', who won the World Heavyweight Championship in 1899 against Bob Fitzsimmons.

The story of Edward O'Baldwin from Lismore illustrates the connections between boxing and crime that have long existed in the world of prize fighting. The Irish Giant serves as an interesting fulcrum between the bareknuckle boxing world that made Dan Donnelly legendary and the Marquess of Queensbury-gloved fighting that we know today. O'Baldwin shows how improvements to one's life can be made if the will and work ethic are there, but also that opportunities that are so sorely chased must be taken before a career dissipates. The Waterford fighter had the world at the feet of his 6ft 6½in frame in 1868, yet just seven years later this gargantuan fighter was six feet underground.

7

Vere Thomas St Leger Goold (1853–1909): Waterford Tennis Player and Monte Carlo Murderer

Born in Waterford on 2 October 1853, Goold became a keen player of lawn tennis in its early days in his native city. He later became a member of Fitzwilliam Lawn Tennis Club in Dublin. In 1878, he won the Men's Singles event of the first Irish Open, which was held in Limerick. The following year, the Irish Open was staged at his home club's courts, and Goold again won the Men's Singles title, receiving a prize of £20. Goold's performance at the Irish Open that year saw him installed as the favourite for the Wimbledon Championship, held a week later. However, he was defeated in the final by the Reverend John Hartley in front of over 1,000 spectators.

Unfortunately, this was to be not only Goold's sole appearance in a Wimbledon final, but also the tournament as a whole. Goold was considered an important member in the administration of the Fitzwilliam Lawn Tennis Club. His most notable tennis achievement until the end of his career in 1883 was winning a doubles match for Ireland against England in what has since been recognised as the first international tennis match between two nations. In 1886, Goold moved to London, and met a Frenchwoman, Marie Violet (twice widowed), whom he married in 1891. After a brief period spent in Canada, they returned to London in 1903. However, an ill-fated venture into the laundry business led them to move to Monte Carlo, trying to achieve wealth through the gambling tables of casinos.

On the 6 August 1907, Goold and his wife were arrested after the discovery of a dismembered body of a woman, named Emma Liven, in their luggage. The trial revealed that Liven was murdered after trying to obtain repayment of a loan she had given Goold and his wife, and was struck when a heated argument erupted. As a result, Goold was imprisoned on Devil's Island, French Guiana, and died a year later on 8 September 1909. His wife was imprisoned and died in 1914. Vere Goold holds the two distinctions of being the first tennis player born on the island of Ireland to contest a Wimbledon final, and also the only Wimbledon finalist to be convicted of murder.

Cover of Le Petit Journal *(No. 875 from 25 August 1907), about the case of Vere St Leger Goold (1853–1907). He was later convicted of murder and sent to Devil's Island, French Guiana.*

8

'Died of Inanition': County Waterford Archery Club, 1860–65

The 1840s saw a renewal of interest in turning the recreation of archery into a modern sport. Early in the nineteenth century the sport was popular among all classes after the Napoleonic Wars, as it was seen as a nostalgic pastime of rural Britain and Ireland. This was further amplified by the popularity of Sir Walter Scott's *Ivanhoe*, which depicted the heroic figure of Locksley winning an archery tournament. The subsequent renewal at the midpoint of the century was aided by festivities, music and gastronomical delights that accompanied such events, as landed gentry and local élites competed with one another, not only with bow and arrow, but also in terms of hospitality and pageantry. Inevitably, this was reflected in Waterford City and County, with the group that would simply become known as the Waterford Archers.

The sport of archery is best explained by local periodical the *Waterford Mail*, which deemed it as a gathering:

'The archer sees the make upon the path of the infinite, and He bends you with His might that His arrows may go swift and far.' Kahlil Gibran.

not one with weapons of war, for the shedding of human blood, nor was it even the gathering of hunters, to arouse the game of the forest, but it was for the more peaceful purpose of trying the skill of combatants, seeing who had the most accurate eye and the steadiest hand, who could send the feathered arrow most frequently to the bull's eye ...

The Waterford Archery Club was only in its infancy, but already by 1860 (which some journals place as the club's first season) was one of the largest formal groups in the south of Ireland, which was equally reflected in its notable membership (frequented by lords and prominent civic figures), pomp and prizes that were hallmarks of its meetings. Among their number were army officers who were quartered in the garrison town of Waterford. Furthermore, it included the local bourgeoisie from hotel chefs to craftsmen, who not only wanted to display their talents in spreads and prizes, but used these events to tout for future business.

In July 1860, the Waterford Archery Club held what was described as an 'annual meeting' at Bellevue, the home of Nicholas Alfred Power. His grandson, the artist and poet Arthur Richard Power, would inherit the property, but sold it in 1940. There, at Bellevue, toxophilites (lovers of archery) were joined by the band of the Waterford Artillery thanks to Captain Glubb, as more than 100 guests sat down to a seasonal dinner, catered for by John Power of the Adelphi Hotel. The *Waterford News* reported of the day as 'charmingly fine, the sun brilliantly shining, all nature gay and smiling, the attendance on the ground in consequence being very large, comprising the rank, beauty, and fashion of the city and neighbourhood, foremost among whom were the fair competitors for the prizes, attired in archery costume'. It would appear from this description that Bellevue bore all the traits akin to Evelyn Waugh's *Brideshead Revisited* on that summer's day. As to the competition, the victors on the day were Miss Meara, who claimed the top Ladies' Prize of a gold bracelet, and Mr Fleming, awarded the Gentlemen's Prize of a handsome set of studs and wrist fasteners.

The burgeoning popularity of the sport is reflected in it being played by both men and women, which gave an added attraction as a social occasion, in trying to impress partners and prospective lovers, as well as the basic nature of the competitive spirit. There was added focus to the spectacle of the day, between hospitality and entertainment, which reflected the classes who were able to participate and enjoy such events, but also the hope that Cupid's arrow could lead to suitable matches in matrimony. During an era when marriages were viewed like business investments, one could say that some of the competitive archers were also touting for business in matters of the heart.

A couple of months later, on 5 September, a second meeting of the Archery Club was held in the city, with the Marchioness of Waterford and the youthful Earl of Tyrone in attendance. Prizes were supplied by a Mr Mosley, with the Ladies' Prize again being a gold bracelet, with opal and diamond pendant, presented in a Morocco box carrying the inscription: 'Ladies Challenge Prize, presented by James Mosley to the Waterford Archery Club'. The Gentlemen's Prize was an engraved and chased claret jug. As the area was sheltered by trees, away from the gaze of the public, a temporary timber structure was erected by Club Secretary John Wall for guests to assemble and later have supper. The *Waterford Mail* noted that 'hanging from tree to tree were flags of many colours and sizes, borrowed from the yachts in the harbour, and they greatly enlivened the aspect of the scene'. Clearly, these were people who had the benefits of great wealth, and the privilege of enough free time to indulge in pleasures that could not be afforded to the working-class population, which numbered salters, sailors and mothers trying to survive in difficult times.

Figures such as James Mosley, jeweller, Sir Robert Paul, Edward Roberts and F.G. Bloomfield were treated to music by the Waterford Artillery band with tunes from Auber, Julien, Verdi and, of course, William Vincent Wallace's 'serenade' from *Don Pasquale*. As the Waterford Archers' first season came to a close in early October, the *Waterford News* proclaimed that its success was due in large part to the great 'excitement [which] prevailed amongst the competitors as the moment for announcing the scores arrived'. The County of Waterford Archers held a ball and supper at the Town Hall on 27 November 1860, with a gentleman's ticket costing 12*s* 6*d*, and a lady's entry being 6*d*. Around 190 people were in attendance, as the dancing started at ten o'clock. At 1.30 they adjourned for supper, and when they returned to the ballroom, the dancing was kept up until morning.

This annual ball would come to dominate the coverage of the Waterford Archery Club, as we see adverts for prize meetings, but much more information on the decoration and dancing at the Town Hall each November. Come the 1863 season, there was a renewed interest in detailing the meets, such as the first of the season held in June on the property of Sir H.W. Barron at Barroncourt in County Kilkenny. Barron was MP for Waterford at Westminster from 1832 to 1841, with a second period from 1849 to 1852, and again from 1865 to 1869. One could argue that such an event could serve as an electioneering exercise or campaigning event, in preparation for trying to obtain a seat in the Imperial Parliament. Also living in Armagh, Barron had held the office of the High Sheriff of Waterford just a few years previously in 1858.

We again see John Wall as secretary, aided by the efforts of Harry R. Sargent, with prizes supplied by James Mosley on Custom House Quay. Wall and Sargent were not only Trojan workers for the Archery Club, but they were also heroes! In early May 1865, during a fire in Bailey's New Street, Sargent was Herculean in his effort to save the many families living in tenement dwellings that were in grave danger due to the ferocity of the blaze. The *Waterford News* noted that Sargent 'was everywhere that help or advice were required, smashing glass with his improtected [sic] hand to effect an entrance where peril was imminent, utterly disregarding all personal danger

'Died of Inanition': County Waterford Archery Club, 1860–65

Henry Winston Barron by George Hayter.

and actuated by but one object, the saving of human life'. He was ably assisted by his archery club colleague, John Wall. It was believed that they, with D. Butler, M. Horne, George Carroll and the local fire services, were able to save five families, which included sixteen children. Sadly, the lone death due to the fire was the youngest child of a Mrs Humphries, it being 18 months old. The *News* reported, 'The cause of the fire is stated to have arisen from the act of a lodger in the house, a carpenter, while inebriated, allowing a candle to fall into a heap of shavings.'

After such a harrowing event, it must have been difficult for Sargent to return to the trivial affairs of arranging archery meetings. The Sargent and Wall families put their efforts into raising funds for the families that were devastated by the fire.

It seems vulgar to turn to look at the third prominent figure in the Archery Club after detailing the destruction from that May day, but returning to Barroncourt, we see the jeweller who was ever present. James Mosley was a popular figure in the city, his window display attracted great admiration, and he was regularly recorded in local papers as donating cups and prizes to various organisations, from the Royal Irish Constabulary to agricultural societies. However, this made him a prime victim of crime, with his premises ransacked and goods being stolen on several occasions.

Barron's mansion at Belmont would host the second meeting of the season in September and a grand ball, where Sargent and the 'Prince of Caterers', John Power, excelled in making the event the highlight of the city's social calendar. The soundtrack to the day's competition was once more provided by the band of the Waterford Artillery, under the direction of Mr Tiffin.

Again, the competition at the archery meets became secondary to the club's annual ball, where in early January 1865, the Archery Club occupied the Large Room of the Town Hall. A correspondent for the *Waterford Chronicle* was taken by the ladies in attendance, writing:

> Dancing commenced at half-past ten o'clock, after which the room began to be filled rapidly. About 11 o'clock, the ball-room was a blasé of beauty, and resembled a moving *parterre* of flowers, the splendid and varied colours of the ladies' dresses contrasting well with more sombre hues of the gentlemen. The votaries of Terpsichore were unceasing in their devotion throughout the night. The beauty of the county appeared to have been assembled within those walls. Brightly the lamps shone on fair women, whose bright eyes sparkled with pleasure, and whose cheeks glowed with animation, as they moved thro' the mazes of the dance, or leant on the arms of their partners.

Later that year, in September, the Waterford Archery Ball was staged at F.G. Bloomfield's Newpark (purchased from the Rev. John Newport, nephew of Sir John Newport), as the Waterford Archers looked to be primarily a dance club with a passing interest in archery, as the pursuit of the sport was clearly waning. And this is the last reference we see to the County Waterford Archery Club, until an article in the *Waterford Standard*, dated 27 May 1868, which read:

> We regret to say that the Waterford Archery Club appears to have 'died of inanition'; for whilst the clubs of Kilkenny, Wexford, and Clonmel are in a most flourishing condition, our local archers appear to have no signs of life. The fault is not due to Mr Harry Sargent who, if energy, zeal, and untiring exertions could avail, would render the club one of the most successful in Ireland, as it ought to be, considering the rank and wealth which prevails in this county. We read periodical reports of the successful meetings of the surrounding clubs, and it is then really to be regretted that our county is so apathetic. Let the ladies only come forward, and we are sure that the gentlemen will quickly follow. We would ask our fair readers to consider the pleasure and excitement of an archery meeting, and we are sure that they will no longer allow Waterford to be an exception to the surrounding counties, so far as archery is concerned.

Having started and flourished so quickly, the demise of the Waterford Archers was just as quick, from being the largest toxophilite group in the south of Ireland, to being overshadowed by neighbouring towns to the north and east of Waterford city.

One suspects that the decline of the group was due to the efforts of Sargent and Wall turning to help the victims of that fire at Bailey's New Street. It is a mark of both these men, and their families, that they used their energies and experiences to help others in need. It serves as an interesting juxtaposition from the pomp and ceremony displayed at Bellevue and Curraghmore to the poverty and neglect apparent to those destitute in Waterford city. If this led to balls being left unorganised and gala events falling to the wayside, Sargent and Wall deserve a silver cup from James Mosley, for they attempted the greatest endeavour of all, to help others.

The Dublin, Cork, and South of Ireland: A Literary, Commercial, and Social Review (1892) recorded: 'JAMES MOSLEY & SONS, Watchmakers, Jewellers, Silversmiths, and Electroplaters, 97 and 98, Quay; and Exchange Street, Waterford. This thriving centre of commercial activity in the South of Ireland possesses no more attractive establishments than that conducted by Messrs. James Mosley And Sons, the well-known Watchmakers, Jewellers, and Silversmiths, 97 and 98, Quay, and Exchange Street, whose extended connection with the trade of the City amply justifies the prominence assigned to them in this work. The history of the house dates back to 1832, when it was founded by the grandfather of the present proprietor. The establishment is centrally situated on the Quay facing the river, and forms a noted feature of the attractions of this fine thoroughfare.'

9

Thomas Joseph Dart Kelly: Waterford Man and Aussie Cricketer

Test cricket has been played since 1877 with around 3,000 men having the title of Test cricketer. Up to 2018, when Ireland played its first Test match, eleven Irish men had played cricket at what is considered the highest level and the spiritual form of the game, with Waterford-born Thomas Joseph Dart Kelly being the second of that group.

Tom Kelly was born in County Waterford on 3 May 1844. As a child, he moved to Bristol, England, with his parents. While in Gloucestershire, Kelly was educated in cricket by the Grace brothers at Durdham Downs. Known as the 'three Graces', there was William Gilbert or W.G., considered to be one of the finest cricketers of all time; Edward Mills or E.M., an all-rounder, and Fred, who died aged 29 of pneumonia as a result of exacerbating a cold after getting soaked by rain playing a cricket match. Quite a collection of luminaries of the game with whom Kelly could hone his ability with bat and ball.

Subsequently, Kelly migrated to Australia in 1863 aged 19 and eventually settled in Melbourne. Chris Rumford and Stephen Wagg, in their study *Cricket and Globalization*, note that 'even if cricket was increasingly viewed as a foreign game in Ireland itself, Irish emigrants to Australia demonstrated not only that they had grown up with the sport but also that they were more than willing to play it in their new homeland, not least as it provided an opportunity to play the English at one of their own games'. Although in Kelly's native land there may have been disdain in some quarters of the game of cricket (cricket was a popular pastime in Ireland prior to the establishment of the Gaelic Athletic Association [GAA] in 1884), his time in England had provided him with a firm grounding in the sport. He would be more than a match to compete with the best talent Down Under.

Waterford-born Kelly made his first-class debut for Parr's XI in 1863–64 and played domestic cricket for Victoria for a total of seventeen seasons as a middle-order, right-handed batsman. Kelly was noted for his fielding ability. In thirteen first-class matches for Victoria, Kelly mustered 446 runs at a batting average of 21.18 runs. An impressive figure in an era when such averages were low compared with today's cricketers. This included five 50s, with his highest total of 86 coming against New South Wales in 1874–75. Of his eighteen catches, the most notable was the dismissal of Billy Caffyn at Melbourne in 1867. Caffyn was an English cricketer who had the honour of bowling the first ball in the maiden match between a team from Australia and England at the Melbourne Cricket Ground on New Year's Day 1862.

Kelly made his debut for Melbourne Cricket Club in 1863–64, with his last appearance for the first XI coming in 1888–89. His second season with MCC saw him top score with 46 in defeating Albert Cricket Club by an innings. Kelly twice topped the club's batting average with 225 runs at an average of 27.50 in 1873–74 and again in 1882–83 with 446 runs at 37.16. Though not noted for his bowling ability, his slow bowling led him to topping the bowling averages in 1875–76 with 73 wickets at a rate of a wicket for 8.35 runs.

Later, Kelly made his Test debut for Australia aged 32 (and is Australian Test cricketer No. 12) in the second test of the 1876–77 season. In the second innings of the test he hit 35, which was his highest total in Test cricket. This included eight successive strikes for four.

Kelly was the second Irishman to play for the Baggy Greens, the first being Tom Horan of Midleton, County Cork. Horan went on to captain Australia and played fifteen times for his adopted country. Kelly wasn't available for the first Australian tour of England in 1878. Kelly played with Horan in the Waterford-born cricketer's second and final test match for Australia. His appearance in this one-off test in 1878–79 was due to him replacing George Bailey, who had broken his arm in a fielding mishap.

Though Kelly's legacy does not rival Horan, the Waterford man can boast being the first Australian cricketer to wear a blazer, which he designed himself. It was red, white and blue with a sash to match. The striped jacket was in the colours of Melbourne Cricket Club and made to Kelly's own specifications. Nicknamed 'The Little Wonder', the blazer was an exemplification of the flair and style with which he played the game. Ken Williams, in *For Club and Country*, wrote Kelly 'was best known for his exceptional fielding, though he was also a hard-hitting batsman with a good record in intercolonial matches. Brilliant and fearless at point, he stood up close to even the fiercest hitters and by general consent was regarded as the finest field in England or Australia in that position.'

Joe Tracy: America's Greatest Race Car Driver

American race car driver and engineer Joe Tracy claimed he was born in County Waterford on 22 March 1873. Very little is known about his early years in the Gentle County, but we know that Tracy emigrated to the United States around the age of 18. From various reports of Tracy in adulthood, he appeared to be a quiet but thoughtful person who was never one to lose his temper, no matter the pressure. He decided to pursue a career as a professional chauffeur and later as a race car driver. Tracy had a notable second-place finish at the 5-mile Daytona Beach Contest in 1904, where he drove a Peerless. The following year he crossed the Atlantic to compete in the Gordon Bennett Race in France, but disappointingly, after travelling so far, only completed two laps after stripping two gears of his Locomobile. The vehicle was given such a name due to its likeness to a locomotive. Locomobile had been established in 1899 and harnessed steam power in its early years before converting to operate on petrol in 1905. The version of the vehicle with which Tracy is fondly entwined with was named 'Old 16'.

Tracy and the Vanderbilt Cup, 1904–06

Tracy was more well known for his performances in his Locomobiles at the Vanderbilt Cup races staged on Long Island. The Irishman was the only driver to compete in the first five races associated with this historic series in American motorsport. This encompassed the Vanderbilt Cup in 1904–06 and the American Elimination Races in 1905 and 1906. The latter event was the qualifier to select the five drivers who could compete at the Vanderbilt, which was the biggest and most prestigious auto race in the United States at that time, until 1910. Tracy competed at these events alongside mechanician Al Poole and the pair's best finish in the Vanderbilt Cup was third in 1905, while they were victorious in the American Elimination Race in 1906.

That third-place finish in Long Island seemed unimaginable to Tracy the day before as the cylinders of his Locomobile had cracked, leading to him having to stay up the night before the showpiece to replace them. He was under such time constraints that his first time testing the new cylinders out was in the race itself. Amazingly they worked, and with Tracy not stopping for fuel he managed to achieve a notable result, not just personally but also for American automobiles as he finished behind two French drivers, showing that the United States could hold its own against its European counterparts. Such a publicity opportunity was not lost by the Locomobile company, based in Bridgeport, Connecticut, as they advertised the vehicle as 'The Greatest American Car'. This was matched similarly by its pricing range, with the cheapest model selling at $3,000 to $5,000 for the Model H. In today's money that is from over $94,000 to nearly $160,000.

The 1906 Elimination Race was held in September and was made up of ten laps around a 29.7-mile course. Tracy completed the race in five hours, twenty-seven minutes and forty-five seconds, more than twenty minutes ahead of his nearest competitors. The *Indianapolis News* noted that:

> Tracy attributes his victory to the excellency of the car, and to the fact that he practiced long and hard for the event, and was familiar with the course. Saturday's time was the fastest he has made over the course, no fast trials having been attempted by him previous to the day of the race.

However, there appears to have been an added incentive to Tracy's imperious driving that day as he continually ignored the Locomobile's owners' commands to slow down. This was due to him promising to marry a Miss Taylor if he won the race. The *Pittsburgh Press* carried the headline, 'Sweetheart Fainted as Her Fearless Lover Safely Piloted Locomobile Across Finish Line'.

Life After Racing: Daredevil in Love?

The year 1906 was to prove to be one of Tracy's last as a professional racer, with him retiring and becoming a consulting engineer in the automotive industry. Having qualified in such style, Tracy failed to place in the Vanderbilt Cup due to suffering eleven tyre faults. It was a pity as commentators estimated there were anywhere upwards of 500,000 spectators present at what could have been the Waterford man's finest moment. To add further intrigue and mystery to the story of Joe Tracy, the woman referred to as Miss Taylor was a pseudonym to protect the individual's true identity. Nearly ten years after the race, it was revealed that the Irishman had invented the name for Fannie Collins Coles, who was married to a wealthy New York broker.

It was claimed that her 'girlhood devotion' to the racer nicknamed 'Daredevil' continually irked her husband. Such stories attracted much attention as the general public lapped up stories of this lively figure.

From 1908, Tracy worked as a consulting engineer for the tyre-making company Diamond Rubber, where he was placed in charge of the racing department. A novel move, as it was the first time that a tyre company had hired an expert driver. It would prove to be lucrative too, leading to Tracy moving his testing plant, requiring more space due to increased demand for his expertise. Sadly, though, the same could not be said for his previous employer Locomobile, which fell into financial trouble in 1919 and was later purchased by William Durant (previously of General Motors). The financial crash of 1929 put paid to the company seeing another decade.

Driven to Win: An Icon Remembered

Even after retiring from professional racing, a story from 1946 demonstrates how the competitive impulse never left Joe Tracy, even into his dotage. The *Kingston Daily Freeman* reported that he took part in an automobile enthusiasts' celebration by competing in a race driving the same Locomobile from that 1906 victory. The white-haired Tracy donning his iconic goggles was aged 74 and he won the race, beating cars such as a 1916 Stutz and a 1912 Mercer. A pair of his racing goggles from around 1905 are housed in the Henry Ford Museum, forming part of their 'Driven to Win' exhibition celebrating racing in America.

Tracy died aged 86 on 20 March 1959.

11

Waterford's First Hurling Revival, 1884–1934

As Waterford reached the Munster final of both hurling and Gaelic football for the first time in the same year (1957), Thomas Drohan, a native of Ferrybank, noted that the footballers were the firm favourites, having defeated Kerry in the previous round. The hurlers were considered as the first to challenge the 1956 All-Ireland Champions, Wexford, by drawing with them in the National League. Since the staging of the first All-Ireland Championships in 1887, Waterford had claimed a solitary All-Ireland title, coming in hurling in 1948. Such scantiness of titles made Drohan surmise that the county was 'the Cinderella of Gaelic Games'. However, he would contend that, 'Despite Waterford's lowly position in the All-Ireland honours list … the Gaelic tradition of the County goes back a long way.'

'The Hurlers of Fahastogeen': Gaelic Games in the Eighteenth and Nineteenth Centuries

In the areas we know today as Barrack Street and Slievekeale, where Walsh Park is situated, was a stronghold of hurling in the early eighteenth and nineteenth centuries. This district was known as Fahastogeen. In local folklore, it is said that it was the hurlers of Fahastogeen who introduced hurling into the North American continent. Waterford's connection to Newfoundland by trade saw emigrants settle in the area. Drohan details that:

> Folk songs of the nineteenth century praise the 'hurlers of Fahastogeen … now on the banks of Newfoundland' … as the first men to strike a hurling ball on the American Continent were the Waterford Sailor-hurlers.

The hurling that would take place at upper Barrack Street on the 'good ould Faha fields' saw many matches, such as one recalled by Thomas Sexton between hurlers from Mothel against Kilbarry and 'the Stogeens' in which sixty men were stripped to the waist in an exhibition of the game.

In the county in 1826, during the election for the county seat, hurling and football matches helped attract and entertain crowds awaiting the arrival of speakers in an election that saw Lord Beresford lose his seat and the momentum of Catholic Emancipation accelerate. Prior to the Famine in the 1840s, hurling and football matches were regular occurrences throughout the county. In 1848, Thomas Francis Meagher had revived hurling in Ballytruckle in Waterford city, and it continued to survive. The games would take place with shouts of 'Ballytruckle abu!', to which their usual opponents, Ballybricken, would respond with a version of 'The White Cockade'. A similar revival attempt that was short-lived would take place in the city in 1865 when a group of Fenians made up of Cashman, Kent, Grennan, Walsh and Kenny tried to evoke the work of Meagher nearly twenty years earlier.

Tipperary vs Waterford: The Game that Changed Football

The county could also count an influence on the game of Gaelic football as we know it today. A match between Waterford (composed mostly of players from Rathgormack and Windgap) and Tipperary led the brothers Maurice and Pat Davin to devise the idea for remodelling the rules of the game. The Davins wanted to rid the 'old style' of thirty-four players aside, with wrestling the norm. The first match played under the new code was between the footballers of Callan and Kilkenny.

John Wyse Power: The Man who Gave the GAA its Name

Born at Knockhouse outside Waterford City in 1859, John Wyse Power attended Mount Sion School and is suggested to have 'put love of country before personal advancement' by his old schoolmate, Councillor McDonald of Waterford Corporation, upon his death in 1926. It seems Wyse Power's association with Edmund Rice's school foreshadows the strong hurling tradition of Mount Sion in Waterford, both school and club, the latter of which was founded in 1932.

A career in the British administration in Ireland was curtailed by his simmering nationalist sympathies (he was also a fluent Irish speaker), which led to a career in journalism and he became the editor of the *Leinster Leader* in 1883. Wyse Power was

Thomas Sexton, Irish Nationalist and Irish Parliamentary Party MP, 1880s.

Maurice Davin.

also being monitored by the British authorities for his connections to the Fenians and Irish Republican Brotherhood. Moreover, it is suggested that he could have become Chief Secretary of Ireland if not for the political career of William Edward Foster, known as 'Buckshot' for his apparent ordering of the police to fire on a crowd. Power was arrested and spent time in Naas Jail as one of 'Foster's Suspects'.

At Hayes Hotel in Thurles on 1 November 1884, Power was one of the participants in the founding of the GAA. Furthermore, his role as one of the first secretaries of the association can be deemed to have set strong foundations that are still felt so vibrantly in twenty-first-century Ireland. Perhaps his position and Waterford connection was one of the factors in Tramore hosting the first All-Ireland Championships three years later. His main interest was in the 'athletic' pursuits of the association, more so than hurling and Gaelic football. Though a fervent nationalist, Wyse Power would resign his role as an assistant secretary in 1887 as a result of the banning of RIC members from the GAA. However, his association with Gaelic games continued as the first Chairman of the Dublin County Board. Furthermore, he would receive similar treatment to that of Michael Cusack by James Joyce, also featuring in *Ulysses* as 'John Wyse Nolan'.

The GAA in Waterford, 1885

Eleven months after the establishment of the GAA (1884), the Waterford branch was inaugurated at the rooms of the Waterford Young Ireland Society (located at the end house on the right side on the corner where High Street leads into Henrietta Street) in October 1885. There had been much talk in the city of the new organisation, which led James Upton to note that 'in these interchanges of views and means for the forming of clubs, the drapers' and grocers' assistants of the city must get the fullest measure of credit for giving ... [the] GAA a habitation and a name in the old Suir-side city'. Two active members in the movement were the brothers William G. (who would act as Secretary of the County Board) and Harry Fisher, who used their newspapers, the *Evening Mail* and *Munster Express*, to promote the development of Gaelic games in Waterford. Meetings of the new Waterford GAA were held at J.P. Kenney's hostel on George's Street.

The early affiliated clubs (from 1885 to 1890) included Waterford Commercials, T.F. Meaghers (known as 'the Salters'), John Mitchell's (Ballytruckle), Thomas Sexton's (Ferrybank), Tim Healy's (Butlerstown), Joe Biggar's (Butlerstown's second team), David Gleeson's (Stradbally) as well as teams from Dungarvan, Ring, Ballinarod, Grange (Ardmore), Kilgobnet, Clodagh Campaigners (Rathgormack & Clonea), Windgap, Carrickbeg, Kilmolleran, Erin's Stars (Kilrossanty), Kill, Fews, Newtown, Fenor, Ballyduff (Lower), Ballyduff (Upper), William O'Brien's (Ballinamella), Ballinacourty, Ballylemon, Callaghan, Home Rulers (Nire), Portlaw, Carbally, Aglish, Dunmore, John O'Mahony Hurling Club, Slieve Gua. James Upton noted that:

> The old survivors of early generations of Waterfordians who knew something of the former prestige of Waterford County in hurling were amazed to find at the inception of the Gaelic Athletic Association that the premier national game of hurling was to all intense and purposes scarcely anything more than a fast fading tradition.

The preference for football saw Ballysaggart win the inaugural County Football Championship in 1885. In 1886, the Waterford County Board was finally established at Kilmacthomas. Waterford was one of only nine counties to compete in the first All-Ireland Football Championship, staged in 1887. The Déise were drawn against Louth, but as neither county had played their hurling championship, only the tie between their respective footballers was to take place.

West Waterford was noted for producing many hurleys of high quality and hurling balls, while in the city an old wheelwright's shop in Johnstown produced hurling sticks and Tom Kelly, a shoemaker on Ballybricken, made balls. Such was the decline of hurling in the county, in February 1888 the John O'Mahony Hurling Club were adjudged the county champions as they were the only club to enter the competition.

Although Waterford was late to the table compared to other counties, Drohan notes:

> The Executive of the Gaelic Athletic Association was pleased with the successful launching of Waterford City and County as an asset in the National revival, and marked its appreciation by allotting Waterford the outstanding distinction of holding the first Gaelic Athletic Championship meeting.

It took place in Tramore on 6 October 1885. Dan Fraher of Dungarvan was one of the notable athletes who won the 'standing jump' at 30ft 8in (as recorded by the *Waterford News*). Fraher was the winner of the 'hop, step and jump event'. Other noted Waterford players, such as in football, included Tom and Jim Nolan of Kilmeadan and Eddie Dee.

Monster Hurling and Football

The early Waterford Executive of the GAA tapped into the city and county's transport services of rail by having special trains arranged to transport supporters to tournaments held in the city and county. One such competition was a 'Monster Hurling and Football Tournament' held at Ballinaneeshagh on 20 November 1887. A special train was arranged from Clonmel, stopping at Kilsheelan, Carrick, Fiddown and Grange before arriving at Waterford. In addition, cities such as Waterford allowed pubs to open between 2 p.m. and 7 p.m. on Sunday, coupled with the stipulation that anyone who journeyed more than 3 miles from their home was entitled to be served in a pub. The proximity of the county to hurling strongholds such as Kilkenny, Tipperary and Cork, combined with a good rail service and the opportunity of a pint or two, made Waterford a very attractive location for matches.

Twelve years later, a similar tournament was held at the grounds of the Waterford Hurling Club based in Ballytruckle. It was in aid of raising funds for the rebuilding of the Christian Brothers Schools of Mount Sion in the city. A report from the *Munster Express* of the day's events is as follows:

> The afternoon was fine up to about four o'clock, with the result that something like a couple of thousand persons assembled to witness the sport. The local railways ran excursion trains to the city, and each carried a very large contingent. The hurling match between Thurles and Mooncoin might be looked upon as the event of the afternoon, as each is regarded as a crack team. The play, which was very fine, lasted for about 40 minutes, with the result that each had scored three goals and three points, but at this juncture unpleasantness began to manifest itself

amongst the players, with the result that the Thurles men left the field, when the match was awarded to Mooncoin. The football match between Clonmel and Vinegar Hill teams followed, but the best of the play all through rested with the Clonmel men, who had no difficulty in disposing of their opponents. The Two-Mile-Borris hardy team easily disposed of the Kilkenny Confederates, but still the play was very interesting for the hour. Taken altogether, the afternoon's sport was most enjoyable. The Barrack street Independent Brass Band played a selection of music during the afternoon.

The Gaelic Field in Dungarvan would stage tournaments that saw sides from Ballytruckle, Middleton, Shamrocks of Clonmel, Kilmacow, Shandon Rovers (Dungarvan) and Gracedieu compete. Such was the appreciation of the Gaelic Field at Shandon, it was used to host the tie between Cork and Kilkenny in the first All-Ireland Hurling Championship in 1887.

Ballytruckle Pioneer Hurling Club and America

In 1897, the Irish in America began preparations to mark the centenary of the Insurrection of 1798. They predicted that a quarter of a million visitors from Ireland would cross the Atlantic in celebrations that would include music, pageantry and sport. Gaelic games were high on the agenda of events, with teams and representatives from all over Ireland looking to take part in what was to be a major cultural event

Ballytruckle hurling team, 1897.

in the history of Irish America. In Waterford, John Garvey of Johnstown and James Moir organised a group of young men and held a meeting in Garvey's parlour. From the meeting they formed the Ballytruckle Hurling Club. Garvey allowed the players to use the field at the back of his shop for training purposes. The side's first game came against a Kilkenny outfit at Kilmacow, where they lost by a small margin. Sadly, events in America were cancelled due to the outbreak of the Spanish–American War. The Ballytruckle club continued for a few years after, but gradually died out with a lack of opposition to face in the city and county.

Erin's Hope: Munster Champions and 1898 All-Ireland Finalists

Although Ballytruckle would miss out on playing in America, the people of County Waterford had plenty to cheer. A club called Erin's Hope reached the final of the 1898 All-Ireland Championship, where they were pitted against Geraldines of Dublin. 'The Hopes' were the first Waterford side to claim provincial honours but missed out on ultimate glory when defeated by a score of 2–8 to 4 points. The team was made up of: J. Wall (captain), Michael Cullinane (vice captain), W. Meade, P. Meade, J. Meade, J. Nagle, James Nagle, J. Healy, P. Sullivan, J. Power, J. Kennedy, N. Noonan, J. Franklin, W. Brien, J. Begley, Declan Flynn and J. Foley.

Although the success that followed Erin's Hope was undoubted, it wasn't all plain sailing to begin with, as in 1895 they demanded £3 and twenty-five free tickets from the Cycling and Athletics Sports' Committee for the use of Captain Curran's field at Shandon. Curran denied the claim that the use of the field was only for the sport of Gaelic football, which led to the *Munster Express* opining of the Dungarvan outfit that 'as Gaels, and following Gaelic sports, they should forward rather than retard the promotion of sport'.

Dan Fraher and the West Awakes

By the early 1900s, Dan Fraher was President of the Waterford GAA and the county could count on nine football clubs and eight in hurling to number their championships. The study *The GAA: County by County* records that 'nobody came close to exercising the influence that Fraher had over the early GAA in Waterford'. The Dungarvan draper with his Gaelic Outfitting Store was a renowned athlete, administrator and was responsible for leasing Captain Curran's field and developing it into a sportsground now known as Fraher Field. The venue has staged more All-Ireland finals than any other outside of Croke Park. It hosted hurling finals in 1903, 1905, 1907 and 1911.

Although Gaelic games were developing in the city and county, Waterford's record at intercounty level left a lot to be desired. In 1888, Na Déise (Carrickbeg being the representatives) played its first Munster Championship match in hurling, losing to Cork (2–8 to no score) in a game held at the Gaelic Field in Dungarvan and refereed by D. Fraher. The following fourteen years were made up of walkovers and first-round defeats, as the county's drought for a win continued into the twentieth century. Waterford's victory came over Kerry in 1903 in hurling on a score line of 5–6 to 2–9, reaching their first Munster final (which took place in 1904) and losing to Cork. Their second hurling championship win would not be until 1925 when Waterford beat Clare to reach their second Munster final. Tipperary were the provincial victors, as the Gentle County remained the only one in Munster not to win an All-Ireland hurling title.

'Rank with the Best in the Country': Hurling Competitiveness in the 1930s

The 1930s would see an upturn in the county's fortunes, with the Waterford Minors winning an All-Ireland in 1929 and the Junior hurlers winning three titles in 1931, 1934 and 1936. Performances also improved at senior level as Waterford drew in the 1931 Munster final with Cork but later lost the replay by 15 points. Back-to-back (1933 and 1934) provincial deciders at the Cork Athletic Grounds against Limerick saw the county reach five Munster finals in ten campaigns (1925–34). *Rover* wrote, 'until the good old Gael from Dungarvan, Dan Fraher, set the West going, and after a few years the game came towards the East, with the result that Waterford hurlers of the present day rank with the best in the country'.

The game of hurling was finally revived in Waterford to a level that made the county competitive, leading it to the cusp of a provincial breakthrough and its first golden age in the GAA.

12

Patrick Street, Pugilism and Preaching: Stories of Arthur Clampett

Arthur G. Clampett and Waterford

Arthur G. Clampett was a well-known figure in Waterford city in the latter half of the nineteenth century. His father had a shoemaker's shop on Patrick Street and was sexton of St Patrick's Church. Arthur attended the Model School and began his professional career at the offices of R.W. Cherry, solicitor, at William Street. His employment there was brief, and when concluded he worked as a clerk to James Lorenzo Hickey, registrar of the Probate Court. Clampett then worked at the Post Office, where he befriended a group of Revivalists and, as was noted by the *Munster Express*, 'evinced a desire for reading the Bible and saying prayers for his brother employees during office hours, which they resented and he was compelled to leave'. His religious acquaintances helped him become a scripture reader, which he wearied of and finally left the city. Throughout his time in Waterford, he membered the choir of the Protestant cathedral.

Aside from his family and career, one of the few certainties we know about Clampett is that he saved a life in September 1876. A young boy named Maurice Reid of John's Hill was watching a dog swimming in the Pill by the park when he lost his footing and fell into the river. Clampett was on hand to rescue Reid from being carried away by the undercurrent. Intriguingly, the *Munster Express* remarks, 'Mr Clampett has risked his life on more than one occasion to draw persons from a watery grave.'

Arthur Clampett: The Myth?

We are not certain where Clampett went or what he did, but when he eventually returned to his hometown he did so as 'Lieutenant Clampett', although it was rumoured in local circles that he had enlisted as an officer's servant and was home on furlough. It appears that his friends bought him out from this service, and he was next seen singing in the Catholic cathedral in Tuam. Clampett is then believed to have joined an opera company and began performing under the name 'Signor Clampetti'. It seems he left Ireland for good in 1882, with his last-known whereabouts being Derry. As you can see from here, it's hard to sift fact from fiction as the rest of the tale permeates from a colourful character who appeared to revel in mischief-making. From his own words, Clampett had travelled the length and breadth of the globe. His noted achievements (by his own telling) were that he had won the swimming championship in New York, swam the Golden Gate in San Francisco and trained Charley Mitchell in his fight against Ned Cleary before arriving in New Zealand in around 1889.

George T. Sullivan: 'Converted Pugilist'

On arriving in Auckland, it appears that Clampett's theatrical opera experience came into play. Described as a 'good-looking, muscular young man, of something over 30 years of age', he represented himself to be the brother of the celebrated champion boxer John L. Sullivan. His story was that he himself was a pugilist who was drinking heavily and penniless when one night he witnessed some Revivalists conducting a mission. Once more the *Munster Express* details, 'he was called in by two gentlemen, and, after a couple of hymns had been sung, he was asked, "Do you believe?" and replied in the affirmative'. He then joined in singing hymns with his baritone voice, and demonstrated the speediness of his conversion by delivering a lecture on 'The New Birth'.

Clampett as George. T. Sullivan became something of a celebrity in New Zealand, as thousands came to hear him preach. After five successful months in Auckland, he went to Wellington and, after raising a considerable sum of money, eventually set up his own mission in Christchurch. Yet, the editor of the local *Telegraph* 'suspected that John L's younger brother was not all he appeared to be …'.

'This Ended the Impostor': The Truth Uncovered

Finally, in late 1890, the suspicions surrounding Clampett's deception were finally confirmed. There are two versions of how it unfolded. One in New Zealand is that he had a drink too many while being interviewed by a journalist, while the Waterford papers carry a more local detection. His photograph was seen in a shop window by a Miss M. Burns, who attended the same school as Clampett and knew him from singing in the choir of Christchurch. Burns had just arrived in New Zealand and upon seeing the picture exclaimed, 'Oh! There's Arthur Clampett'. She was informed that the image was of the converted pugilist George T. Sullivan. Word spread that Sullivan was actually the Irishman Arthur Clampett, which led to him departing for San Francisco in a hurry. It is believed that in nine months he made well over £1,000 from his preaching. Certainly a colourful figure, it's hard to differentiate between what is true and what is a flight of fancy, although we can confidently assume like the Irish and New Zealand papers that Arthur Clampett was 'the greatest religious impostor of the day'.

13

Dungarvan was his Hometown: Shaw Desmond (Author and Spiritualist)

Charles Nathaniel Lowe Shaw was born in Dungarvan on 19 January 1877 to James and Emma Shaw. James was the governor of the local prison, with his son Charles claiming the doubtful distinction of having been born in Dungarvan Jail (though the *Waterford News*, dated 20 December 1929, suggests James Shaw was the 'manager of the Gas Works there' in the Old Borough) and was a Methodist, though his son Charles was baptised in the Church of Ireland. Born to an Irish father and English mother, Shaw is believed to have been educated by the local Christian Brothers. Young Charles attended both the Methodist and Anglican churches, though a rebellious streak saw him leave school aged 15 to begin a business career in London. Retrospectively, it was self-proclaimed that by his early 20s he had become a secretary and director of several public companies in the English capital. In his semi-autobiographical work *Nathaniel* (1950), the protagonist's success in the 'get-rich-quick' financer firm of Alexander Jupiter O'Dowd is noted.

Such an apparent profile led him to contest an election to Westminster for the Battersea seat against the English trade unionist and Liberal Member of Parliament John Burns; the man more well known today for having coined the phrase 'the Thames is liquid history'. Unsuccessful in his campaign for election, Shaw returned to Ireland to take up farming. Furthermore, it is believed that during that time he sailed around Cape Horn in a windjammer, traversed 7,000 miles in Africa and boarded a trawler to the Arctic. Not much time for cultivating or harvesting there! After his spell in agriculture (and travelling), Shaw again ventured to London in 1911 to explore a career in journalism and literature, leading him to adopt the nom de plume 'Shaw Desmond'. Of this decision, the *Waterford News* commented:

Nowadays young authors seem not to prefer the blonde Saxon system of nomenclature: they 'fall for' an American cacophonous style. I suppose America is the spiritual home of the psycho-analysing sentimentalist.

His work can be found in many leading European newspapers and periodicals of the time. Subjects he looked at included the opportunity for Labour to capitalise if Irish Home Rule was passed and the decline in English athleticism to the Ulster Question and the decline of oratory skills in the political arena.

In the same year as he returned to London, Shaw married the Danish writer Karen Ewald in London, and the pair later moved to Copenhagen. They would have two children together (both of whom were born in Dublin), a boy and a girl, although the boy tragically died aged 10. After a prolific period writing for the *New York Herald*, Shaw published his book *The Drama of Sinn Féin*, which the *Irish Independent* described as 'a record of Easter Week in the style of Carlyle's "French Revolution"', which received a mixed response in 1923. Nevertheless, he continued to publish novels. Shaw even wrote a film script entitled *The Mountains of Mourne* about Ireland of yesteryear. It was to be set during the Land War, while the film would pivot around a heroine who was left homeless after being evicted from her property. It was planned for the 'talkie' to be filmed in County Down and New York, with Herbert Wilcox serving as producer.

A lecture given by Shaw to the Irish Literary Society in 1932 entitled 'The Irish Fairy in Literature and Life' saw him detail that when he was a child in Dungarvan, he heard a banshee. Yet, this wasn't his only experience with such 'extra-human' creatures, as he saw a fairy in Richmond Park (Surrey) in 1928. Shaw noted the abundance of testimony he had gathered as far away as America on the subject. Twelve months after his talk, Shaw stayed with friends on a visit to his native Dungarvan. He met his good friend Tommy O'Mahony (Bridge Street) and spent many evenings and nights fishing on the Colligan together. While there, he gave a lecture in the Town Hall on Friday, 22 September 1933, speaking of his writings on Arthur Griffith, Michael Collins and Sinn Féin, his journeys in Africa and meeting Zulus, and finishing with the advice that in any future war (with poison gas being the decisive factor) Ireland should keep out of it. The purpose of the lecture was to raise funds for local charities.

This was followed by a lecture at Ulster Hall, Belfast on Tuesday, 28 November on the subject 'You can speak with your dead', Shaw having made an exhaustive study in relation to the claims of Spiritualism and coming to the conclusion that communication between the living and the dead was a reality. Shaw Desmond believed the three questions that concerned the dead were 'whence, why and whither?' The Dungarvan native detailed how he had communicated with the 'so-called dead' and believed that 'Man would never die'. He stated that death was the necessary entrance into another world.

River Colligan, Dungarvan.

In 1934, Shaw Desmond and Mrs Dawson Scott co-founded the International Institute for Psychical Research, which investigated and published papers on alleged psychic phenomena, using photographic and sound recording to investigate such incidences. The council of the institute was made up of both believers and non-believers in spiritualism as a means of guaranteeing impartiality (although if you didn't believe, would you really join such an organisation in the first place?). Five years later, the institute merged with the British College of Psychic Science to become the International Institute for Psychic Investigation, which operated until it was disbanded in 1947.

During this time, Shaw continued to write and published the book *Chaos* in 1938, which prophesised what would happen to Europe if war unfolded in the 1940s. Such forecasts included 'enemy planes – conical shells, smooth and polished without wings' trying to penetrate 'a spider's web of electrified defence wires suspended balloons over London ...' It was described as a grim novel of the future. Post-war, Shaw Desmond believed that no major government would ever use the atom bomb again as he believed countries were developing 'effective, but cheaper and quicker in production' weapons.

Over the course of his writing career, Shaw Desmond published seventy-five books. He frequently lectured around Britain and Ireland and told stories of conversations with Arthur Griffith, Cathal Brugha and Darrell Figgis and of meeting international figures such as Pope Pius XI, Adolf Hitler, Benito Mussolini and Count Ciano.

In his later years, Shaw noted his recreations as including 'ju-jitsu, dancing, cricket and tennis' and that on his 82nd birthday he was 'a crazy dancer'. Shaw Desmond obtained a black belt in ju-jitsu in late 1937 and had previously met the sport's World Champion, Nageika of Tokyo on the mat. Every day he did yoga exercises, 10-mile walks and spent a good deal of time yachting. Even into his mid-70s, Shaw stated that he continued to swim the Thames, even in the cool of January. Another passion of his was collecting folk songs and stories across Ireland, which, in collaboration with Ella Young, were published in the United States. Upon his death in Twickenham in 1960, aged 83, Shaw remembered his hometown of Dungarvan in his will, which read:

> ... in my native and beloved Ireland in recognition of the four years I spent there [at the Monastery of the Christian Brothers, Dungarvan, Co. Waterford] as a pupil a copy of each of the following seven of my published books for their library, 'Windjammer', 'African Log', 'The Edwardian Story', 'The Story of Sinn Fein', 'Personality and Power', 'London Pride' and 'Life and Foster Freeman'.

The story of a life less ordinary, which certainly poses more questions about the validity of the testimony of the man concerned. His tales of the great and influential of London and Dublin to conversations with figures on the international stage was matched by a prolific career in journalism and writing. It was a long way from young Charles' early days by the River Colligan, but the man who became Shaw Desmond never forgot that it was Dungarvan from whence he came.

14

To the Waterford Coast and Along it: Arthur Ignatius Conan Doyle (1859–1930)

Arthur Ignatius Conan Doyle was a Hibernian Scot who was born in Edinburgh in 1859. Doyle would proceed to create the Sherlock Holmes character over the course of four novels and fifty-six short stories, and is widely regarded as the pioneer of crime fiction as we know it today. Of his Irish connections, Conan Doyle noted in his memoir entitled *Memories and Adventures* (1924), that, 'I, an Irishman by extraction was born in the Scottish capital after two separate lines of Irish wanderers came together under one roof'.

Arthur's grandfather was John Doyle, who was born in Dublin around 1797. He was from a wealthy Irish Catholic family who moved to England because of the Penal Laws. He wrote political cartoons and caricatures under the name H.B. John's son Charles Altamont Doyle was an illustrator and watercolourist, and Charles' brother Dicky designed the covers of *Punch*. Charles Altamont, the father of Arthur Conan Doyle, moved to Edinburgh in 1849 to work for the Scottish Office of Works. He became disillusioned with this and eventually became an alcoholic, which ultimately led to him being institutionalised. There has been much more written and commented on the paternal side of the Sherlock Holmes author's family compared to his mother's lineage.

The Foleys of Lismore, Co. Waterford

In earlier and much happier times Charles was a lodger in the home of Kilkenny woman Mrs Catherine Foley (née Pack, a widow, her husband was William Foley, a medical doctor from Lismore, Co. Waterford, who died in Clonmel 1841 around 37 years of age) and went on to marry her daughter Mary on 31 July 1855.

Mary Foley was born on 8 July 1837 and came from Glencarin, Lismore in County Waterford. The Foley family had a long association with Lismore with Conan Doyle's great-grandfather, Thomas Foley, appointed as an agent for the estate of the Duke of Devonshire by the River Blackwater in 1748. They have been described by the author Andrew Lycett as 'essentially upwardly mobile creatures of the Waterford soil'. The family's wealth derived from having the rights to fish on 11 miles of the river, which contained the best salmon in Ireland. 'Black Tom' Foley, as he was known, had a ruthless streak when maintaining order, and with his son Patrick killed a member of the agrarian agitator group the Whiteboys in the latter part of the century.

Patrick's half-brother was Thomas Foley, who became a lawyer and lived comfortably at Tourtane, Lismore, Co. Waterford. Thomas's second wife, Hannah Lowe from Cardiff, gave birth to William Foley (Conan Doyle's grandfather), who attended Trinity College Dublin in 1825, where he is recorded as being a Roman Catholic. An unambitious doctor, he married Catherine Pack of Kilkenny in 1835, with her family forming part of the Anglo-Irish establishment there. For love, Catherine converted to the faith of her husband.

'An Ideal Mother for a Literary Man': Mary Foley Doyle and her Son Arthur

After her husband died, Catherine taught in Edinburgh and started a governess placement service. To supplement her income, she took on boarders such as Charles Altamont. After marrying the daughter of his landlady, they started a family. Arthur was the couple's third child, but their first son. The *Irish Press*'s Tom O'Dea wrote that Mary Foley Doyle 'was an ideal mother for a literary man. Cultivated and sensitive, she developed her eldest son's taste for reading and the art of self-expression while he was still very young'. She took care of her son and brought him to visit her homeland on numerous occasions, including visits to Ballygally near Glencarin and Ballylin on the other side of the River Blackwater. The splendid environs of west Waterford would be the setting for his hunting, shooting and riverside pursuits.

Jess Faraday writes that, 'Mary was well-educated, and herself a gifted storyteller.' Arthur described his mother as 'the quaintest mixture of the housewife and the woman of letters, with the high-bred spirited lady as a basis for either character'. Her storytelling talent was accentuated by her ability of 'sinking her voice to a horror-stricken whisper' at the climax of her tales of intrigue. Conan Doyle tried to emulate these vivid stories when he devised his own dreams and narratives. The poverty the Doyle family endured in Edinburgh was offered brief reprieves with holidays at Ballygally, paid for by the Foleys based there, who would then support the young Arthur's education.

Doyle: Lismore Cricketer?

Even as an adult, Conan Doyle continued to visit his mother's home county, visiting Lismore in 1881 during the early years of the Land War. The Parochial House on the South Mall in Lismore is believed to have been where he stayed.

While there he played cricket for the Lismore club against the 25th Regiment on 1 July, scoring 3 runs and taking 2 wickets in a rather unremarkable display. At a social event at Ballylin Gardens, Lismore, he met Miss Elmo Weldon, who became his first serious girlfriend. Weldon was staying at her relation's property in Bellevue. It appeared to be a real summer of love for Conan Doyle, as he described Weldon as 'such a beauty', but claimed to have his eye on marrying two or three other women while in Ireland.

One of Conan Doyle's visits formed the basis of his semi-autobiographical photographic essay entitled 'To the Waterford Coast and Along it', published by the *British Journal of Photography* in 1883. Another notable composition of his inspired by Lismore was his short story called 'The Heiress of Glenmahowley' (which was first published in 1884). But our attention turns to his travelogue along the Waterford coast.

'To the Waterford Coast and Along it': 1883 Travelogue

Conan Doyle boarded the *Rathlin* in Dublin to journey along the east coast before turning to enter the mouth of Waterford Harbour. The journey got off to a rather ignominious start when the vessel was impeded by a mud bank, which delayed the voyage by three hours. Travelling overnight, the vessel reached Duncannon by six in the morning and made its way up the River Suir towards Waterford city, which of its first viewing Conan Doyle remarked, 'A sudden bend of the river brought us right up to the town – a long, thin straggling line of grey houses with a few steeples here and there, and a sprinkling of shipping in the river in front of it, the whole giving rather an impression of decay.' As he and his travel companion settled into their hotel, they rambled around Ireland's oldest city and were shown the spot where 'some English conqueror had landed' but it couldn't be clarified whether it was 'Cromwell or Richard Strongbow' who was the figure in question, although the guide seemed to intimate they were one of the same person.

Next on their tour of the city, they were shown a hypothetical site of where the first potato planted in Irish soil was supposed to have been placed by Sir Walter Raleigh (although numerous locations boast the same feat, with Youghal being another and probably the most famous).

After one night spent in Waterford, they made their way to Youghal by rail. Noting of the east Cork town, 'Here the Blackwater river opens out into a considerable estuary, which in turn opens out into the Irish Sea. The town itself is a quaint, old-fashioned place, with an amphibious population who live principally by fishing for the salmon as they try to ascend the Blackwater, and capturing them in long drift-nets.'

There Conan Doyle met the cousin of his friend Smith, whose yacht was waiting in order to show them views of Youghal. After returning to land they made their way to a local concert, where the song 'Buckshot Forster' appeared to be the most popular tune of the day. They stayed in the Crown Hotel and the following day attempted to traverse between the fishing trawlers to get some images of the coast, although the choppy sea made photography virtually impossible. After collecting a great haul ranging from hake to molluscs, their attention turned back to photography. They ventured closer to shore where the water was calmer and went around the rocky point north of Youghal and eventually reached the bay of Ardmore. They cast anchor and went ashore in a dinghy.

Conan Doyle described Ardmore as 'a primitive village which has stood where it stands now for at least two thousand years without apparently altering very much one way or the other'. He noted the white cottages but was most taken by the iconic round tower of the area. In his article he wrote, 'Behind the village there is the most perfect specimen in Ireland of that mysterious edifice known as the round tower. This one was about 70ft high, built very much like a modern lighthouse. Though its erection is entirely pre-historic, the mortar between the stones is as firm now as ever, and the stones themselves do not show the least symptoms of decay.'

Ardmore is believed to be the oldest Christian settlement in Ireland. According to tradition, Saint Declan lived in the region in the early fifth century and Christianised the area before the coming of Saint Patrick.

After some dinner, they went to visit the 'black stone of Ardmore', which was believed to provide many cures from touching it or crawling through the hole in it. That night they stayed on their yacht in Ardmore Bay and had initially planned to make their way to Queenstown for Ramsay and Smith (two of his three travel companions on the journey) to make their way back to Scotland to settle a business matter. Conan Doyle with his friend Cunningham were invited by the captain of the yacht to come along the Blackwater with them. Like the great novelist he was, Conan Doyle decided to keep what they saw and visited there for another paper. He concluded, 'suffice it that the short excursion along the Waterford coast was a thoroughly enjoyable one, and that our only grief was that it should have been so curtailed'.

Conan Doyle never hid his Irish lineage. In a response to Edmund Downey, the editor of the *Waterford News*, in 1914, he noted on a postcard sent from his home in Sussex that his relations were 'Foleys of Ballygally near Lismore'. The original postcard is part of the collection of Waterford County Museum in Dungarvan.

15

'The Palm of Superiority': Handball in Waterford, 1887–1911

Gaelic handball was once deemed the most Irish of sports, as it was popularly played across the island in the sixteenth century. Over the centuries, it was used as a means of training by pugilists, because of the practising of hand-eye co-ordination and endurance. Handball came to renewed prominence in Irish society with the formation and promotion of the sport by the GAA. However, like all movements, there would be teething issues as hurling and Gaelic football came to the forefront of this organisation. The seaside town of Tramore was regarded as occupying 'a position second to none in Ireland as regarded handball playing'. Having a fine court, it was hoped the facility would help cultivate a champion handball team in the county. The game would capture the public imagination in 1887, when the American Champion Phil Casey (born at Mountrath, residing in Brooklyn) defeated the Irish Champion John Lawlor (Dublin) to become the World Champion.

The twilight of the 1880s saw Carrick-on-Suir lead the way in staging handball contests as they played teams from Owning, Waterford and Youghal. One of the games of 1888 was staged at the ball alley in Spring Garden Alley in Waterford, between Shea and Cuddihy (Carrick-on-Suir) and Treacy and Coughlan (Youghal). It was seen as the contest to act as the springboard for resurrecting the game in Ireland's oldest city. The ball alley was built by the Goggin family, with Thomas Neary the last tenant. Neary was born on Spring Garden Alley, and came to prominence by defeating Irish Champion John J. Bowles (Limerick) in the early 1900s. As the family looked after the ball alley, Tom worked as a gas fitter. Other career roles included working in the British Prison Service, on the staff of Waterford Post Office, and even running as a candidate for Waterford Corporation. He died aged 70 in May 1951. The

Neary family played in the ball alley, which was subsequently described as 'one of the oldest recreation grounds in Waterford' by Ald. Jones in 1933.

Such was its popularity, the *Munster Express* noted that:

> ... it was the most popular game played in Ireland, and in no part of the country did better men strip than in Carrick-on-Suir, Kilkenny city, Waterford city. During the year county contests for the palm of superiority in the art of play were looked forward to for weeks before the events came off so great was the rivalry that centred in them; indeed, the local racquet court in Spring Garden Alley and the fine Tramore alley were thronged to excess and at stiffish prices to witness play.

The new decade saw American Champion players such as Casey, Bernard McQuade (undisputed Champion of New York), John Dunne, Eddie Moran, Philip Smith (former Champion of St Louis), Richard Cronin and Michael Gillen tour Ireland, including playing exhibitions at Waterford. Sadly, by 1896 the playing of racquets or handball at Spring Garden Alley were near extinction as they were so rarely played in an area that looked initially to form a hotbed for its pursuit. The local alley was almost deserted all week round. It appeared the only area in the south-east of Ireland where handball was kept alive was at Piltown through the efforts of James Anthony.

There was a revival of the sport in Waterford in 1899, where the court measured 76ft in depth and 26ft in width as the sport deserved 'from an athletic stand-point a much higher position'. Ironically, this came at a time when, upon the expiration of the alley's lease, Mr Dobbyn sought to turn it into backyards for some of the houses adjoining. For thirty years, the Neary family (who were the tenants of the handball alley) remained undefeated at that court in Spring Garden Alley. Another two players leading the effort were John and Michael Regan. A match was planned for Sunday, 13 August between Waterford and neighbouring Mullinavat, with Thomas Neary and James Regan in the city, competing against R. Walsh and P. Veale. The tie was the best of five games, as the Kilkenny pair won 3–2. Three of the games finished 21–20 (two to Kilkenny, and one to Waterford). After the match (which was well attended), Tom Neary requested to play any man in Carrick-on-Suir. However, his sights were firmly set on meeting Cuddihy, who was regarded as one of the best ball players in the district.

Later that summer, the promotion of handball in the city saw the *Evening News* (Waterford) detail:

> Handball is one of the oldest of games. It is probably what may be called an essentially Irish game, for the reason that two hundred years ago, or more, it was played in this country, when they only had turf to play upon.

'The Palm of Superiority': Handball in Waterford, 1887–1911

As game play had evolved from smashing the ball against the main wall awaiting the return to more subtlety, the sport was being extolled as the best kind of exercise for developing muscles. It was a staple addition to training for pugilists, working on the muscles of the chest and encouraging proficiency in both hands. The advocacy of the sport by 'Gentleman Jim' Corbett provided the impetus to increase its popularity in the Victorian era.

Unfortunately, one of the barriers to handball in Ireland was the uncertainty concerning the weather. Waterford had planned to visit Mullinavat on 6 August 1899, but the game was called off as heavy rain had broken up the handball alley's floor. One of the most well-known proponents of the sport on Suirside was the 'cycling policeman', Constable Torsney, who had taken up the sport and had a successful season. He was no match for the pair of Patrick and Thomas Neary, who were the 'Champions of Waterford'. The following year, Thomas issued a challenge to play any man in Waterford City or County, for the best five out of nine games, from £1 to £5 aside.

The sport would receive negative publicity, such as at the Portlaw Petty Sessions in January 1900, when Constable Finnigan summoned Cornelius McGrath, George Heffernan, Nicholas Connors and Edward Wall on a charge of 'ball-playing [handball] on that part of Portlaw adjoining Mrs Harney's Hotel'. They were each fined 1*d*, with 1*s* 6*d* in costs. If the group persevered in playing handball, they were told by the Chairman of the Sessions, W. Malcolmson, that they would be dealt with most severely. While Mullinavat staged a handball tournament for local youths on St Patrick's Day 1901, further reports of 'nuisances' surrounding the sport would be reported in Carrick-on-Suir, Kilmacthomas and Waterford city in the years to come.

In April 1901, Mullinavat defeated Waterford 3–2 at the Racquet Court at Spring Garden Alley in Waterford. Patrick Clarke and Joe Marmion defeated the brothers Neary. The game, officiated by Sergeant Eager (RIC), was described by the *Evening News*, 'The play on both sides was fast and scientific, and the keenest interest was taken in it by the spectators, who mustered a big crowd.' A month later, Thomas Neary (Waterford) beat Joseph Marmion (Dublin) 3–2 in a match-up that received attention from across the island. The referee was Mr McGuire (Strokestown, Co. Roscommon), with Patrick Clarke as stakeholder and James Barron serving as marker. Not to be outdone, a strong rivalry developed between Kilmacthomas and Kilrossanty in the sport, with the pair deciding to have contests at neutral grounds such as Clonea. A year later, Cappoquin sought to cultivate the playing of handball with demonstrations and workshops on the art of the sport.

The purses for games continued to increase, such as James and Patrick Neary (representing Waterford) facing James Aldridge and Michael McSweeney (Kilkenny) at the Kilkenny Handball Court in 1903, with a stake of £10 and two silver medals up for grabs. It was proving to be a rather lucrative pursuit if one was proficient at the sport. A 1903 Double Handed Championship of Ireland was claimed by Thomas and James Neary, who defeated the Limerick pair John J. Bowles and John Brown (incidentally an Irish Champion) as they won five games in a row. Such games would see a discussion about the development of an open draw All-Ireland Championship, which would take place in 1904. The Neary family continued to spread the game by playing an exhibition game at the Tramore Racquet Court on Sunday, 23 October 1904. The venue was to hold a championship contest the following month, but this was cancelled due to inclement weather.

The key to the transformed interest in handball was the effort and success of Corkman Oliver Drew in claiming the Irish Championship, and travelling to meet figures such as Ordozgoitis, the French and Spanish Champion. They faced one another in New Jersey on 12 January 1905, with a purse of £100 aside. Drew defeated the Spaniard 4–2 in the best of seven series. Meanwhile, in County Waterford, players such as John McQueal and Joseph Torpey (both Tramore) challenged the city pair of Patrick Neary and John Power for the right of being deemed the best players in the Gentle County. In June 1905, a handball match at the ball alley attached to the Military Barracks saw William Ryan (Emmett's Place and former Champion of India) compete against two soldiers, whom he outclassed.

As the first decade of the twentieth century progressed, De La Salle College would further enhance the game, with players such as M. O'Doherty and P. Fogarty taking on figures like P. Mordaunt and James Walsh. The college also boasted individuals such as William Regan and James Carroll, who would lead to Spring Garden Alley again attracting enthusiastic spectators to watch handball. Westwards, Lismore would get caught up in the craze, leading to a group of young men seeking to renovate the old ball court at Church Street. A meeting presided over by Waterford County Council Chairman Patrick O'Gorman saw a subscription list created, which raised £3 10s. This would be supplemented by a town collection on Monday, 29 June 1908.

The rather unformal arrangement of the sport in Ireland would come to an end in November 1911. The *Kilkenny Journal* reported that:

> The handball game continues to attract increasing numbers in Tipperary in connection with other counties, and at the forthcoming convention for the southern Division, a motion will be on the agenda urging the necessity of at once starting a county handball championship, and there is every reason to believe that the motion will meet with the unanimous approval of Gaels concerned. Handball is one of the oldest and most efficient forms of exercise in Ireland, and it is regrettable to find that the Association cannot be induced to take anything beyond a very passive interest in popularising it in the manner it deserves. At the All-Ireland Convention Mr Walter Hanrahan proposed a number of well thought out rules to further facilitate the game; the rules were adopted, but we want more than that, we want the Association

to work the game into the same popularity as hurling and football have attained under the G.A.A. code, and if the Association cannot see its way to do so, then let us have county and provincial handball committee established under the G.A.A. auspices, who would have control of the game and formation of county, provincial, and All-Ireland Championships annually.

Handball would follow another direction after a solid decade of growth in County Waterford and across the country.

Sadly, in 1933, Thomas Neary was served a notice to quit the ball alley at Spring Garden by Waterford Corporation for no apparent reason. Locally, Ald. Jones felt that this closure was due to 'not spirit enough among the Gaels of Waterford to preserve the Alley for the ancient game of handball that Waterford men in the past had distinguished themselves throughout Ireland with their prowess at the game'. However, John J. Neary felt that Irish games were 'wasted on the patriotic members of Waterford Corporation'. J.J. Neary was noted as the man who 'tells the world about Waterford', serving as the curator of Reginald's Tower from the mid-1950s. Previously, he had worked for Waterford and London County Councils, and was noted as a handball exponent and boxing enthusiast.

Reginald's Tower, c.1900.

Heavyweight Boxing: Champion of the World Visits Waterford, December 1887

The last bare-knuckle boxing Champion of the World was Irish-American John L. Sullivan. He formed the link between the old style and modern boxing under the Queensberry Rules. While still Heavyweight Champion of the World, Sullivan toured Ireland in 1887. On Tuesday, 13 December 1887, he departed Dublin for Waterford on the nine o'clock train. At each stop on the journey he received a warm reception, and it is believed that he had time to visit Donnelly's Hollow, a natural amphitheatre in County Kildare where Dan Donnelly defeated Englishman George Cooper in 1815.

Hundreds gathered along the Quay to get a glimpse of the 'Boston Strong Boy' as he made his way to the Imperial Hotel (now the Tower Hotel). That evening, Sullivan sparred with his sidekick Jack Ashton in an exhibition at the Theatre Royal. The *Freeman's Journal* noted that 'whilst the men were on stage the spectators seemed to be simply spellbound'. After the sparring session, Sullivan told the crowd that his trip across the Atlantic had originally been to allow him to fight the English Champion Jem Smith, but now he had to settle for a bout with Charlie Mitchell, though he remarked to the crowd that it didn't matter who he fought. Sullivan was to leave Waterford for Cork the next day to fight local amateur Frank Creedon.

The Quay, once termed by historian Mark Girouard as 'the noblest quay in Europe'.

17

Jack Mitchell: 'The Man with the Plate in his Head'

Waterford watchmaker John Mitchell and his wife Lizzie welcomed the birth of their baby boy Jack on 16 November 1889 at Manor Street, which leads you to the gateway of the old city walls built by the Anglo-Normans. Young Jack attended the Protestant Bishop Foy's School in the townland of Grantstown as his family lived in Bath Street (just off the east side of the street where he was born). The road was named after baths established there around 1819, which had become a fine terrace by the time Mitchell turned 10. It appears that Mitchell was a boarder in the 'Blue School', which had a proud sporting tradition until its closure in 1967. One such student was Dungarvan's George Henry Cooke, who played cricket and rugby for the school before joining the Indian Civil Service.

Around 1906 the 'Bould Jack', as he was known in his youth, joined the British Army and initially served as a member of the Flying Corps. In the early years of the First World War, Mitchell was a sergeant in the Irish Guards and was promoted to second lieutenant. A flying accident in 1915 saw him needing a steel plate inserted into his head and he was considered unfit for flying. Local lore has it that Mitchell fell out of the plane and landed in a tree by a one in a million chance. One imagines that in relation to his soccer pursuits, this hidden steel made the army man a tough opponent on the playing fields. I, for one, wouldn't fancy going up for a header against him.

A year after his near-death experience, the Waterford man was made a captain in the Royal Artillery. It was this military title that he would be known by in his native city: The Captain. Mitchell was awarded the Military Cross for 'conspicuous gallantry' at the Battle of Shaik Saad in Mesopotamia in 1916, and after he received the MC he departedfor duty in Cairo for five years, returning to Waterford around 1923.

Mitchell wasn't just confined to his military career while in England. As a centre-half, the Waterford man played for Reading and Leicester (it appears that his competitive appearances for both teams are in the single digits), while he could be counted on as an opening batsman for Hampshire County Cricket Club. Mitchell's other sporting endeavours included rugby and cricket, which he played and coached during his lifetime, such as at Newtown School. While in Cairo, he managed to become Squash Champion of Egypt for three years in succession.

When he returned to Waterford, he was a member of the first committee of the Waterford and District Junior League in 1924 and membered the squad of O'Connell Celtic, who were by far the strongest team in the early years of the Junior League. A large part of that side's success was down to the ability of Tommy Arrigan, who later captained Waterford FC to their first Free State Cup victory in 1937 over St James's Gate. That entity, joined by leading players of rival teams in the locality, became Waterford Celtic, who entered the Munster Senior League. It is an important club in the history of the city by the River Suir in not only playing senior football but signing cross-channel professionals such as left-full Billy Hoss and inside left Davy Haywood. Another star was the centre forward Jack Doran, who served in the 17th Middlesex Regiment (1st Football Battalion) and who previously played for Newcastle United, Norwich City, Brighton and Hove Albion and Manchester City. The early 1920s saw Doran receive three caps for Ireland. Around the mid-1920s, Mitchell was officiating soccer and rugby matches and captained Grantstown cricket XI. In July 1927, he scored 84, his highest total for the season. He was described by Leo Dunne as a 'polished bat[tter] and superb fielder'.

Celtic developed into Waterford FC and entered the League of Ireland in 1930, with Mitchell lining out for the Blues' first game in the league at Kilcohan on 2 November with the home side losing 3–1. Mitchell maintained strong connections as a trainer and secretary for the club. Local papers often carry reports of Mitchell playing full-back in a rugby match and refereeing a soccer match on the same weekend. One of the notable fixtures that he was tasked with overseeing was a Free State Shield tie between Cork and Drumcondra at the Mardyke in October 1935. Cork supporters attacked the referee, who had to be escorted to a pavilion by Civic Guards 'amid a shower of sticks and stones'. One imagines that after surviving the atrocities of the First World War, Mitchell was more than able to cope with Leesiders lobbing missiles.

Mitchell passed on his enthusiasm for sporting endeavours to his children (particularly hockey). Unusually, Mitchell defeated his own son John in the final of the annual billiards handicap at the Waterford YMCA Hall in May 1949 by a score of 150 to 102. His later years were spent in Sallypark, also known as 'the town which disappeared' as the railway industry declined over the course of the twentieth century. Mitchell died in early March 1966 aged 76.

18

'*Urbs Intacta* was Supposed to be at Stake': Oxford and the Waterford City Regatta, 15 July 1890

On Tuesday, 15 July 1890, the renowned Oxford and Liverpool (Mersey Club) crews were scheduled to compete against All-Ireland with notice of numerous entries promised from Clonmel, Dublin, Limerick and New Ross in a regatta on the River Suir. The events were going to be accompanied by music from the Band of the Manchester Regiment playing from the grandstand of the Waterford Boat Club. All the action was to be followed by a dinner at City Hall on the Mall, with tickets costing 10*s* each. It was the most eagerly anticipated event in the history of Irish rowing, as the Waterford City Regatta was about to play host to several high-calibre teams that would compete against one another in exciting races. Previewing the excitement, the *Waterford Mirror & Tramore Visitor* noted:

> … some of the crews are famous. An unprecedent fact is that of two English crews having entered, viz: Oxford and Mersey (Liverpool). The former is, of course, world-famed as the cradle of rowing, and the crew which will compete at Waterford, will probably, be a carefully selected one.

It was considered the first occasion on which a crew from Oxford competed in Ireland, although the best teams on the island of Ireland were to be equally well represented with Dublin University sending several crews as the hotly anticipated race for the senior fours being described as 'a ding-dong one' on a day filled with many attractions. Nevertheless, there was pragmatism about how Waterford representatives would get on against high-calibre opponents, although that didn't rule out hope, with the *Waterford Chronicle* concluding, 'However, on their own [Waterford rowers] water the blue with white hoop will make a great race, and it will take a "nailing" crew to beat them.'

'An Occurrence of Peculiar Moment …': Oxford University Boat Club in Waterford City

The appearance of the Oxford crew led the *Standard* to pronounce of the Waterford Regatta:

> Within modern times it was always an event of importance in the rounds of amusements of the season, but this year it was regarded as an occurrence of peculiar moment, in which the reputation of the oarsmen of *Urbs Intacta* was supposed to be at stake.

Hospitality was provided for the Oxford crew and several of the boat club men, who were entertained and housed at the residence of Mr Richard Hassard at Rockenham. He was the son of Michael Dobbyn Hassard of Glenville, who had represented Waterford City in the Imperial Parliament at Westminster. Richard had previously membered several of the Dublin University clubs and lived just outside the city centre in Ferrybank. Richard practised as a solicitor in Waterford, but died at the young age of 33 in late 1892 as a result of contracting typhoid fever. However, the *Waterford Standard* reported that the Oxford men were the guests of Charles E. Denny at his residence in May Park. The rest of the crews stayed at the Adelphi Hotel, which overlooked the course on the Suir for the day's races.

Such was the anticipation, many watched the crews' final exercises that Monday evening before the day's competitive rowing when the numbers of spectators were increased due to trains (which the *Standard* evocatively described as 'iron horses') bringing many visitors to the city to witness the day's events. Many businesses in the city decided to give employees an afternoon off, with the *Standard* reporting 'from one to two o'clock there was a partial suspension of commercial transactions, thus letting free a considerable number whose energies for the rest of the day were directed to securing the best view of the races'. Crowds lined the quayside from the Milford hulks as far as past the Market House. For those few hours on that July day, the atmosphere would rival the crackling anticipation of the world's great sporting arenas, from the Circus Maximus in Ancient Rome to the banks of the River Thames on boat race day.

'A Rare Combination …':
The River Suir, Sunrays and Soaking Rain

The *Waterford Chronicle* report of proceedings opened with the following:

> And Waterford, as it appeared to me from the boat, which was floating me across from the ferry steps, under the welcome effulgence of that returned prodigal, the Sun, and on a magnificent tide which exhibited to striking advantage the splendid stretch of the Waterford Course, and as if inviting people to come forth and make the most of such a rare combination of the elements.

Despite such idyllic conditions, it wasn't long before the rain arrived in flourishes and eventually there was a torrential downpour for the rest of the regatta, which saw many of the women in attendance depart as they were dressed in 'summer costumes' that were not practical for the lashing precipitation that had engulfed that summer's day. The Manchester Regiment's band played at the boat house as a precursor to a local amateur band playing at the Mall later that evening. The Waterford Boat Club's grandstand was decorated with many flags, which was matched by bunting on many vessels anchored at the port. However, not everything was as serene – there was no rest for the ferry, which was nearly brought to a point of complete exhaustion. This was partially due to the ferry boat not being fit to cater for such huge volumes, with one local paper suggesting it was of antediluvian origin. Thus, in evoking Genesis, it seemed appropriate that the day's racing was drenched by such torrid rain and a west to south-westerly wind blowing.

The evening banquet held in City Hall to honour the visit of the Oxford crew to Waterford (you'll note the lack of Mersey representation in the day's events, which would point to a change of plans) saw many well-known local figures and competing oarsmen hosted by Alderman Mahony, High Sheriff of Waterford in the absence of the Mayor. Sadly, we lack descriptions of the day's racing, as the local Regatta Committee did not provide the press with the adequate facilities to witness the action and provide suitable reportage in their subsequent publications. The big race of the day was the Waterford Challenge Cup, valued at £50, with presentation prizes valued at £20, for any class of four-oared boat with the course stretching to around 1½ miles. Nevertheless, with an absence of colour to the rowing proceedings (other than the *Munster Express* recording that the races were 'fairly well contested'), we know the result was:

Dublin University Boat Club (black and white)
N. 'Kaye' (bow), A. 'Catesby', R. Bleasby, H.A. Elgee (stk), H.A. Cowper (cox) ... 1
Waterford Boat Club (navy blue and white)
T.F. Sheedy (bow), C.W. Mosley, B.C. Manning, W.J. Manning (stk),
A. Farrell (cox) ... 2
Oxford University Boat Club (dark blue)
A.W. Mahaffy (bow), C. Parker, R.P.P. Rowe, J. MacLachlan (stk),
A. Cowper (cox) ... 3

The Waterford Boat Club crew didn't disgrace themselves in obtaining a runner-up position that was made even more illustrious by the crew they pipped in the form of Oxford. The most notable member of the Oxford crew at that Waterford meet was R.P.P. Rowe, who competed in the famous Boat Race from 1889 to 1892, winning three of the four races over Cambridge. Rowe attended Clifton College in Bristol (where he would form connections with the Old Vic) and Magdalen College at Oxford University. He later became President of the Oxford University Boat Club in 1892. However, this fails to adequately convey what a generous and remarkable figure the Waterford Boat Club hosted that summer.

Sir Reginald Percy Pfeiffer Rowe (1868–1945): Oxford Oarsman and Published Philanthropist

Reginald Percy Pfeiffer Rowe was born on 11 April 1868 in West Derby, Liverpool. The Rowe family later moved to Paddington and after attending Clifton, Reginald obtained a Bachelor of Arts in 1891 having read history. Three years later, he completed a Master of Arts degree. In 1896, he applied for membership as a 'jobber' in the London Stock Exchange and came to reside in Kensington in London. We know from the 1911 census that he then worked as Secretary of the New University Club at 57 St James Street in Westminster. Upon the outbreak of the First World War, R.P.P. Rowe, at 46 years of age, joined the committee of the United Arts Volunteer Force and after two months' drilling he was gazetted as a captain in the 6th Battalion, the Queen's Own Royal West Kent Regiment, in December 1914. After finishing serving with the Military Intelligence Directorate, Rowe published a book titled the *Concise Chronicle of Events of the Great War*. For his military service, Reginald Rowe was awarded the 1914–15 Star, the British War Medal 1914–1918 and the Victory Medal.

An eternal student, Rowe later qualified as a barrister and resided at 16 Old Square, Lincoln's Inn, and served as Under Treasurer of Lincoln's Inn at the New Hall. From 1900, Rowe served as Chairman of the Improved Tenements Association and was the Founder and Honorary Treasurer of the Sadler's Wells Fund. A man of many talents, Rowe wrote two novels, a play titled *The Worst of Being William* and many poems. Other publications included *The Root of All Evil* (printed by the Economic Reform Club, of which he served as president for a time) and a popular book on rowing produced by the Badminton Library. In the 1934 New Year's Honours List, he was made a Knight Bachelor for his services in combating slum conditions in London and across England. Rowe died aged 76 on 21 January 1945 at Charing Cross Hospital in Westminster.

Epilogue

One ponders what a loss it was to the city of the razzamatazz of the regatta at the Old Boat Club clubhouse that allowed spectators to form along the city's Quayside and created a spectacle and an occasion that even saw businesses shuttering their shops to witness the day's rowing and racing. We see how sport had increasingly become a huge part of the public and social life of Ireland's oldest city, and is reflected in the important civic figures that supported and organised such events. Furthermore, in the form of R.P.P. Rowe we have one of the great figures of British sport, who went on to become a hugely influential personality in a crusade to improve the living conditions of the poor. It seems more than appropriate that Sir Reginald competed in one race for Oxford in the shadow of the iconic Reginald's Tower; you could say it illustrates the modern concept of 'game recognises game'. If that fortified tower was built as a statement of power and defence then Reginald Rowe was certainly a worthy namesake in his crusade in housing and sporting endeavours.

19

'A Cycling Carnival': Ireland vs England, People's Park, Waterford, 11 August 1891

The sport of cycling has a long tradition in Waterford city and county. Some believe that the first known cycle club in Ireland was the Dungarvan Ramblers, established in 1869 (in fact, they would appear to be the third behind Dublin's Amateur Cycling Club and the Earlsfort Terrace Machinery Court Club, with its Dungarvan counterpart formed in June 1870). Nevertheless, this pre-dated the formation of a national body to govern the sport by around fifteen years. The Irish Cycling Association (ICA) was created in 1884. However, more certain is that Dungarvan would continue to be at the forefront of the development of competitive cycling by staging Ireland's first bicycle race for a challenge cup in September 1869. In August 1874, two members of the Waterford Ariel Bicycle Club, R.W. Rose and W. Carden, cycled from Waterford to Wexford to attend the Royal Agricultural Society's show, making newspaper headlines as the Gentle County could 'boast of bicycle feats second to none in Ireland', as noted by the *Waterford Standard*.

The growth in popularity of the sport was mirrored in Waterford city, where in the 1890s the Waterford Bicycle Club competed across the island in search of silverware and attempted to promote the sport in its own area. It was formed in January 1880 by solicitor J.B. Cherry at his home on William Street. It was a male-dominated pastime until the 1890s, which saw races from Waterford to Tramore being particularly popular. The successful club was frequented by figures such as Laurence A. Ryan, mayor of the city from 1880 to 1882. The late 1880s saw members of the Urbs Intacta Cycling Club (formed in 1881 but continually hampered by the Irish weather in staging events) such as Dr George Mackesy and W.G.D. Goff join the club.

On 11 August 1891 a 'cycling carnival' was staged in Waterford in what the *Munster Express* noted as a date that 'will be memorable in the history in the south of

'A Cycling Carnival': Ireland vs England, People's Park, Waterford, 11 August 1891

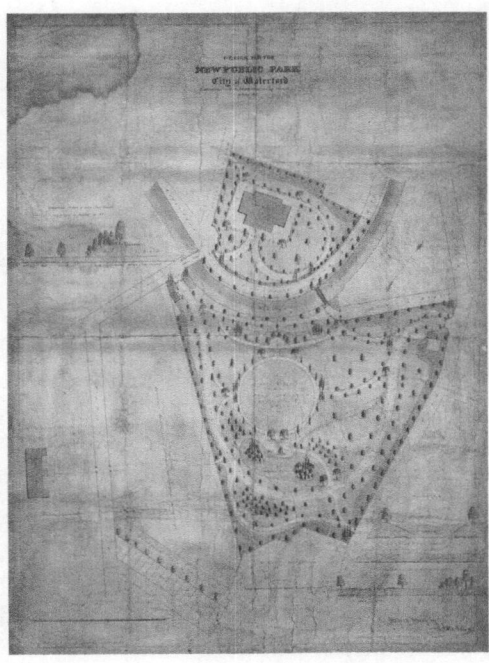

Map of New Public Park designed by Alexander Nimmo in 1855. The amenity would become known as the People's Park. (Courtesy of Waterford City & County Archive)

Ireland as the first occasion of a visit from English cracks'. The English group was made up of Osmond (described as Champion of the World at all distances), Adams (London), Edwards (London), Jones, Parsons and Mole (Polytechnic BC) to name a few, while the home side numbered Arthur and Harvey DuCros, Mecredy, Martin (Dublin), McAdam (Limerick), Kenna, O'Callaghan, Fielding and Williamson. The meeting was to be staged on the new track in the People's Park, with the event promoted by the Waterford Bicycle Club. The enclosure had been enlarged to accommodate thousands of spectators. Admission was priced at 1s.

In previewing the race, the *Munster Express* said the track 'measures four laps to the mile, has good long straights, and the surface is magnificent, while the trees and hillocks which surround it shelter it from the wind'. Anticipation built in the expectation that not only would Irish records be lowered but that world records would be broken. The three men central to the attraction of the event were the English cyclists Adams, Jones and Osmond. They were described as 'the fastest riders in the world' and as holding honours such as Adams, winner of the 25 miles' Ordinary Championship of England; Jones, previous holder of the mile record; and Osmond, English Champion of both the 5 and 50 miles distances. Jones was also the holder of all the world's records from 1 to 50 miles while his time for the mile was noted as two minutes and sixteen seconds.

Again, the local papers promoted the event:

> The Waterford public will have a chance of seeing the best men in the world and the finest racing ever put before the public, and we trust that they will assemble in their thousands to welcome the visitors and to support the Club which has worked so hard to give this treat.

A previous cycling race in Tramore was described as taking 'the blooming cake', while this race between Ireland and English teams 'will take the whole bakery'. Yet, this doesn't reflect the fact of the Tramore meeting being abandoned due to the failure of the English cyclists to show up for the race.

Even the competition among the Irish contingent was eagerly awaited, as Arthur DuCros and Mecredy were going to slog it out for the bragging rights of best of the Emerald Isle. Mecredy had strong form going into the race, although DuCros had the 'Indian sign' over him by winning each event in which the two competed. It was to be a busy year for the Galwayman R.J. Mecredy, who invented the game of 'bicycle polo', which closely followed the rules of horse polo. The first match of this was held on 4 October 1891 between Rathclaren Rovers and Ohne Hast Cycling Club at The Scalp in County Wicklow.

Local support favoured Williams of Annestown, who was described as 'a road rider of no mean order', having won the Power's medal in June, covering a distance of 122 miles in ten hours and forty-five minutes. Yet, there was an even more international dimension due to the presence of Count Konstantin Norbert Stadnicki, a Polish national who was an Irish Cycling Champion. Stadnicki was from Podolia, a predominantly Polish-speaking area of the Russian Empire, and was taught English by an Irish tutor. He was later educated at Beaumont College in Berkshire. It appears his love of cycling began while in Torquay in 1883 before moving to Ireland to study engineering at the Royal University of Ireland in around October the same year. His story and rivalry with Mecredy is brilliantly elaborated by the historian Brian Griffin, formerly of Bath Spa University, in *The Boneshaker: The Journal of the Veteran Cycle Club*.

The new track at the People's Park was a gift from Mr Goff to the Waterford Bicycle Club and considered to be one of the best in Ireland. Yet it was noted that:

> The last of the English Championships for 1891 has passed, and the Irish riders have not succeeded in winning even one. One of the causes of the recent ill-success of those to whom was allotted the arduous task of bearing the Irish standard lies in the fact that there is not in Dublin a track on which men can acquire the form requisite to compete successfully against such a highly-trained mettlesome flyer as Osmond.

'A Cycling Carnival': Ireland vs England, People's Park, Waterford, 11 August 1891

Certainly, the financial support from figures like Goff was central to the development of the sport in Waterford. Two years after gifting the track, he funded the building of a club pavilion, dressing room and grandstand that could hold up to 500 people in 1892. There is also the Goff Challenge Shield, a solid silver trophy that was estimated to be worth 40 guineas.

From all of this, you can see that Waterford was certainly a hotbed of cycling. As for the race results of 11 August 1891, we will follow the time-honoured tradition of *L'Auto* when detailing the early years of the stage finishes of the Tour de France by publishing the results at a later date with some colour. For more on cycling in Waterford in the meantime, it is worth consulting the *Decies* journal of 2019, where Brian Griffin contributed a detailed article on the sport in the city and county in the Victorian and Edwardian eras. One piece of information that piqued my interest was that around the same time Waterford could boast of having one of the biggest and heaviest cyclists in the world, a Michael Manning, who reached 6ft in height and weighed around 22st. Family connections? No comment, but if anyone has seen me cycling the comparison makes sense.

Waterford People's Park, 1891.

T.O. Jameson: The Captain at Cappoquin

Described as 'a fine all-rounder', Tom Ormsby Jameson was born in Clonsilla, Dublin, on 4 April 1892 and attended Hazelwood School until March 1906. When leaving Hazelwood for Harrow, the former school magazine noted that Jameson 'will find at Harrow the right training ground for his talents in every branch of sport. He has shown abilities as a cricketer second to few or none.' He went on to play for the Harrow XI in 1909 and 1910. The latter year he played in the renowned 'Fowler's Match', where he was twice dismissed for single figures. Jameson opened the second inning by scoring 2 runs in fifty minutes.

However, his sporting endeavours weren't limited to cricket. While at Harrow, he played rackets and continued to play the game with much distinction while serving in the British Army (which he joined upon the outbreak of the First World War). Mobilised as a second lieutenant with the 3rd Battalion, he was subsequently promoted to lieutenant and later captain on 1 January 1917. In September 1917, Jameson was seconded to the West African Frontier Force before returning to his old battalion and serving in Ireland from 1919 to 1922. Such was his athletic prowess that he won the amateur Squash Rackets Championships in 1922 and 1923.

Jameson and Joan Musgrave: A Couple in Cappoquin

Even with such a hectic career and sporting endeavours, there was time for romance. On 11 June 1920 Jameson married the artist Joan Moira Maud Musgrave, the daughter of Sir Richard John Musgrave, 5th Baronet of Tourin. Joan had studied art at the Académie Julian in Paris. On his retirement from the army in 1924, Jameson moved back to Ireland and ran a family farm at Cappoquin, Co. Waterford. The couple split their time between Waterford and London until 1929, when upon the death of Joan's father, the couple moved to Tourin.

Between 1919 and 1932, Jameson played fifty-three matches for Hampshire, scoring over 2,000 runs (including 105 not out against Somerset in Portsmouth in 1926) and taking 77 wickets (his best figures were 5 for 18 against Kent at Southampton in 1925). During the same period, the Dubliner played for MCC (his first appearance coming in 1919) and the army (in 1920, the year in which he was also elected a Free Forester). Jameson numbered in the Tennyson XI that toured South Africa in 1924–25 and played in three games against the hosts, as well as scoring 90 not out against Rhodesia at Bulawayo and reaching his highest score in his first-class cricket career of 133 against the Orange Free State at Bloemfontein.

After the South African tour, Jameson played for the MCC side that visited the West Indies, reaching figures of 110 against Jamaica at Kingston and 98 against the West Indies at Bridgetown. He was a part of Marylebone's trip to South America in 1926–27, excelling with both bat and ball as he took 5 for 27 and 5 for 29 against Argentina at Belgrano. When the opportunity arose, Jameson also played for his native Ireland and in 1928 was part of the team that inflicted a first defeat of the tour on the travelling West Indian side.

From Touring to Tourin:
A Revival of Cricket in West Waterford

Two years after moving to Tourin with his wife, Jameson was one of the individuals behind the revival of cricket in Cappoquin after a thirty-year lapse of the playing of the game in the west Waterford town. Jameson tutored the club's players, who in their first month of existence in July 1931 played three matches, two against Cahir (a loss and a draw), and were victorious over the well-established Lismore club by 107 runs to 58. Subsequently, they played a Hearne's XI made up of the employees of the building contractor John Hearne and Son, with the west Waterford side losing by 18 runs.

For the return fixture, the Cappoquin side's Jameson, the captain, and J. Lacey managed to bowl the Waterford city side out for 9 runs in the first innings. Over the 2 innings, Cappoquin comfortably won by 2 wickets and 40 runs. Jameson took 7 wickets over the 2 innings and scored 12 runs (dismissed by lbw) in the first innings.

Jameson's interests weren't just limited to cricket as he was also patron of the Cappoquin Rugby Football Club. Over the next couple of years the Cappoquin Cricket Club played the Hearne's XI, Cahir, Curraghmore and Woodstown cricket clubs regularly. However, Jameson appeared to be more absent than present for the matches. When he was available, Jameson's bowling efforts were unable to compete with a continually improving Hearne's side as it appeared that the game was slowly petering out in Cappoquin by 1935. Jameson's own life was nearly extinguished when in August 1935, when driving near Cappoquin, the steering gear of his car became locked and the car struck a fence. The vehicle was wrecked but he managed to survive with a few scratches.

Decline of Cappoquin, Rise of County Waterford Cricket

In 1936 the Cappoquin Cricket Club ceased to function for that summer, with many of its prominent members becoming involved with the Lismore club. But the club would return briefly again by the end of the decade. In 1937, aged 45, Jameson was selected for the Lord Tennyson side in India, but poor health saw his performances hampered.

Waterford city and county could boast nine clubs by May 1939, namely Bishop Foy School, Cappoquin, Christendom, John Hearne & Son, Killea, Lismore, Newtown School, Tramore and Woodstown. It was the intention of the latter club's captain, P.L. Dempster, and J.E. Lloyd Lewis (headmaster of Bishop Foy School) to form and develop a County Waterford team. The following year, Jameson was selected for a Waterford County XI to face the Phoenix Club of Dublin at Woodstown Cricket Club grounds. The creation of a Waterford County side was part of the growth in the game in the south-east of Ireland, with Cork very much being a stronghold in the province of Munster.

Jameson was described as 'a tall, stylish batsman and a particularly fine driver' by *The Cricketer* in April 1965. Upon his death, *Wisden* recorded of Jameson that, 'In all first-class cricket he hit 4,631 runs, average 31.71, with leg-break bowling took 241 wickets for 23.92 runs each and, chiefly at slip, held 86 catches.' Prior to his death, Jameson had been residing at Rock House in Ardmore, having moved there with his wife in the early 1950s. It's an unfamiliar tale of one of the great all-rounders making his home in west Waterford. Jameson brought his love of the game of cricket to Cappoquin, but it was his love for Joan Musgrave that brought him to Cappoquin in the first innings.

21

Dan Cooney (1892–1940): 'Our Dan' from Near Dungarvan

Born on 22 November 1892 at Carrigroe in Carriglea near Dungarvan, Daniel Cooney was the third oldest of the Cooney family and the eldest boy according to the 1901 Census. Daniel's father John (a farmer) and his mother Ellen both spoke Irish and English. The family were nationalistic in their outlook and supported the cause of Irish Freedom. This would influence Daniel's efforts during the Anglo-Irish War, 1919–21. Five of the children who were of school going age were able to read and write, so would have known the words of Wolfe Tone and Emmet by sight and sound. Young Dan was a great follower of sport, but developed an early affection for the fistic arts. So much was his devotion to pugilism that Cooney was a well-regarded name on the Irish boxing scene by the age of 16. The *Munster Express* noted that, 'He became renowned for his amazing vitality and his stamina, which kept him to the forefront when often faced with tremendous odds.'

Trained by Irish Boxing Champion Jem Roche

Under the tutelage of Wexford's Jem Roche, Cooney went from strength to strength in the ring. Roche had fought for the World Heavyweight title in 1908, but was defeated by Tommy Burns by first round knockout. Roche's manager Tennant noted his record as 30–7–1. After his time inside the ring, Roche ran a pub on South Main Street in Wexford before becoming a bookie and later manager of a commission agent's establishment in his native county. It's fair to say, there would be few better placed than Jem Roche to advise and train Dan Cooney. Roche was in high demand as he was also trainer of the Wexford Senior Gaelic football team, which went on to win four All-Ireland titles in a row from 1915 to 1918.

The Carrigroe boxer's earliest recorded fight was a draw against the heavier 'Buck' Reilly at the Erin's Hope band rooms in Waterford city on 13 September 1913. Cooney forced the fighting from the start, although Reilly defended well but was not as alert as the Dungarvan fighter. Cooney's February 1914 fight against Waterford's 'Duck' Daly at the Town Hall in Dungarvan in front of hundreds of spectators was the bout that caught people's attention. Daly was 2/1 favourite and weighed 10lb more than his challenger. Advertised as a twenty-round, three-minute per round contest, many had travelled from Waterford with many more placing bets on Daly, who was a staple of the lightweight division in Ireland. Cooney put himself on the pugilistic map by knocking Daly out in two minutes and seven seconds. The *Cork Examiner* wrote of the decisive blow:

> ... both men coming to close quarters, where exchanges took place, when, with surprising swiftness, Cooney landed one on the solar plexus, and Daly went down on his side. As the count went on, he turned on his back, and lay there helpless being counted out.

Cooney was talked about as the coming fighter in Irish featherweight circles, and a real test came on 20 October 1914 at the Ancient Concert Rooms in Dublin against County Cork's Featherweight Champion Paddy Buckley. This was followed by notable performances against Mitchell, a draw with then undefeated Lightweight Champion Dubliner Pat O'Shea (who weighed 2st more than Cooney) on Monday, 12 July 1915 in Dungarvan, a bout against Dublin's Frank Dillion, and a fight against noted English Featherweight Champion Jack Levene.

The latter fight for the Featherweight Championship was staged at the Coliseum in Waterford city on Saturday, 11 August 1917 and saw Cooney disobey doctor's orders to stay in bed to battle the Englishman. The bout went the full fifteen rounds, with the *Munster Express* recording that Cooney 'to his credit in the fistic arena that he was never knocked out, but by sheer staying power and an ability to assimilate terrific punishment, often wore down and defeated a superior opponent'.

Cooney's Preparation for Featherweight Title Fight

Cooney's focus wasn't just on the ring, but also on legal matters. Just a few days before the bout for the Featherweight Championship, at a sitting of the Kilmacthomas Petty Sessions, a Patrick Lawlor and Cooney prosecuted ex-Recruiting Sergeant Maurice Barron (who was wounded in France) for assault on 11 July. Lawlor and Cooney were among a group celebrating the East Clare by-election when Lawlor was struck on the shoulder with a stick. Barron, in his cross-examination, noted that Lawlor was carrying a flag and used the expression 'To hell with the King and country and those who fought for him.'

A record of the defendant's convictions noted arrests for drunkenness, riotous behaviour and assaulting members of the Royal Irish Constabulary. It was decided by Royal Magistrate Orr that Barron be fined 2s 6d and costs in the case brought against him by Lawlor while Cooney's case was dismissed.

Remarkably, on the same page of the local paper detailing the civil proceedings against Barron was a preview of the fight against Levene, which was garnering plenty of attention due to its international flavour. The *Munster* highlighted:

> All who saw this game lad [Dan Cooney] concede a stone to Kid Doyle, the best light weight in Ireland, and then make a brilliant aggressive fight right through took him to their hearts as the 'beau ideal' of a boxer to watch-clever, fast, rugged and carrying a heavy punch, he possesses all the attributes of the champion, which his manager hopes to make of him ere long. Experience, which can only be obtained in the course of many ring battles, is the only thing he lacks, in common with all young boxers; this failing his connections are certainly going the right way to eradicate, in matching him against such class men as Levene.

As already noted, Cooney went against doctor's orders by taking to the ring, and surely, his condition wasn't helped by the late start of 10.25 p.m. The first round saw Levene strike first blood with a nasty cut over the Kilmacthomas-residing man's left eye. The next few rounds were even until the fifth when the cut started to create issues for Cooney that the Londoner capitalised on. There was a brief reprieve in the next round before Cooney was floored in the seventh, but recovered quickly. The ninth, tenth and eleventh rounds saw the Waterford fighter take plenty of punishment but he responded with 'a wonderful amount of pluck and staying power.' As the fight wore on into the championship rounds, Cooney was showing visible signs of the punishment he received, with the referee declaring Levene the winner on points. The *Waterford Star* concluded its report with, 'We understand that Cooney was somewhat indisposed prior to the contest, and this, coupled with bad luck in the opening round, doubtless mutated against what would have been a more even contest.'

Cooney Nears End of Lightweight Prime, Moves to Welterweight

Cooney would also fight at Waterford's Theatre Royal in late 1917 against the rugged Lar Roche (brother of Cooney's coach, Jem) from Wexford in a scheduled bout of twelve rounds of three-minute duration. The contest between the pair from the south-east of Ireland was described as 'the best of the night' as Cooney was awarded the verdict after going ten rounds. Of the fight, the *Munster Express* recorded that:

Cooney throughout was master of the situation notwithstanding the fact that Roche was a strong, rugged fighter and full of gameness. Cooney was more scientific and was able to elude the Wexford man's punches. He was punished very severely by Cooney from the fourth round and went to his corner several times appearing very groggy.

Though still in his prime, Cooney was absent from the ring for two years until he returned to training in the summer of 1919. It appears that in the early 1920s he was recorded as the Welterweight Champion of Munster.

From Cooney the Boxer to Cooney the Nurse: Helping 'the Real Chief' Liam Lynch

Cooney was to the fore in the cause of Irish Freedom during the War of Independence, with his finest hour being in giving aid to the IRA Chief of Staff Liam Lynch. This was after the Fermoy Ambush in September 1919, when a wounded Lynch was brought to Youghal, but the column was tracked by an observing aeroplane. Cooney's home at Carrigroe was used to house Lynch, which the *Munster* detailed 'so cleverly and secretly was this good work done that even the neighbours and friends of the district were not aware of what was going on'. Cooney was actually on holiday at his homeplace when this all occurred, but gave an invaluable service to help Dungarvan's Dr Moloney nurse Liam Lynch back to good health. It is believed that Lynch stayed in Carrigroe for around two weeks before going to James Kirwin's on the slopes of the Comeragh Mountains. The Limerick man then returned to Cooney's homestead for another three weeks before seeking shelter elsewhere.

Business Interests and Personal Beliefs

Cooney had gone into business in Kilmacthomas during the First World War and later ran a shop on The Square in Dungarvan. Dan became a prominent figure in the Old Borough's community and was on the Catholic Truth Society Dungarvan Parish Committee, which in spring 1926 adopted the motion, 'That the practice of supplying intoxicating liquor through licensed bars at dances is an added danger, and seriously detrimental to the morals of our young people, and we strongly recommend that the local authority and all who are responsible should exercise their influence in future to have this abominable practice discontinued.'

Sadly, Daniel was predeceased by his father just a few months prior to his own death, as the younger Cooney died on 5 August 1940 at the Bon Secours, Cork, due to tuberculosis.

The Wild Man from Borneo: Grand National Winner 1895

The Widger family in Waterford were horse breeders who supplied horses to cavalry regiments across Europe, primarily in England, Italy and the Netherlands. Joe Widger had an ambition to have success in the horse-racing industry, and rode his first winner aged 13 at Bangor. He and his brother John bought a horse named The Wild Man from Borneo (so-called after two well-known stuntmen) in 1893 with a view to competing at the Grand National at Aintree in the following year. On his first run in the hardest race in the National Hunt, he came third, having taking the lead at the penultimate fence. The Widgers and The Wild Man from Borneo were back at Aintree in 1895 with Joe Widger guiding the horse to contention coming up onto the last fence. Under his guidance, the horse won the race by one and a half lengths, with celebrations aplenty in their hometown. The horse would compete two more times in the Grand National in 1896 and 1897 and was pulled up in the latter race.

23

'The First Waterford Men to Win All-Ireland Medals': Jack Dwan and Larry Tobin, Tipperary Footballers

The 1900 All-Ireland Championship saw the introduction of a new format for the competition, where the four provincial winners would play a Home Championship, with the victors of that final playing London in *the* All-Ireland final. As County Championships were played off to decide their respective representatives for the intercounty series, the headache of the fixture calendar saw Cashel play host to the 1899 County Tipperary Football final on 1 April 1900. The decider in one of the most competitive local Gaelic Football Championships paired Clonmel Shamrocks with Arravale Rovers, with the latter representing Tipperary in the Munster Championship, where they were beaten by Cork after three games were staged to decide the Provincial Champions for 1899. It was one of many sagas to be faced by Tipperary football in the years to come.

It was a golden era for the local Tipperary Championship, as Bohercrowe and Arravale claimed All-Ireland glory in 1889 and 1895 respectively. Both clubs would have faced a Clonmel Shamrocks side that had a formidable reputation as they would go on to win four county titles outright in five years. This led Shamrocks to represent County Tipperary, which defeated Cork initially in 1897. The Rebel County eventually progressed and reached the All-Ireland final for reasons off the field of play. For a second consecutive year, again Clonmel Shamrocks would represent Tipperary against Waterford for the following campaign but were defeated due to playing a weakened team as some of their players did not travel for the match.

It would prove third time lucky in the province for the south Tipperary club. Clonmel Shamrocks would represent Tipperary for a third time in the Inter-County

Championship for 1900 – which was staged between August 1901 and late October 1902 – with them defeating Cork (represented by Fermoy) as Shamrocks were short seven players from their starting team, for their tie in Dungarvan, Co. Waterford, in the Munster quarter-final. It was a great start to a campaign that saw them beat Limerick, Kerry (in the Munster final staged at Limerick's Markets Field in May 1902), and Kilkenny (after lodging an objection having lost the game in Carrick-on-Suir) to reach the Home Championship final, where they would face the Connacht Champions Galway. However, like all sporting journeys, the results don't always tell the full story of how a side got to the pinnacle of their sport.

Tipperary vs Kilkenny:
Battles on the Field and Objections Off It

The objection surrounding the semi-final against the Leinster Champions Kilkenny was that the Cats were represented by the Slate Quarry Miners, who for the game turned out to number eleven Grangemockler players who were disgruntled at being defeated by Clonmel Shamrocks earlier in the Tipperary Championship. The Quarry Miners club was made up of men from the border between Tipperary and Kilkenny who worked in the local slate quarry (hence the name). A local derby thus had an added edge to proceedings; the Kilkenny side wore emerald-green jerseys with a yellow sash and won the match on a scoreline of 1–6 to 7 points. After the objection was lodged, it was concluded that the Kilkenny side had played five illegal players. Furthermore, the Shamrocks felt they had won the match anyway by 2 points, but managed to overcome such trying circumstances by hammering Galway (represented by Tuam Krugers) in the 'Home Final' by 2–17 to 1 point at Terenure, which *The Nationalist* reported Tipperary 'won by a huge score, literally "making lanes" through the Galway men'.

Shamrocks added a third All-Ireland title to the Premier County's roll of honour when they beat London 3–7 to 2 points in front of 2,000 spectators at Jones's Road. That day, the London Hibernians numbered Sam Maguire, who lost the first of three finals he competed in for London. Nevertheless, the flattering scoreline didn't reflect the difficulty Tipperary had in getting to the game, as the train to Kingsbridge Station (now Heuston) was an hour late. Far from an easy route to win an All-Ireland, but one imagines it was made all the sweeter by the travails, trials and tribulations they overcame that had bordered on epic proportions akin to Fenian legend. Further history is attached to this achievement by two Waterford men playing for the Clonmel Shamrocks that formed the bedrock of the team that won Tipperary the ultimate honour of the 1900 All-Ireland Championship.

Clonmel Shamrock's County Waterford Players

The victorious Tipperary team had eight players from Clonmel Shamrocks, two from Arravale Rovers, five from Grangemockler (one can imagine a rather frosty response when these lads showed up for training after the semi-final debacle), two from Clonmel Commercials and Jack Hayes from Fethard. Interestingly, two of the Clonmel Shamrocks contingent were Waterford men, Jack Dwan (Fourmilewater) and Larry Tobin (The Nire). In a letter in the *Irish Press* of 2 December 1964, Sean O'Donnell noted that Dwan and Tobin were 'the first Waterford men to win All-Ireland medals'.

Jack Dwan (1880–1962): 'One of the Greatest Sportsmen Ever to Come Out of Fourmilewater'

Jack (John) Dwan hailed from Fourmilewater, Co. Waterford, and along with being a prominent footballer with Clonmel Shamrocks, he was also a founding member of the Aughavolimane Coursing Club. The Fourmilewater native was known for having scored a goal from 78 yards out for Tipperary against Dublin at Waterford in 1904. The athletic genes ran in the family as he was a cousin of the sporting Kirwans from Kilmacthomas. Dwan lived just an 8-mile walk from Clonmel, which was seen as a sporting hub. The teenage Dwan was adept at athletics (along with his brother Larry) but it was in the sphere of Gaelic football that he would make his name.

From that Tipperary All-Ireland winning team, Jack Dwan was its youngest member, when in his early twenties. He later worked in the grocery business in Limerick, where he played for the Limerick Commercials club, whom he would win a county title with during his three-year playing spell there. Aside from his efforts in Gaelic games, Dwan played rugby for Clonmel and the famous Garryowen club. The *Munster Tribune* noted that, 'He was a two-footed player, but it seems he had a lethal left and invariably played in the left half back position, left centre in rugby', which was demonstrated by his monster goal strike against Dublin in 1904. The same periodical concluded that Jack Dwan was 'one of the greatest sportsmen ever to come out of Fourmilewater'. Dwan lived into his early 80s and died at his residence in Ballymacarbry in 1962.

Larry Tobin (1878–1939): 'One of the Best Wing Forwards in the Game'

Jack Dwan's Shamrocks teammate and fellow Waterford native Laurence (Larry) Tobin came from Glendaloughin in the Nire. Tobin lived in Clonmel for nearly fifty years and was associated with many movements and organisations in that Tipperary town. He was considered the chief figure in the establishment of the new Gaelic grounds in Clonmel and was a director of the Sportsfield Company. He served as an alderman and councillor on Clonmel Corporation and had roles with Clonmel Board of Guardians, South Tipperary County Council and the Clonmel Mental Hospital Committee. His business interests included a grocery and spirit store on Parnell Street, the development of the Slievenamon Hotel and owning a drapery and boot store on Gladstone Street. During his playing days, he was considered one of the leading footballers in the country. The *Munster Tribune* described Tobin as 'of average height, but he possessed a stock, hardy build, and was of the best wing forwards in the game'. He died aged 61 on 1 August 1939.

Clonmel Shamrocks Continued Sagas

From the moment of the Shamrock side's greatest triumph came a bitter fall. The Clonmel club were in dispute with the GAA's Central Council, as players that represented Tipperary from Grangemockler, Fethard and Tipperary town stayed in Clonmel on the eve of the final when the club were promised extra expenses from the GAA, who later refused to pay the £7.50 that had been incurred by the Tipperary club. Shamrocks sued the Council and had a decree issued against the General Secretary for the sum that was owed. The GAA retaliated by imposing a two-year suspension on the club, which was eventually overturned, but by that point the club had disbanded as it proved an obstacle too far for a battle-hardened group. It was nearly thirty years before a Clonmel Shamrocks team would claim the Tipperary County title again, in 1932.

As All-Ireland winners in Waterford are rare things and as the county has yet to lift the Sam Maguire Trophy, it's worth acknowledging the role of two Waterford natives, Jack Dwan and Larry Tobin, in achieving such history and they should be recorded as the first men from the Gentle County to win All-Ireland medals in Gaelic football.

'Battling Brannigan': The Story of Gerald Hurley

In 1901 by Lake Michigan, Gerald Hurley was born in Chicago, Illinois. His grand-father was John Hurley, who had taught at Dunhill National School and later Banagher in Co. Offaly before migrating to the United States and settling in Denver, Colorado, where he died aged 83. Gerald's uncle was also a teacher, working at a school that was attached to St Patrick's Hospital in Waterford. Gerald Hurley was a stepbrother of Mrs F. Matthews of Marian Park, Waterford. Gerald would move to the city where he had such strong connections when he was 3 years old.

The young Hurley lived with his grandmother Bridget at 26 Castle Street. He was most associated with living in adulthood at Grange Terrace in Waterford. Growing up in the south-east of Ireland, Hurley loved singing, handball and, in his late teens, became the Softball Champion of Waterford. One of his favourite haunts was the handball alley and boxing club at Spring Garden Alley, which was popular with athletes on Sunday mornings.

Boxing Career: 1919–29

The incident that began his journey in professional pugilism occurred in 1919 in the ball alley in Waterford. The owner of the alley, Thomas Neary, decided to settle an argument between Hurley and a local boxing hero named Jackson by giving the pair boxing gloves and in the ensuing scrap the youth knocked Jackson out cold.

Neary was an All-Ireland Handball Champion who had trained a young John L. Sullivan, and after returning to Ireland saw that Hurley had some potential that he could harness. Hurley fought under the name of 'Battling Brannigan' and began his boxing career, aged 18, as a lightweight. The adoption of the alias was due to him fighting against the wishes of his parents. For the purposes of exploring his professional boxing career this piece will refer to Hurley as 'Battling Brannigan' up to his retirement from the ring in 1929.

Brannigan's first bout in the ring came against Warrington lightweight Ted Hughes at the old Liverpool Stadium, which he lost after six rounds on points. It was the first of nearly 100 fights, although the Waterford boxer told the *Sunday Independent* in 1977 that he couldn't remember the exact record but admitted 'to having lost more of the bouts he engaged in across the water' than he won. His most notable victory in Britain was a seventh-round knockout of the Tommy Burns protégé Hyman Gordon at Newcastle. Gordon had never been floored until his fight against Brannigan.

Even with such a successful career developing, it did not prevent the young Waterford man from witnessing great tragedy. During the siege of Waterford in July 1922, while watching the hostilities with his companions John Long and Paddy Moloney, their group was caught in the cross-fire. When a hail of bullets from Hall's Store sprayed them, it ended with Moloney wounded by a piece of shrapnel to the back and Long shot dead. Another death that took place during the siege was that of Joe Dwan at Olaf Street, whom Hurley/Brannigan worked with when putting up the wooden poles for when the first electric lights were introduced to Waterford.

During the 1920s, professional boxing shows were regular attractions in Ireland, too, with bouts taking place in Belfast, Dublin and Waterford. Brannigan had three fights with the Belfast Irish Lightweight Champion Billy Gilmour, finishing with one win, one draw and one loss. Brannigan went on to become an Irish Champion at that grade. In addition to this title, Brannigan added the Welterweight Championship (in 1927) and, as the *Munster Express* noted in a 1972 interview with him, 'his name had already become a household word, with packed "houses" turning out to see him fight in cities, towns and villages all over Ireland'.

Brannigan graced the surrounds of Croke Park in 1926 when he faced the B Special and then reigning Irish Lightweight Champion Ken Webb in a ten-round contest on the bill of the Tom Heeney and Bartley Madden fight card. Hurley came out as the winner of the bout, having been considered the underdog prior to the contest.

One of Brannigan's most cherished memories was fighting Sam Minto at the Theatre Royal in Waterford on 12th October 1928. Minto was an adept operator in the ring, who had lost narrowly to the European Champion Featherweight Charles Ledoux. Brannigan defeated the Bahamian-born Minto on points after 15 rounds of brawling. The Cork Examiner's report of proceedings recorded:

The big fight was expected to prove thrilling, and it did. Brannigan fought to the last nine rounds with one hand, having badly sprained his right wrist in the sixth round. Thereafter, to those who knew, it was a marvel his 'k.o.' did not come at any moment ...
...Brannigan seemed to anticipate every move of his opponent. For one second he dare not lose his concentration. The strain for 15 rounds was heavy, and though there were many who disagreed with the referee's decision, those who followed the contest intelligently will agree Mr Jim Roche gave an honest verdict.

Battling Brannigan's last fight came in 1929 when he fought Louis Sloan in Belfast's Ulster Hall. Sloan was being hailed as a future champion, with Brannigan tipped as a rank outsider, with odds of 50/1 given by local bookmakers. The Waterford boxer managed to knock Sloan out in six rounds. Neither fighter would compete in the ring again after that bout.

A Battler and a Singer:
Hurley, the Ex-Boxer and Pro Singer

After retiring from the ring in 1929, Brannigan/Hurley worked as a P.T. instructor and boxing tutor for forty-two years in several schools in Dublin, such as St Columba's College, and retired from that career in 1970. Hurley was also a trainer and coach in the early years of the Waterford City Boxing Club in the 1930s. Furthermore, he could note positions as athletic coach at Trinity College Dublin, and a physical education instructor at the Garda Depot in the Phoenix Park. For a time, he worked as a representative of the Lucan Dairy Co. During his time as a physical instructor with University College Dublin in 1938, Hurley was interviewed by the *Munster Express*:

> He expressed the view [on amateur boxers in Waterford] that in most cases they needed training on scientific lines ... they did not develop the 'manly art of self-defence' as much as they did their fighting prowess ... [he] would have stood no chance in the ring because of his rather light build but for his superior ring craft against heavier and stronger opponents.

In the early 1930s, Hurley lived in Parnell Street in Waterford and later settled with his wife in Rathgar, Dublin. He was described by the *Munster* as 'an expert and highly polished exponent of the fistic art, in the fulfilment of which, incidentally, he did not have the benefit of a manager: he was also much sought-after as a professional classical singer', appearing in concerts all over Ireland.

Reverting to his birth name, Hurley was trained as an alto for the Westminster Cathedral Choir by Professor Murray of Newtown, Waterford, who was the organist at St John's Church. Known as 'the boy with the phenomenal voice', he sang with St John's and later the Dominican Church on Bridge Street. He continued to sing during his boxing career. Venues that he performed at included the Ancient Concert Rooms in Westland Row, the old Queen's Theatre and the Tivoli on Burgh Quay. While in Dublin, he was a part of the church choir at Harrington Street.

Hurley also sang at a club run by Delia Larkin at Langrishe Place, Summerhill, and became acquainted with her brother Jim. The socialist and trade union leader Jim Larkin used to frequent the club known as the Irish Workers' Club, where his sister organised meetings and performances there with the help of Sean O'Casey. Jim became a friend of Hurley and wanted him to go to America to pursue his boxing career with Benny Leonard. Hurley noted that, 'I never did but I was privileged to box for Jim and also sing at concerts he ran.' In an interview with the *Sunday Independent*, Hurley stated that 'one of the great regrets of my life [was] that I didn't seriously pursue my singing career'. Even in Dublin, he maintained strong connections with Waterford; his brother Tim lived on Barrack Street and his nephew Michael Butler was a hairdresser on Manor Street.

The man born Gerald Hurley who came to national renown as 'Battling Brannigan' died in Dublin in late November 1985 and was buried in Skerries. Perhaps the words of Tom Cryan sum up the importance of Hurley/Brannigan in the story of Irish boxing, 'a sort of trail-blazer for Cork's enigma Jack Doyle. Years before the "Gorgeous Gael" made and lost a fortune combining a certain boxing expertise with a fine singing voice, silver-haired Gerald was doing the same.'

25

An American Millionaire at Waterford Harbour

The eccentric American millionaire Howard Gould was described by the *Evening Herald* (Dublin) as 'not born famous. [But] He has [had] fame thrust upon him …' Howard was the son of American railroad magnate Jay Gould, who was described as a 'robber baron', amassing his fortune through unprincipled business practices, making him one of the wealthiest individuals in the late-nineteenth century. The controversial New Yorker was unpopular for his unscrupulous ways, which led to a famous cartoon depicting Wall Street as his 'Private Bowling Alley'. Howard (born 8 June 1871) was the fourth child of six born to Jay Gould and his wife Helen Day Miller. He attended Columbia College and matriculated with the class of 1894, but records of the undergraduate college of Columbia University show that he did not graduate. Four years later, Howard purchased a seat on the New York Stock Exchange, with his offices located at 195 Broadway. It was a seat he maintained until his death in 1959.

Two Yachts Named *Niagara*

The younger Gould's real passion (aside from money) was competitive yachting. A year after entering the New York Stock Exchange, Howard acquired the 65ft (20m) sloop yacht *Niagara*, built by the Herreshoff Manufacturing Company of Bristol, Rhode Island, in 1895. It was in this vessel that Gould won Lord Dunraven's Castle Yacht Club Challenge Cup. Skippered by John Barr, in her first racing season she won twenty-nine first prizes, nine second prizes and one third prize. In the twenty-rating class, *Niagara* sailed at the Thames Yacht Club Regatta and at the end of the 1895 season was left at Fay's yards in Southampton for the winter.

In addition to his sloop, Gould owned a large (282ft) steam yacht also known as the *Niagara*, which was built in 1898 by Harlan and Hollingsworth in Wilmington,

Delaware. Coincidentally, the acquiring of both vessels coincided with romantic entanglements. Prior to buying the sloop yacht, Gould was engaged to actress Odette Tyler, who performed a number of Shakespearian roles such as Desdemona, Juliet and Portia. However, both families objected to the engagement, which was subsequently broken off as a result. One wonders if the purchase of the sloop was a way to cheer up a broken heart and to get away from the United States by competing at regattas in the United Kingdom?

The same year that the steam yacht was built, Gould married the actress (he certainly had a type) Katherine Clemmons on 12 October 1898. One review described Clemmons as having 'a beautiful profile and a lissom figure, but was devoid of any acting ability'. While married to Gould, it is believed that Clemmons was having an affair with 'Buffalo Bill', aka William F. Cody, who subsidised a major portion of her acting career.

Gould and *Niagara* at Waterford Harbour

On Sunday, 21 July 1901, Gould put into Waterford Harbour aboard his magnificent yacht for the purpose of visiting various castles and country residences to form an understanding of 'what a nobleman's house is like'. As the *Nationalist* (Tipperary) put it, 'His ostensible object is to see some of our [Ireland's] famous castles to find a model for the grand new mansion he is about to build in [the] New York suburbs.' The plan was for Gould to sail from Waterford to Queenstown (Cobh) with a coaching tour through Kerry in mind. However, like all things in Ireland, this was subject to change, and with the riches Gould could spend to cover such excursions, why wouldn't it?

The *Evening Herald* surmised:

> As Howard Gould's magnificently appointed yacht, bought out of the millions that he never earned, lay anchored between the Waterford and Wexford shores, he might have visited many a place whose memories would broaden his mind, and give him knowledge which, in the long run, might be of no more use to him than suggestions for building a palatial residence of marble, stucco, and gliding that is to lick creation.

Anchored at Passage East, the *Waterford News* noted that the *Niagara* was 'much admired by those who had the opportunity of seeing the graceful outlines of this splendid vessel even at a distance, for no visitors were allowed aboard'. Tuesday, 23 July saw Gould and his party travel to Waterford in one of the steam launches and lunch at the Imperial Hotel on the Mall. The local paper described:

> The luncheon was served in the splendid drawing-room of the Imperial Hotel, the spacious proportions of which were much admired by the visitors, and the beautiful

ceiling of the apartment which is an exquisite work of art attracted very special and most appreciative attention.

After lunch, the party, made up of Mr and Mrs Gould, Mr W.A. Perry, Mrs Perry and Mr H. Perry Jr of New York and A.H. Lery (London) took the 1.30 train from Waterford to Kilkenny. Before leaving the Imperial Hotel, Gould was presented by William Murray (proprietor of the hotel) with a copy of the *Waterford News*' publication *Beauty Spots*.

From the Marble County, the American party travelled to Limerick and took a coach from the Treaty County to Listowel en route to Killarney. While they travelled through Munster, the *Niagara* was making its way for Bantry Bay. Stops in Kerry included Tralee, Dingle, Valentia to visit the Knight of Kerry, Sir Maurice Fitzgerald, Waterville, Parknasilla, Kenmare, Glengariff, Bantry and Cork before the party departed aboard their yacht for Le Havre.

While at Queenstown, Gould's yacht was not the only American millionaire's vessel to arrive there that week. The morning after docking there, those aboard the *Niagara* would have witnessed the White Star steamer *Majestic* arrive from New York. Aboard was W.A. Vanderbilt, whose fortune was made through steamboats and railroads. A few years previously, Vanderbilt had built the largest privately owned home in the United States in the form of the 250-room mansion named Biltmore Estate. The Staten Island native with his party boarded his yacht *Valiant* and they made their way to Southampton.

Six months after Gould's visit to the south of Ireland, it was reported by Mr J.J. Comerford in the *Royal Magazine* that Gould planned to build a replica of Kilkenny Castle in Long Island. He was able to obtain photographs of the castle while engineers and architects planned to build a larger version with modern comforts and improvements across the Atlantic. This was known as Castle Gould, although it was not to the couples' liking and they decided to build another larger house in a Tudor style

The western façade (looking east) of Castle Gould within the Sands Point Preserve.

and called it Hempstead House. After the completion of the estate in 1912, Gould sold it to Daniel Guggenheim.

Debts, Divorce and the Déise

Though everything seems to have been cordial between the Goulds and their connections with Ireland, it would not always be the case. In 1906, the Cork painter Henry Jones (Thaddeus Walsh) brought an action against Mrs Gould, who would not pay the contracted price on a portrait she was dissatisfied with. The court found in favour of Jones, with Katherine Gould having to pay $5,675. A year later saw the beginning of the process of judicial separation between the couple, as Katherine accused her husband of bribing detectives in the public service to shadow her movements and gather evidence against her for court proceedings. The matter was finally settled two years later when the court granted the separation, exonerating Clemmons of Howard's charges of impropriety and habitual intoxication. She was granted an allowance of £7,200 a year.

Gould married one final time in 1937, to German actress Grete Mosheim (whose most notable credit was her role in the 1930 film *Dreyfus*, based on the events of the Dreyfus affair). However, the couple divorced ten years later. Howard was the last surviving son of Jay Gould and Helen Day Miller, and he died in 1959 aged 88 at Doctors' Hospital in Manhattan. Of the two vessels named *Niagara* that he was most associated with, the sloop was broken up in England in 1960 while the steamer was bought by the US Navy on 10 August 1917. She was converted into an armed patrol yacht and commissioned in Tebo's Yacht Basin, Brooklyn, under the command of Commander E.B. Larimer. After the First World War she cruised off the coast of Mexico and on 17 July 1920 *Niagara* was reclassified as PY-9, patrolling the Caribbean. Finally, the steam yacht was decommissioned at Philadelphia on 21 April 1922. Recommissioned as *Niagara*, the vessel was used to survey in the Caribbean and from 1924 charted the Gulf of Venezuela and the coast of Central America. She was decommissioned a second time in 1931 and sold for scrapping two years later.

Howard's visit to the south-east was not the last connection between the Gould family and Waterford. In 1911, nearly ten years after Howard's tour of the castles in the south of Ireland, his niece Helen Vivien Gould married John Beresford, 5th Baron Decies. Sadly, Helen died tragically of jaundice and a heart attack in London in February 1931.

One would imagine today that if an American millionaire docked in Passage East, there would be a frenzy on Twitter and Instagram as a wealthy celebrity party toured Ireland, a grand tour in search of grand designs. You could say it was 'by hook or by crooke' that Gould ended up building Kilkenny Castle on Long Island. An unusual story concerning the auld sod and the New World. Although the tale has largely been forgotten, you could say silence was Gould's end.

'Aesthetic Appeal': The Many Lives of Edward Augustine McGuire (1901–92)

'The Catholic Middle Class': McGuire Family and E.A.'s Education

Edward Augustine McGuire was born at his grandfather's house on Priest Road in Tramore on 28 August 1901. Edward Augustine (known as Ned) was the eldest of five sons and two daughters. His father was John Francis McGuire, a draper who was the managing director of Hearne and Co. on the quay in Waterford city, while his mother was Mary (née Moloney). The family were supporters of John Redmond and sympathetic to the Home Rule tradition. The elder McGuire not only supported the Irish Party, but was an adjutant of the Waterford Battalion of the National Volunteers. Ned attended the Ursuline Convent and Waterpark CBS and later went to Clongowes Wood College. He spent 1916–17 at Douai School in Berkshire. In 1919, he entered University College Dublin but left after twelve months to pursue a career in business with his father. The family formed part of the new ascendancy in the Irish Free State, of the Catholic middle class, as the family sought to

Clery's clock.

further themselves in the Jazz Age filled with modern styles and immersed in the cultural life of the capital of the fledgling state.

Master of 'Aesthetic Appeal': from Merrion Row to Brown Thomas, Grafton Street

By 1920, the family had moved to Dublin, operating their own enterprise at Shelbourne House on Merrion Row. Three years later, Ned's father, John Francis, had become the managing director of Clery's department store and transformed the ailing business into a thriving operation. This was due largely to the father and son duo applying modern marketing methods combined with innovative trading techniques to appeal to a mass market as they sought small profits with a high turnover of goods.

However, in 1933, a rift between the board of Clery's and the McGuires saw the latter purchase Brown Thomas on Grafton Street from Gordon Selfridge. The Selfridge family were financially pressed as the effects of the Great Depression began to have a further impact. Under the guidance of John Francis, Ned developed the jaded store to become the most fashionable in Dublin. The McGuires sought to compete with Switzers, as they introduced a new hairdressing and beauty salon, as well as a new fleet of delivery vans to cater for the suburbs of Dublin. John Francis was the shrewd business brain, while his son was 'entrusted with its aesthetic appeal'. Around the time of these developments a commentator from *The Standard* wrote, 'Brilliant lights showed up the glitter and colour of women's weaknesses ... The store was gay, it was alive, it was smiling.'

The younger McGuire introduced new brands to Dublin consumers, such as Dior and Fontana. They continued their policy of novel marketing with unique displays calling on the artistic abilities of Norah McGuinness. McGuinness' eye was noted by the *Irish Times* as permeating 'the windows and interiors of Brown Thomas ... every aspect of the shop took on a Paris chic and a New York air of fantasy'. Employing McGuinness was a masterstroke by McGuire. She was a young modernist painter who had worked under Andre Lohote in Paris and had lived in India, Egypt and New York. The story goes that she was inspired to design windows when one day, travelling on a bus up Fifth Avenue in the Big Apple, she saw an irate Salvador Dalí ejected from a department store by police. He had attempted to throw a bath through a window after customers objected to his displays. A week's trial that literally stopped traffic on Grafton Street led to a full-time career with Brown Thomas.

During the same period of operating Clery's and later owning Brown Thomas, McGuire married Bridget Patricia Neary of Newry in July 1926, and they went on to have four children (two daughters and two sons), one of whom was the painter Edward McGuire (1932–86). From the 1940s, the family resided at Newtownpark House in Blackrock until 1976. McGuire was in control of Brown Thomas (first as MD and later chairman) until 1970, when it was sold to Galen Weston.

'The Premier Player in Ireland': E.A. McGuire – Irish Singles Champion and Davis Cup Tennis Player

McGuire was very much an all-rounder when it came to sporting pastimes, and excelled at tennis. He was noted for his drop shot and was a member of the Irish Davis Cup team from 1924–26, 1928–35 and on two of four teams in 1936 and 1937. He achieved an Irish Singles Championship in 1931 and was a Men's Doubles Champion on four occasions (1928, 1929, 1931 and 1937). McGuire was also twice winner of the Hardcourt Championship. One of his earliest selections for Ireland was against France in the second round of the 1924 Davis Cup. That was the second season in which Ireland participated in the premier international team event in men's tennis.

The same year, he entered the Wimbledon Men's Singles Championship and Doubles, with his partner being M. Ritchie. McGuire would lose his first-round tie to the American R.N. Williams, 6–1, 6–4, 6–4. Williams was a formidable opponent, having previously won the US Open in 1914 and 1916. The American right-hander went on to reach the semi-finals of the All England Club in 1924. In addition, Williams was a survivor of the RMS *Titanic* disaster in 1912. He helped free a trapped passenger just after the ship's collision with the iceberg. It is said this incident inspired one of the scenes in the James Cameron epic film of the disaster, starring Leonardo Di Caprio and Kate Winslet.

In the Men's Doubles, McGuire and Major Ritchie reached the second round but were beaten by the Alonso brothers from San Sebastián in four sets. The Tramore native's partner (Major was his first name and not a military title) was reaching the end of his playing days but had previously reached the final of the Singles in 1909 and

R.N. Williams *was described by* New York Times *tennis writer, Allison Danzig as, 'At his best he was unbeatable, and more dazzling than Tilden.'*

'Aesthetic Appeal': The Many Lives of Edward Augustine McGuire (1901–92)

Anthony Wilding's Olympic biography notes, 'He won the Wimbledon singles title 1910–13 when the defending champion had to play only a challenge round, helped the combined team of Australasia win the Davis Cup three times, and won a bronze medal at the Stockholm Olympic Games in the covered court singles. Wilding won the Australian Championships in 1906 and 1909. In doubles he won Wimbledon titles in 1907–08, 1910, and 1914 and an Australian title in 1906, adding a mixed doubles title at Wimbledon in 1914. Wilding also won the World Hard Court Championship in 1913–14 and the World Covered Court Championship in 1913, both of which were considered major championships in that era. He was a successful and popular figure on the world tennis circuit that was then centred on the tourist spots of Europe.'

twice won the Men's Doubles in 1908 and 1910. The Englishman's partner for those two titles was the New Zealand-born Anthony Wilding, a two-time winner of the Australian Open and four-time winner of the Wimbledon Singles Championship.

McGuire's next appearance at the fabled Wimbledon Championships was in June 1927, when he reached the third round of the tournament, where he was defeated by the French left-handed player Christian Boussus. Boussus would become a successful Davis Cup player, winning the competition four times with his country. In 1930, he reached his highest ranking of ninth in the world, but would never claim a Singles Grand Slam crown. The closest he came was in the French Open in 1931, losing to four-time Grand Slam winner Jean Borotra.

Following the conclusion of Wimbledon in July 1927, in an international exhibition between England and Ireland, McGuire gave his most impressive display to date. The *Irish Independent* detailed that although Ireland lost the tie 4–2 the:

> philosophical can find solace even in defeat, and thus we can console ourselves in some measure through the fact that our one victory on Saturday was the result of a fine display by one of the younger generation. E.A. McGuire, whose play in the last couple of years has hardly been up to expectation, showed definite advance in winning his match against M.V. Summerson in straight sets. Hitherto his chief failing has been a lack of confidence in himself – a tendency to play tentatively and

allow his opponent to dictate the course of the match. On Saturday, however, he hit the ball with vigour tempered by discretion, and, against an erratic opponent always held the upper hand. His visit to Wimbledon this year has obviously done him much good, for he played more purposeful tennis than he has hitherto produced.

He won 6–1, 6–3. To place the result in context, Ireland's record in the Davis Cup from 1923 was a single victory over India (R1, 1923). The Irish endeavour was for competitiveness at an international level, while players such as McGuire and George Lyttleton Rogers sought to promote the game further in the Free State.

In 1928, McGuire returned to the Irish Davis Cup fold after defeating G.W. Scroope in straight sets, 6–2, 6–1, 6–1 at trials at the Fitzwilliam Club. The *Sunday Independent* outlined that McGuire:

> was untroubled by the nervousness which generally attacks him on big occasions and in consequence played the tennis of which we all know he is capable ... McGuire defended skilfully from the back of the court until the inevitable short one came back, and he then scored the winning ace with a hard, deep drive to either corner, or a well-angled volley.

This new-found confidence aided McGuire on his journey to reaching the final four of that year's Irish Championship. However, Ireland's search for a first-round Davis Cup victory was denied by Hungary by a score of 5–0.

Another of McGuire's impressive displays came in a Davis Cup tie against Italy in 1929, in which he was defeated by de Stefani, 6–4, 4–6, 8–6, 4–6, 8–6. A clip from this game can be seen on British Pathé News on YouTube. The following day, McGuire was again defeated by Baron H.L. de Morpurgo by three sets to one. CAM of the *Irish Independent* noted:

> No one can deny it was the best display given by an Irish team for a number of years, and it is all the more encouraging for the fact that we were not depending upon men who next season might be thousands of miles away from Fitzwilliam Club. In G.L. Rogers and E.A. McGuire we have two young players who should be available for a number of years to come, and perhaps this match with Italy marks the turning point of our fortunes in International tennis ... McGuire has never played better than he did on this occasion, and this despite the fact he was suffering from a badly blistered toe.

Ireland had reached the second round after receiving a bye in the earlier stage. The Italian pair that McGuire faced were the top two Italian players, with de Morpurgo having achieved a silver medal at the 1924 Paris Olympics. The same year, McGuire again participated in Wimbledon but was defeated by the German Heinrich Kleinschroth, losing in five sets.

So many near misses were finally pushed a side when McGuire sealed victory for Ireland over Monaco in the first round of the 1930 Davis Cup at the Fitzwilliam Club. This gained them the right to play Australia in the next round. The Aussie selection included superstars such as Jack Crawford, who would win six Grand Slam titles, and Edgar Moon, winner of that year's Australian Open. Against such a calibre of player, McGuire and his country's hopes were ended at that stage.

In 1931, McGuire won three Irish lawn tennis titles, winning the Singles Championships for the first time, defeating young Cork international H.F. Cronin, 6–2, 6–2, 6–3; the Men's Doubles and retaining the Mixed Doubles with Miss Fleming. Another appearance at Wimbledon saw him reach the second round, where he was defeated by Ian Collins in five sets. McGuire's first-round victory came when leading by two sets to one over his opponent Teddy Higgs, who retired due to injury. McGuire was pivotal in Ireland's first-round victory in the Davis Cup over Switzerland (scoreline 5–0), winning both his matches against Hector Fisher and Charles Aeschliman. They were defeated in the next round by South Africa 4–1.

McGuire's fine form continued as he added hard court titles to his extensive collection in May 1932, with the *Irish Press* deeming him to be 'the premier player in Ireland without any doubt'. It was to be a golden year, as he formed part of the team that defeated Hungary 4–1 in the second round (again receiving a bye in the first round) of that year's Davis Cup. They were knocked out in the next round in Berlin by Germany. In one of the ties, McGuire was defeated by future two-time French Open Champion Gottfried von Cramm. At the County Wicklow Championship meeting in Bray in August 1932, McGuire had the distinction of reaching three championship finals, of which he won two. He defeated A.E. Fannin in the Men's Singles final and the Men's Doubles with his partner being D.D. O'Sullivan.

McGuire's period of supremacy in Irish tennis came to an end in April 1933 when he was defeated by Trevor McVeagh in three sets at the National Hard-Court Championships. 'Permel' recorded in the *Irish Press* that McGuire was 'dead off colour and has seldom before played such patchy, mistake-laden tennis'. This would lead to a debate over who should have a place on the Irish Davis Cup team, McGuire or McVeagh. Both were selected, as the *Evening Herald* hoped 'for the sake of Ireland's best chance that our second-best player, which undoubtedly McGuire is, will have come back to his best form by the time the Davis Cup begins against Denmark in Copenhagen'. This faith was to be rewarded as Ireland recorded a spectacular victory, with McGuire's defeat of the Dane E. Ulrich being key to the team progressing to the next round. Ireland were beaten in the next round by Japan, although Ned shone in the doubles test.

Nearing the end of his playing days, McGuire was not only the Honorary Secretary of the Fitzwilliam Lawn Tennis Club but also described tennis games on the radio in 1937. He was elected to the Leinster Council in January 1934. A headline in the *Irish Press* in July 1934 noted that, 'McGuire is still a force', with 'Permel' writing:

> I am afraid that I have perhaps been doing my friend E.A. McGuire, Ireland's Davis Cup player, something of an injustice by stating that Ireland's team requires younger blood.
>
> McGuire has been at the forefront in Irish tennis for such a considerable time now one could be forgiven for regarding him a veteran.
>
> As a matter of fact, he is only 32 years of age, which is an age at which many former Irish international tennis players had not been chosen to represent their country for even the first time.
>
> I should like to draw particular notice to a feature of McGuire's play this season, which calls for special comment, and which quite unjustly has not been stressed up to this. McGuire's fine displays in doubles have been one of the outstanding features of the season.

McGuire would continue to play, focusing on doubles tennis, but was recalled to the Irish set-up in 1937 as he was one of the few players to get in a lot of 'winter tennis'. He was an advocate of promoting winter lawn tennis to increase the playing and popularity of the sport in Ireland. The era in which he played proved to be the heyday of Irish tennis. McGuire was against the sending of young Irish players to play and learn the game on the Riviera. In March 1939, Edward McGuire was elected captain of the Irish international team. Sadly, the playing of tennis internationally was interrupted by the Second World War.

'From Country Drapers into the Aristocracy of the Free State': Ned the Senator

Ned McGuire was asked to help organise Dublin employers to deal with the growth of the trade union movement. He was a high-profile figure in the Drapers' Chamber of Trade and in 1937 became Chairman of the Federated Employers Ltd Industrial relations were modernised as the organisation took on a much more modern and professional approach to industrial relations in line with the stipulations of the Trade Union Act of 1941. The following year saw the Federated Union of Employers created, and McGuire's guidance was central in the formation of the main employers' negotiating group in the Republic of Ireland. He served as president of the group until 1967 when he was given the title of 'founder patron'.

The Tramore native was a supporter of the Cumann na nGaedheal party in the 1920s and as it morphed into Fine Gael, McGuire was later nominated as a Senator in 1948 by Taoiseach John A. Costello. He would hold his position in the Senate until 1965 (elected on the Industrial and Commercial panel). McGuire felt that the party wasn't openly pro-business but served as the main fundraiser of the organisation, acting as a link between the party and the business community. Maurice Manning attributes the loss of McGuire's seat in 1965 to 'carelessly spending most of the campaign on a continental cruise'.

Anne Haverty, in her history of Brown Thomas titled *Elegant Times*, writes that 'within a generation the McGuires had been transformed from country drapers into the aristocracy of the Free State'.

'Technique of Expressionism': The Artist and Collector

McGuire was considered an adept painter, evoking the style of Jack B. Yeats. E.C. Curran in *The Bell* of September 1941 noted that 'his work has shown in different degrees the influence of Yeats, Roualt and Vlaminck, and he has finally adopted the technique of expressionism'. He was a member of the Dublin Painters' Group and the Academy of Christian Art. McGuire built up an impressive art collection and was an early advocate of good design in industry. Such was his expertise, he had been appointed to an advisory committee on design in industry by the Minister for Industry and Commerce in 1939.

McGuire was a member of the Board of Governors of the National Gallery of Ireland for thirty years and served as its chairman for sixteen years. In 1951, he was appointed as an inaugural member of the Arts Council by Éamon de Valera. Sadly, two years later, McGuire's wife Brigid died, in February 1953. In 1957, his eldest son John Francis McGuire, was engaged to Birgitta Wennerberg, the daughter of the then Swedish Minister Folke Wennerberg. They would later divorce and the younger John Francis would marry a second time and later established the A-Wear chain.

Noted in the pages of the *Munster Express*, McGuire never forgot his Waterford roots and in the mid-1960s donated 'a most valuable dinner set of Old Waterford Glass to the Old Waterford Society', which apparently met in City Hall in the 1970s. Around the same time as donating the Waterford glass, McGuire attended the annual Waterpark College Past Pupils' Union dinner in 1964 and said that he 'cherished the happiest of memories of his boyhood years in Waterpark College'. Yet in addition to this, the *Southern Star* reported he thought it 'was wrong for workers to seek more money and shorter hours'.

In September 1976, a three-day fine art auction was held at Newtown Park House and realised £320,000, with the collection of paintings, tapestry and porcelain of the former senator being sold. The auction was handled by Christie's of London and Hamilton and Hamilton of Dublin. On the final day, the highest price was £6,000, paid by a Dublin dealer for a late seventeenth-century Mortlake tapestry panel symbolising autumn. Part of the sale was due to McGuire moving to a modern home nearby. The family home for nearly forty years was to be demolished to make way for a housing development, while the golf course was to form a car park for residents.

Later years saw McGuire spilt his time between his homes in Dublin and Spain. He died on 27 October 1992 and is buried at Deansgrange cemetery. One of Tramore and Waterford's forgotten sons, he represented his country in the Davis Cup, adept on both grass and hard courts, yet his style and progressiveness were displayed in his business acumen and love of the arts. Ned McGuire lived many lives and his legacy continues to encompass the social, sporting and cultural life of Ireland.

Jack B. Yeats. The Irish Museum of Modern Art (IMMA) details, 'Irish painter Jack Butler Yeats was born in London and grew up in Sligo with his maternal grandparents before returning to London in 1887 to live with his parents. He briefly attended the Government School of Design and the Westminster School of Art and went on to work as an illustrator for sporting periodicals and newspapers. A visit to the west of Ireland in 1898 inspired his first solo exhibition 'Sketches of Life in the West of Ireland'. It would remain his theme for much of his artistic career. By 1910 he had moved permanently to Ireland, living in Greystones, Co. Wicklow and later Dublin. Yeats was elected a member of the Royal Hibernian Academy in 1916. His painting 'The Liffey Swim' won a silver medal at the 1924 Olympic Games in Paris. The broad fluid brushstrokes of that work mark the change in his technique during the 1920s, from that decade his work became more expressive and experimental. Yeats's work is held in numerous national collections including IMMA, the National Gallery of Ireland, Dublin City Gallery The Hugh Lane, Crawford Art Gallery and the Model, Sligo.'

27

'I Fail to See Why We Cannot Play Polo': Waterford Polo Club, 1904–06

On Friday, 3 June 1904, an inaugural meeting of members and those wishing to join the Waterford Polo Club was held at the Imperial Hotel at 12 noon. The governance of the club and various rules were to be discussed, with the meeting arranged by Club Secretary Captain E.H. Holmes. He had convened the meeting at the request of several gentlemen keen to develop the sport in the city. A large gathering at the Imperial saw Dr Staunton propose George F. Malcolmson to the role of chairing the foundation meeting, which was seconded by J.J. Stafford, and passed unanimously. Malcolmson noted that though it was late in the season, if the proposed club was to succeed then it was paramount that a president, secretary, treasurer and committee were appointed for the effective functioning of the organisation. Once these roles were filled, it was important for the club to find suitable grounds for the following season. They initially settled on the old drill field at Ballinaneeshagh. Although too small, it was the best site available at this juncture to get things off the ground. The long-term plan was to obtain the use of a field at Mullinabro (which would have required an hour's walk from the city, and crossing Timbertoes Bridge) which a Mr Jones was willing for the polo club to have the use of for 1905.

Holmes detailed to the gathering that he had received a letter from the Marquess of Waterford, which noted that the peer would consent to become president of the new club if established. Those assembled were keen to have both playing and non-playing members form part of the fledgling club. This led to the matter of annual subscriptions being discussed, which saw Staunton propose a fee of 2 guineas for playing members, and a guinea for non-players, which was agreed upon. It was noted that in attendance were twelve members who wished to be players. Turning to costs,

Holmes highlighted that it would cost £10 to put the parade ground in order, as the surface had rocks at the centre of it, which needed to be removed. For the field at Ballinaneeshagh, the lease would amount to £35 for six months, with Holmes concluding, 'but that need not deter us. I fail to see why we cannot play polo in Waterford as well as they do in South Africa or India'.

The following officers were elected:

President: The Most Noble the Marquess of Waterford, K.P.,
Vice Presidents: Alderman Sir James A. Power, Mayor of Waterford; Captain Palliser, Sir William Paul, Bart., Mr P.M. Power, Faithlegg, Mr John Widger and Alderman W.G.D. Goff, J.P.
Hon. Secretary: Captain Holmes,
Committee of six (elected by ballot): Messrs G. Malcolmson, Chairman, G.P. Fitzgerald, J.J. Stafford, W. Robertson, W. Richardson and Dr. Staunton.
Hon. Treasurer: Dr. Staunton

The committee arranged an opening day for the club, which was held at Mullinabro on Saturday, 18 June, with the *Evening News* reporting:

> This afternoon the members of the Waterford Polo Club held their first practice on their admirably laid out grounds at Mullinabro, which is one of the most conveniently situated and picturesque venues in the South-East of Ireland. There was a large and fashionable attendance, and the interest evinced in the meeting, gave ample proof that the club has a splendid future before it. It was not thought that this fine ground could have been secured this season, but thanks to the courtesy and characteristic kindness of Mr Jones, certain difficulties which at first appeared insurmountable were overcome, and the Waterford Polo Club have not only acquired its name, but a first-class habitation as well. It was too late this afternoon when the practice was concluded to enable us to do more than to say that it was all that could be desired, but we hope later on to have the opinion of an expert on the subject.

We learn that on that Saturday afternoon, a practise match was held on the 15-acre site, with the pitch matching a billiards table. Around 3.30, two teams took to the field, the Reds, who numbered Dr Staunton, Ralph Cartwright, P. Kenneally and Captain Holmes (back), against the Whites, who fielded J.J. Stafford, Widger, Groome and Captain Harpur (back). The game was refereed by W. Richardson and Captain Holland. The first goal came for the Reds, and was scored by Kenneally. The same individual scored again after an interval, as the Reds led 2–0.

Before playing again, the Reds were considered too strong for the Whites, so Cartwright and Stafford swapped sides to make it a more competitive affair. The

Whites pulled a goal back through Captain Harpur in the fourth chukker (a game is usually made up of six chukkers, with each lasting seven-and-a-half minutes). It was concluded by the Monday edition of the *Evening News* that:

> Considering that three of the players were novices, the game was fast and interesting throughout, and before the season is much older we expect a team of Waterford players will compete with success against the neighbouring clubs, Kilkenny and Carlow.

It was decided that after 8 July, the Polo Ground would be open for play on Tuesdays and Saturdays at 3.30 p.m. to members. Just over a week later, vast improvements were noted in the playing standard, as players improved with very few calls of 'off-side' or 'foul' heard. Unfortunately, the new club would lose the services of Captain Holmes as he was moving with the troops. He had left the young organisation on a sound foundation, and it was hoped that, in the words of the *Waterford Standard* it would become 'a flourishing club, which will afford excellent amusement to the members and public alike'.

Holmes was replaced by the pair of J.J. Stafford and G.T. Groome as honorary secretaries, as practise games were increased during the summer to late August, with games on Mondays, Wednesdays and Saturdays. On Saturday, 30 July 1904, a match between Red and White selections witnessed a good crowd at the grounds in Mullinabro. The Reds were listed as Jack Widger, J.J. Stafford, Captain Holmes, and Captain Musgrave (back), while the Whites included G.F. Malcolmson, Percy Kenneally, Dr Staunton and E. Winston Barron (back). The Whites took the lead through Malcolmson, and it remained that way until the third chukker, when Stafford drew level for the Reds. Two more goals in the last chukker couldn't split the sides, as the game finished 2–2. A variation of the two teams played again on Monday, with the Reds winning 3–1.

Later that week, the Waterford Polo Club faced an 'Odds and Ends' side that included Captain Musgrave, Ruggles Brise, Kilkenny, George Smithwick, Kilkenny and H.W. Barron, Woodstown. These visitors to Mullinabro won comfortably, 3–0, as the Waterford group faced the Carlow club next (on Tuesday, 30 August 1904). The Waterford side that travelled to Tiny Park in Carlow included Stafford, Widger, Kenneally, G.G. Malcolmson (alternate), and the Marquess of Waterford (back). At half-time, the County Waterford Polo Club had a commanding lead, as they were 3–1 with two chukkers to go. The visitors stretched their lead to 6–2, but collapsed in the last chukker to see the game finish 7–7. The *Standard* reported that:

> As Waterford had to get away by the afternoon train there was no time available for a deciding issue, and the game was a drawn one. The feature of the match was the

fine playing of the backs on both sides. The Waterford team is to be congratulated on having such an ardent sportsman for their captain, and on the manner the several players acquitted themselves in their first public match.

Immediately, a return match was arranged, and was set for Wednesday, 21 September, with Carlow demonstrating why they were considered one of the best clubs in the country, winning by 11 goals to 2. However, this would be dwarfed by the arrangement of an American Tournament Sealed Handicap taking place at Mullinabro on Saturday, 24 September, with the participants including:

Waterford: Messrs J.J. Stafford, J.W. Widger, G. Malcolmson, E.W. Barron.
Kilkenny: Messrs Carew, A. Smithwick, Pilsworth and Lindsay.
Slocock's Team (Carlow): Messrs A. Stoney, W.F. Slocock, B.M. Slocock, and Dr. Coghlan.
Enniscorthy: Messrs Chambers, Captain Mowbray, J. Deathe, Captain Loftus, and A. Bryan.

A prize would be presented to the winning team by E.W. Barron, and Mr Greer on Michael Street in the city had been appointed caterer for the event. It appears that the Enniscorthy selection pulled out of the tournament at short notice. However, the hosts were well beaten in two games, with Slocock's side winning 6–1, and the same score for Kilkenny. The *Evening News* concluded that:

> ... it is to the credit of the youthful Waterford Polo Club that the large crowd of spectators who journeyed to the grounds of Mullinabro were able to witness such an interesting exhibition. To the Waterford team, the majority of whom never handled a polo stick before the formation of the club, the congratulations of our sport-loving citizens are due. They possess an excellent ground, they are full of the best of spirit, and plenty of material to draw upon, what is more in this game, they know a good opponent when they meet one.

Still a long way off from being truly competitive (certainly when the Marquess of Waterford wasn't present on the playing field), the Polo Club had a terrific organisational ability, which would see it grow to match the events staged in Carlow. The Waterford club held its first annual general meeting on Saturday, 11 February 1905, at the Imperial Hotel. The main issue considered costs, which Committee Chairman Malcolmson noted as a net deficiency of £15 16s 6d, the majority of which were initial expenses that the group would not have in the future. Such purchases included £28 for a lawn mower, £12 for the erection of a shelter and £15 for the crop of hay that was on the grounds, and these were three expenses that the Waterford Polo

Club would not have to countenance for the season ahead. The committee remained largely the same, although the notable change was Major Dobbin and W.A. Murray appointed as honorary treasurers.

A couple of months later, in April 1905, the club sought to increase its membership by attracting lady members to the organisation, with their annual subscription set at 10s. The *Waterford Standard* believed that this effort was 'to have the advice and assistance of the lady members in so far as commissariat arrangements are concerned'. By mid-May, we see that Winston Barron (Woodstown) had acquired Geneva Barrack in Passage East, with the intention of developing it into a polo ground. On the field, a practise match was staged at Mullinabro on Tuesday, 9 May 1905 between the Waterford club and a Lord Waterford side, with the latter claiming victory. Despite the apparent fragmentation caused by Barron's plans at Geneva and Lord Waterford putting his own side together, a general meeting was called by the Waterford Polo Club for Monday, 29 May.

The course of the discussion held at the Imperial Hotel concerned the arrangement of a polo and bicycle gymkhana at Mullinabro for Whit Monday (12 June 1905). Previously, a great park carnival was held for the amusement of locals and visitors on the public holiday, but this subsequently waned as people's interests changed. At the same gathering members were made aware of arrangements being made for a leading Welsh club to play a Waterford selection in the season ahead. The following month saw the Waterford Club Grounds host the 3rd Dragoon Guards from Ballincollig, as anticipation continued to increase surrounding the club's activities in the area. The visitors from Cork ran out 5–2 winners, with the local *Standard* concluding that, 'Waterford made a good stand against their first military opponents and in their first game of the season, and before the close of the summer we hope to often see their colours hoisted in victory.'

Just over a week out from the gymkhana, the local polo club had put together a comprehensive programme, which included pony races, cycle events, a fancy dress parade and novelty 'bending races' (which entailed eight laths, 10 yards apart, starting from one end and returning, passing laths alternatively on right and left) to provide entertainment for all comers. Of the day, one periodical recorded:

> The weather was brilliantly fine, and as a consequence the scene was a most brilliant one, the exquisite dresses of the fair sex adding colour and effect. The programme was a very lengthy one, but so well were the ground arrangements carried out that there was not a tedious moment, the intervals being enlivened by the strains of the fine band from the Clonmel Industrial School.

This was before the polo club faced their greatest test, as a team from Pembrokeshire came to play them on Saturday, 30 June. The visitors could count on two of the best players in England, and another member who had played in nine All-India Cup finals in a row. The fixture was refereed by George Smithwick. The visitors, who numbered Lord Kensington, D. Harrison, H. Allen and F.C. Hunter, ran out easy winners on a scoreline of 11–1. The group wished to play the 3rd Dragoons at Mullinabro. Other sides the Waterford Polo Club faced that summer in 1905 included Co. Kilkenny Nos. 1 and 2, 'skirmishers', Wanderers and Malcolmson's team, while Club Secretary S.T. Groome organised a contest in Tramore on 1 September to finish the polo club's season.

The second annual general meeting was held on 3 May 1906, where Major Dobbin provided an extremely detailed treasurer's report, which placed the club's available cash in bank at £12 18s. Subscriptions amounted to £79 18s, with around £33 still to be received or collected. The property the club owned was valued at £71 14s, which when factoring in deprecation, placed the Waterford Polo Club's property and cash at around £70. Aside from a healthy bank balance, Club Secretary S.T. Groome reported of the season to be 'a very disastrous one to the Polo Club, owning to the outbreak of epizootic lymphangitis in this part of the country. A great number of people were afraid to bring their ponies into Waterford.' The disease that devastated equines was eradicated from the United Kingdom later in the year. Of the club's finances, Groome placed the increase in funds by the club down to the successful gymkhana, which raised £12 4s 7d. The secretary posed questions concerning the future existence of the club, with the need for future gymkhanas, and the possibility of adding a croquet club to the polo group.

After the group agreed to continue for another season, a resolution was passed that the playing members' subscription would be increased to £5. The biggest event to be staged was the gymkhana at Mullinabro on Friday, 29 June 1906, and in preparation for it, the polo club hosted Tenby from Wales, and the Waterford side claimed a notable scalp with a 4–3 victory. Turning to the gymkhana, prizes were presented by the Marchioness of Waterford, while the band of the Royal Irish Regiment under the baton of Mr Chammings provided the soundtrack to a Victoria Cross Race, Housewives' Stakes over 30 yards, a bending race on ponies, tent pegging and a pig stick competition. A notable prize was a valuable antique silver trophy, won by Richard Stafford, which would later be displayed in the window of C.W. Mosley on the Quay. Returning to the sport, Cambridge Wanderers and County Wexford were to play an exhibition match at the Waterford Polo Grounds on Thursday, 16 August, with E. Winston Barron playing an important part in staging the event.

Over just two years of its existence, the *Waterford Standard* deemed that the efforts of the Waterford Polo Club had popularised the pursuit:

> In support of this we have it that the street arabs [sic] of the Irish metropolis gathering along the boundaries of the Nine Cres can be heard day after day discussing the various points of the game with a knowledge and a zeal that could hardly be

'I Fail to See Why We Cannot Play Polo': Waterford Polo Club, 1904–06

approached by polo veterans themselves. The Waterford Polo Club, as at present constituted, is only a short time in existence, but they have one of the best arenas in Ireland, and are doing their part to cater for the tastes of the sporting public of the district.

Later in the month, the Waterford Club faced Cambridge, but were resoundingly beaten 9–3, even with the help of Wexford players Captain Moubray and Mr Chambers, as the defeat brought the polo club's season to a close. It would turn out to be the last full year for the Waterford Polo Club.

It appears that there were so many different efforts in playing polo in County Waterford that they in turn came to be competing against one another, as the Waterford club couldn't unite enough figures to make it viable in the longer term. While Kilkenny, Carlow and Wexford had cohesive and competitive sides, in Waterford we have reference to teams under the auspices of Barron, Malcolmson and Lord Waterford, while the continual movements of the local military meant that the club had no core that would help it gather momentum on the playing fields. We see the field at Mullinabro no longer maintained by the club, and without a tournament that was held there in September 1907, it is very unlikely any polo would have been staged there that year. The competition arranged by E. Winston Barron was notable in no side carrying the Waterford name, with the entrants including County Carlow, County Wexford and 'the Triflers' side put together by Barron.

And with that, a club that appeared to have started off on the right course would disappear from the local scene, with very little disappointment surrounding its demise. It was a sport played by lords, baronets and wealthy merchants, involving a small number of players who did not distil their own aspirations, as personal ambition saw a community (which in a few decades' time would become much maligned in Irish society) come into conflict with itself. It lacked the military discipline that would see other sports such as rugby and soccer become popular in Waterford city.

Patrick Joseph Mahon: Forgotten World No. 1 Golfer?

Early Years: The Mahons – a Family of Golfers

Patrick Joseph Mahon was born on 7 November 1906 in Dublin and named after his father, Patrick, who was born in Sligo, and served with the Royal Irish Constabulary in Wexford, Belfast, and later in Kilkenny. After his career in the RIC, Paddy Jr's father was recorded as working in insurance and living at Laytown when he received slight injuries when hit by a motor vehicle while cycling in September 1937. One certainty was that the younger Patrick was educated at Mount Sion CBS in the heart of Waterford city. Paddy's brother Charlie attended the same school and excelled academically, receiving a scholarship with CIÉ (at one stage it appeared that Paddy would become a railway clerk) and later lived in the Glen, just a short distance from the city's quays. Yet, Paddy Mahon was to follow a different career path completely by becoming a professional golfer.

We know that, as a young man, Mahon caddied in Tramore and Waterford and was a student of P.J. O'Sullivan (later captain of Tramore Golf Club). His first steps into golf as a career were as an assistant professional at Waterford Golf Club, followed by professional positions at Rathdowney, then Birr, Co. Offaly, and eventually settling at the Royal Dublin Club around 1934. Paddy wasn't the only member of his family to leave a mark on the Irish golf scene. His brother J.A. Mahon would take up duties at Castlebar links in April 1938, while two years later, in June 1940, his other brother C.P. competed in the Irish Close Championship.

His Game: 'Very Smoothly and Very Surely'

Mahon was of diminutive stature, reaching 5ft 3in tall and weighing 9½st. From subsequent conversations the author has had with Paddy's grandson, Kevin McArdle, the success that Mahon enjoyed was even more remarkable, as he was born with a disability – having one leg shorter than the other – which led him to wear callipers. Kevin details that Paddy wore a calliper on one leg until the age of 7, and on the other until he was 14 years old. Aged just 17, Mahon was diagnosed with Type 1 diabetes, which severely impacted his golf career. Long periods of sickness and lethargy were further exacerbated by hypoglycaemia, resulting in uncontrollable tremors. It certainly wouldn't aid putting on the green. Kevin describes his grandfather as a natural lefty, but this would have been considered an aberration in children when schooled, often resulting in it being 'caned' out of them. Mahon could play off both his right and left.

The *Irish Independent* noted that 'few players of his time had greater length with a wooden club'. Mahon stressed to the *Irish Press* that the core aspect of his game was 'timing … and that the power comes from the hips'. A later showing at the Irish Professional Championships in August 1944 saw the *Press* reminisce 'his driving showed all of unique – sweetness', while he 'hardly raises his left heel off the ground in the backswing', a technique he did not pass on to his students. His style was noted as one possessed by few professional golfers, with his pitching and approach play a great strength.

However, Mahon's weakness was putting, and later in his career stamina and confidence would become issues that impeded him from destroying the field and claiming more championships and tournaments. With the information provided by Kevin McArdle, the reason for all of this becomes much clearer. When his putting was going well, it was described by 'Machrie' as 'he seems to slide the ball on the green very smoothly and very surely'. Though the *Press* believed, 'he had that unfortunate habit … of shooting the whole works on the first couple of rounds and blowing up after that'. The *Irish Independent* again noted that Mahon had a 'cheerful temperament [which] was unruffled by success or failure'.

From Competitor to Contender:
1935 Western Isles Champion, the First Irish Golfer
to Win a Tournament in Britain

From 1932 to 1936, Mahon finished runner-up four times (1932 at Royal Dublin and 1933 at Castlerock) at the Irish Professional Championship. In 1932 he represented Ireland in matches against England and Scotland. His best performance at a major British tournament came in 1934 when he finished in a five-way tie for fourth place at the Dunlop-Southport tournament held at Southport and Ainsdale Golf Club. Mahon made his first appearance in the Open Championship in a quest for the Claret Jug but missed the cut by a single stroke (his first round of 72 had him placed in tied tenth position). His move from Birr to Royal Dublin was the start of his greatest performances to come for the remainder of the decade.

In 1935, he won the Western Isles (North of Scotland) Championship on Islay in a field comprised of American and British players. This made him the first Irish professional to bring a British title across the Irish Sea. His aggregate score of 283 saw him four shots ahead of the chasing pack to claim the prize of 150 guineas. The *Glasgow Herald* concluded that Mahon was 'one of the most promising young professional golfers that Ireland has produced since the war'. Two weeks later, he competed at the 70th Open Championship at Muirfield and hit an impressive first round of 71 to place tied seventh on one under par. His challenge would fade as he would finish in a tie for fortieth place. A breakthrough year was a signal of further successes to come in the following two years.

Peak Years: 1936–37

It is acknowledged that his peak years were 1936 and 1937. The latter year was to be his most golden. In 1936 he qualified for the *Daily Mail* tourney (which he would finish in tied twenty-seventh) and won the Dunlop-Irish tournament at Royal Belfast with an aggregate score of 298. His quest to qualify for another Open Championship started well with an opening round of 73, but heavy rain led to the abandoning of play and the earlier scores in qualifying were cancelled. His last two rounds of 78 saw him miss qualifying by a single stroke. Once more, he finished runner-up in the Irish Professional Championship, finishing four shots behind Joe McCartney. At the same tournament, his brother J.A., then an amateur at Birr, made a hole in one with his tee shot at the 125-yard twelfth at Galway. In September 1936 Paddy finished third at the Morecambe-Penfold Northern Open Championship, six shots behind winner Percy Alliss.

Mahon opened his remarkable 1937 season with a tied for third finish at the *Daily Mail* tournament. His golfing ability was further illustrated in April 1937 when he finished as runner-up in the Silver King £1,000 professional golf tournament at Moor Park, Rickmansworth. Mahon was one off the lead of the winner, former Open Champion Henry Cotton, with the Royal Dublin golfer's skill and ill-luck typified by his play on the sixteenth hole. The former Mount Sion student needed two shots under par from the remaining three holes to claim a momentous victory. This appeared against the odds on the 480 yards, which was uphill and had to be played against the wind. The *Irish Press* recorded that, 'Mahon's seemingly frail physique appeared to be unequal to the task – but he put all his heart into a glorious brassie shot which finished on the green and the problematic four seemed a certainty.' Having put himself in position for the win, his 4ft putt ran around the lip of the hole to stay on the edge, meaning a fifth stroke was needed and thus ending his chance of winning.

This was far from a failure though, as the Irish press concluded that it was one of the best performances by an Irish golfer up to that point. Returning to Dublin with a £100 cheque from his efforts at Rickmansworth seemed to signal bigger things ahead and the possible departure of Mahon from being a regular presence on the Irish golfing circuit.

One of his most notable rounds of his greatest year was a 66 (second round) on the Hesketh course at Southport in the Dunlop-Southport £1,600 tournament, where he finished in a more than respectable sixth place.

1937 Ryder Cup Controversy

Mahon was being touted as making the Ryder Cup team for 1937. George Duncan was being suggested as a non-playing captain (as he was supposed to have the 'Indian sign' over Walter Hagen, his US counterpart), while Henry Cotton, Charles and Reggie Whitcombe, Dick Burton and Dal Rees were all nailed on to make the team. Mahon was considered a certainty except for the issue of the residency rule. The Ryder Cup Deed of Trust had been reviewed and revised to stipulate that players had to be born in and resident in their respective countries. The deed referred to Great Britain, which the PGA took as a literal interpretation of excluding those born and living in Ireland. The Royal Dublin golfer missed out on selection, while the American team claimed their first Ryder Cup victory in Britain.

Ryder Cup.

French to British Open Championship: Highs and Lows

Yet, Mahon was not content with just competing at Irish and British tournaments. June 1937 saw him enter the French Open Championship and as a result he became the first Irish professional to compete in a foreign championship. He travelled from Ireland to Leeds for a tournament at Moortown before making his way to Paris to play at the St Cloud course. With an aggregate total of 288, Mahon finished ten strokes behind M. Dallemagne (who retained his French title) in sixth place.

The following month, Mahon defied doctor's orders to play the first day of the qualifying stages for the British Open Championship at Carnoustie (he played a round of 70 at Burnside, which was a new record at the time). Of this round, the *Herald* of Glasgow noted that Mahon 'would probably have been selected in the Ryder Cup team but for his Irish nationality, and who is regarded here as a possible winner'.

Mahon didn't make the cut at Carnoustie as the *Munster Express* detailed that he suffered from a severe cold. On the first two nights he went straight from the eighteenth green to bed and that it was noticeable that his 'hands shook as he putted'. A consequence of this was that he had to pull out of the Irish Open at Portrush for what was described as 'a long holiday'.

'Mahon is the Most Talked-of Golfer this Year': World No. 1?

The *Irish Independent*, in recording his absence from the event, highlighted that 'apart from Henry Cotton, Mahon is the most talked-of golfer this year'. Nevertheless, statistics published by the *Irish Press* in July 1937 of professional golfers who had completed eighteen rounds or more at major tournaments placed Mahon top of the list with an average of 71.95 strokes over twenty-two rounds, a fraction ahead of Open Champion Henry Cotton. Of this astonishing statistic, the same publication concluded that Mahon had done 'much to put Irish golf on the map ... He has ... the distinction of having led the world's greatest golfer over half a season's tournament play'.

He returned to action in August 1937 to win his first Irish PGA Championship, finishing with an aggregate score of 298, ten shots ahead of tied second place J. McCartney (Holywood) and J. McKenna (Bundoran). It appears Mahon's ability to keep the ball on the fairway with length was the key to his success. His increased confidence and an improvement in his short game had seen him grow in stature by taking the opportunities that presented themselves.

In September, he would finish in second place at the 6,701-yard course at Wentworth, which was won by Arthur Lacey. It was his third round of 68 that brought him into contention as he moved up the leaderboard from sixth place to tie third with Henry Cotton going into the final round of play. His putting again deserted him in a round that saw him three putt twice on both the fourth and twelfth hole. His final round of 69 saw him as the only player to break 70 twice in the last two rounds. The season saw Mahon finish second in the

Harry Vardon.

Harry Vardon Trophy competition with a final average of 71.90, missing out on the prize by 0.28 of a shot behind Charles Whitcombe. This finish saw him invited to the Penfold Professional Golf League for 1938. He would finish bottom of the twelve-man league on 5 points (one win and three halved games).

Commercial Activities: Classes at Clery's

Mahon was now giving lectures and lessons on golf in the sports department of Clery's. He would also contribute articles to the *Irish Sports Review* concerning golf swing and technique. The *Cork Examiner* noted in November 1937 that 'it will be readily conceded that Mahon is the greatest golfer that Ireland has yet produced'. Such was his renown, Irish papers of the period frequently featured advertisements in which Mahon promoted Dubtex elasticated trousers.

It appeared that 1938 would be his busiest year to date, playing all the big English tournaments as well as having a number of exhibition matches pencilled in. However, the heavy schedule would be blamed for his lacklustre performance in finishing runner-up in the Michael Moran Memorial Cup of Royal Dublin to Pat O'Connor (Woodbrook Club). The same year, Mahon married Moira Coleman and the couple would have four children together.

At the Open Championship at Royal St George, 18-year-old James Bruen of Muskerry, Co. Cork, was tied for the lead after shooting a 70 in the first round. Mahon was three shots further back. However, the Cork junior would shoot an 80 the next day to miss the cut. Mahon, who was still plagued by health issues, was putting in a gallant performance, being only seven off the lead. The *Evening Echo* suggested, 'as he proved several times last year, he is capable of a very strong finish, and he can be depended upon fully to uphold the prestige of Irish golf'. He finished in tied twentieth in what would prove to be his best performance at the most prestigious and historic event in golf.

Later Career

Ill health would appear to plague Mahon for the rest of the decade and into the 1940s. As he battled Fred Daly to win a fourth Irish Professional Championship in a row in August 1940, his challenge faded. 'Onlooker' remarked in the *Cork Examiner*:

> The champion showed not alone that it was possible to get good figures but that it did not require any spectacular efforts to do so. He played run-up shots to every green, except at the sixteenth, where he had to pitch: he was sometimes short, never

too strong, and he was always putting for his fours. They were not the kind of shots you would marvel at in retrospect, but they yielded the figures, and the figures are the only things that matter in a championship. Mahon's subsequent loss of confidence was the most amazing feature of the championship. He missed enough short putts to give him the title by several strokes.

The *Irish Press* in August 1943 noted an item on the agenda of the Leinster branch of the Golfing Union, 'which should and will probably be raised at this meeting is that concerning Paddy Mahon, the Royal Dublin professional, who now finds himself virtually out of a job and certainly without a home. Doubtless the G.U.I. will give sympathetic consideration to a man who has done so much for Irish golf.'

Mahon's last great showing came at the Irish Professional Championship, with the *Irish Press* in August 1944 noting that 'his driving showed all its usual almost unique – sweetness. His approach play was grand, and on the green he avoided those lapses, which put black marks on the cards of the majority of the players.'

Legacy

Mahon was a well-known figure in both Britain and Ireland prior to his untimely death aged just 38 in 1945. He had won the Irish Professional Championship three years in a row – 1937 at Portmarnock; 1938 at Portrush and 1939 at Bundoran. In the five years previous to his first win at Portmarnock he was runner-up on four occasions. His five professional wins and the fact he was the first Irish golfer to win a tournament in Britain is not a fair reflection of a man who did so much to promote the game and lead a path that Fred Daly would follow and surpass subsequently. Perhaps if he had played in that 1937 Ryder Cup things could have been so very different. When one looks at Mahon's achievements through the prism of his disability and ill health, his achievements are elevated further. Paddy's story should be more widely known today, for the sheer inspiring nature that is at the heart of it. One doubts we will ever see the likes of Paddy Mahon again. His tragically young death has allowed his story to be lost in time and, sadly, left a young family without a father, the greatest tragedy of them all.

'Old Men and Novices': Roller Hockey in Waterford, 1910–85

The first recorded game of 'roller hockey' (using a hardball) was at the Denmark Rink in London in 1878. Four years later, the sport was introduced embryonically to the United States with the creation of the National Roller Polo League in Dayton, Ohio. Initially, players used polo mallets before eventually adopting hockey sticks. The sport continued to evolve over the course of the nineteenth and early twentieth century, with many teams in continental Europe by 1901. Two of the most famous individuals to play roller hockey were silent film stars Stan Laurel and Charlie Chaplin. The game comprised of five players a side and was akin to hockey on skates. Such was the thirst to develop the game in Waterford that on Tuesday, 1 November 1910 (just a few days after a plot was foiled to kill the Kaiser), a meeting was held at the Rink on Adelphi Quay to form the Waterford and District Rink Hockey Association with representatives from Carrick, Clonmel, Dungarvan, Enniscorthy, Kilkenny, New Ross, Tramore and Wexford in attendance. It was the first step in the formal organisation of what was also known as 'rink hockey' in Waterford city.

Waterford and District Rink Hockey Association at Adelphi Quay, 1911–12

At the meeting in Adelphi Quay, it was agreed that the 'Waterford and District' would comprise or include sides in areas within 50 miles around Waterford city. Practise sessions for gentlemen were to be held on Mondays and Fridays, with practices for ladies taking place every Wednesday. This was to be enhanced with two public matches a week with a view to forming the Waterford Rink Hockey Club for fixtures against sides from Cork, Dublin and Limerick. Meanwhile, the league was to be organised by

Waterford Rink Secretary J.C. Ferguson, with a set of gold medals already in place for the competition's winners.

On Thursday, 24 November 1910, the first public rink hockey match in Waterford was held at the Waterford Rink, with the teams being:

The Scarlett Pimpernels: Bertie Poole, W. Torrie, Gray, McIntire and W. Brabason (goalie).
Dreadnoughts: J.T. Chapman, G. Mitchell, T. Pender, Joseph Spencer and E. Harris (goalie).

The twenty-minute match saw the Pimpernels claim victory by two goals to no score, as Gray scored the pair in front of a substantial crowd. The momentum for the development of the sport in the city was further accelerated with the arrangement of several Cork City rinking teams to play in Waterford over the Christmas holidays.

Other teams in the local league included the Bachelors and Woodpeckers. Come the following spring, the Waterford Rink at Adelphi Quay staged an Intercity Rink Hockey match between Limerick and Waterford on Tuesday, 14 February 1911, with a 'bully off' time of 9.15 p.m. and an admission charge of 6*d*. From this exhibition, a team would be selected for the South vs North Munster Competition. As the Waterford Rink's first league season came to a close, the Pimpernels were all but assured of the title with only four fixtures remaining. The following season saw the Scarlett Pimpernels face a side named Teddy Bears for the honour of the rink's colours, but coverage of the sport dwindled to no reports come the winter of 1911. As the rink struggled financially, it closed in 1912 and later reopened as the city's first cinema, named the Rink Picture Palace and later known as the Coliseum Cinema. One imagines the loss of the venue, combined with the outbreak of the First World War put paid to any longer-term plans for the playing of 'rink hockey', as it was then known in Waterford.

Olympia (Roller) Hockey League, 1939–57

During the interwar years, there was renewed interest in playing roller hockey and such was the sport's popularity that the first World Championship was staged in 1936 at Stuttgart in Germany. Thus, it should serve as no surprise that the global trend was reflected in the south-east of Ireland, in the island's oldest city of Waterford. The greatest impetus to the progress of the playing of roller hockey in Waterford was the development of the Olympia Ballroom on Parnell Street, which opened as a skating rink on Saturday, 22 October 1938. From early on in the history of the Olympia there was the intention to stage rink hockey competitions as a means for the people of Waterford to keep fit, with the *Munster Express* (16 December 1938) noting the benefits for men and women, such as:

> ... for the ladies. They can get no better exercise for slimming and also acquiring a graceful carriage. For the men it hardens the muscles considerably and reduces the weight making them physically fit.

The inaugural Olympia Skating Rink Hockey Championships took place in 1939. The tournament included sides such as Blues (made up by the Hodge family), Olympians (Tramore), Pirates (Messrs Graves & Co.), Redskins and Tigers (possibly a Hearne's selection) competing for the league title. The top two sides appeared to be Pirates and Tigers, with the most notable player being Douglas McBride, who captained the Pirates five. The final was held on Wednesday, 19 April 1939 at Parnell Street, where the Redskins defeated the Tigers by one goal to no score. The eventual winners dominated the first half but could not beat P. Dowling until E. Gilligan netted with a hard strike from a goalmouth melee. Tigers tried to battle back in a thrilling game, but would regret their flat opening-half performance.

Waterford Ladies 5–1 Dublin Ladies, Summer 1939

In summer 1939, a Waterford Ladies' team defeated a Dublin selection 5–1 with a side made up of E. Cronin, M. Keller, L. Iddon, E. Iddon and M. Kelly as captain. The men's team that drew 1–1 with their capital counterparts lined out as follows: T. Ryan, J. Kiely, J. McDonald, P. Daly and J. Quinn (captain). The Rink Hockey League began its second season on Tuesday, 6 February 1940 in rude health, with the majority of the original entrants returning to take part. The opening round was held on Shrove Tuesday with a brilliant atmosphere cultivated by carnival novelties and confetti battles as rink manager J.F. Costen and rink instructor Michael Bohill conducted a raffle. Once more, the development of the sport was impeded by difficulties surrounding the Second World War and that was reflected in local paper coverage, which whittled away to next to nothing.

Tramore Dominate Olympia Hockey League, 1942–57

After the Second World War, we can note the development of teams such as the Bohemians and Allied Ironfounders as we again see the important role played by local industry and business in the Suirside sporting sphere. Furthermore, Tramore continued their strong tradition in the game by submitting both men's and women's

The Metal Man, Tramore.

teams into the Olympia Hockey Cup. The men's team would enter two sides, while the women's selection were defeated by a city selection. Thus, it is no surprise to note that Tramore were Hockey League Cup holders on three occasions as the twentieth century reached its midpoint. The staging of the Olympia hockey season was held during the Lenten season, which again serves as a reflection of the times in which roller hockey was most popular.

Furthermore, it is worth noting that going into the 1950s, there was a Waterford team known as The Blazers, possibly alluding to Saint Blaise. Just as the spring beckoned the old Five Nations Rugby Championship or September saw the staging of the All-Ireland finals, the roller hockey league coincided with Lent. The Munster Express reported that on 9 March 1950, 1,500 spectators (one of the highest attendances noted in local papers) packed the Olympia Ballroom to see Tramore A's victory over Bohemians in the League Cup. The Seasiders first round victory was a further statement of their championship credentials. The Tramore side would achieve three titles in a row in 1951. *The Tatler* highlighted that, 'The hockey matches provide some thrilling spectacles, and the speed at which these games are played, must be seen to be believed.' There was renewed competition with sides such as C.Y.M.S, the Foundry, Hotspurs (probably named after the 1951

English First Division winners, Tottenham), Panthers and Ramblers challenging the Olympia League's most dominant side in Tramore.

Of the Hockey Rink Cup semi-final in April 1952, the *Munster Express* reported of the Seasiders' 1–0 victory over Hotspurs that, 'the game had much of the needle element.' Once more, Tramore were victorious, claiming a sixth title when they defeated the Ramblers 4–3 in an exhilarating final. However, it appeared that a team that were once lauded were now being loathed. In their final match report, the *Munster Express* noted:

> It is to be deplored that the staging of the final was, to say the least, marked by 'scenes' of a regrettable character. 'Targets' for the occasion seemed to be visiting Tramore players who had to endure the indignity of frequent cat-calling and booing. It was a poor display of sportsmanship on the part of those responsible, and it was the type of conduct which, it is to be hoped, will not be repeated on any future occasion.

This would appear to have been the last hurrah for that Tramore side as it disbanded prior to the 1953 season; however, some of its members would join the Olympians team. It is no shock to note that the Olympians won the Hockey League that season when they beat Ramblers in the final.

The next few years saw intercounty competition come to the fore, such as an exhibition game between Waterford and Dublin Arcadians on Thursday, 9 April 1953. It was a sport that was becoming increasingly popular in Ireland and is reflected by a national team defeating Egypt in Geneva in the World Rink Roller Hockey Championships in May 1953. A local league was staged at the Olympia, with the Ramblers defeating a Waterford Foundry side in the competition final in 1954. The following campaign would see a reverse of fortunes as the Foundry defeated the Ramblers, a side that had lost three of the four finals it had reached in a row. The games continued to draw huge crowds, with notable sides including Waterford Glass A, Night Owls, The Chancers and the Nockin' Rangers competing with the aforementioned Ramblers, Shamrocks and Grannagh United. Tramore continued to be a hotbed for roller hockey (bar a brief break in the mid-1950s) from when its first club was established in 1942 by James Quinn and Kevin O'Connor.

Skating proved a popular pastime in the late 1950s into the early '60s as the Olympia had skating on Sundays, Tuesdays and Thursday nights with roller hockey matches each night. Admission was 2s for skaters, while spectators were charged 6d. The evening's activities would last from 8 p.m. to 11 p.m. Chancers had taken over Tramore's mantle, as the former retained the Olympia Rink Hockey Cup in 1956 when they defeated Waterford Glass in the final 6–1. The staging of the games at the Olympia faced competition from the Silver Slipper in Tramore from 1957, although the Olympia Rink Hockey Cup continued as Ramblers added to their 1954 title by defeating Waterford Glass. The women's competition received less attention, but we know games were held regularly between Waterford and Tramore selections. One of the most prominent figures involved was Tessie Power, who ran a grocery.

Sadly, from the 1960s, the game locally was surpassed by a Waterford Roller Hockey Team playing Bray and Dublin sides as the playing of the sport eventually went from dwindling interest to petering out by the 1970s.

Flyers Roller Club at O'Connell Street, 1981–84

The early 1980s saw the establishment of the Flyers Roller Club at the site formerly known as Coakleys at 63 O'Connell Street, which would have roller hockey facilities for both men and women. The club opened on Friday, 3 July 1981 and sought to tap into the roller disco-mania craze that had swept across the United States and reached Europe. The development, headed by Nicky Cahill, who used to use the Old Gymnasium at De La Salle, arranged for sides from Dublin and coaches from the capital to exhibit the game and provide expert coaching to teenagers in the south-east. The end of the month saw a Flyers selection representing Waterford defeat Dublin's Star Club 9–8, with the O'Connell Street side numbering Dan and Busty Sullivan, Michael Fitzgerald, Billy Murphy, Colm Adams and Eoin Troy. One of the defeated Crumlin team said after the game:

> We thought we were coming to Flyers to give an exhibition but it was the other way around. We had no answer to the skill of the local lads. How are we going to tell them back at The Star that we were well and truly beaten by a team of old men and novices?

The Flyers Club would face several sides from Dublin and a Waterford Glass Factory team as the early years of the 1980s saw a brief increase in interest in roller hockey, but it never reached the same popularity as it did from 1939 to 1957 when the Olympia League was dominated by a Tramore team. Now as names such as the Coliseum Cinema and Olympia Ballroom have been added to the local lore lexicon for their roles in providing entertainment to fans of the silver screen and the Royal Showband, it should be remembered that a sport such as rink, skate or roller hockey played a significant part in both places' stories and the development of sport as a leisure and entertainment activity in the mid-twentieth century.

30

Danny Morgan: Cheltenham Gold Cup-Winning Jockey and Trainer

Danny Morgan, born on 17 April 1912 in County Waterford, came from strong horse-racing stock, with his lineage made up of Morgans, Murphys and Widgers (his grand-uncle being Joe Widger, who won the 1895 Grand National on The Wild Man from Borneo). Danny's father John was one of eight brothers who were jockeys and the only one to hold amateur status.

Danny's uncle Frank Morgan was an adept trainer who achieved Cheltenham Gold Cup success in 1925 with Ballinode, becoming the first Irish-trained winner of the Gold Cup. Known as the Sligo Mare, it was also the first mare to win the race. However, John Randall and Tony Morris, in their book *A Century of Champions*, would consider the chestnut-coloured horse to be a 'poor' winner of the illustrious race. Ballinode was named after the Sligo village where its owner, Christopher Bentley, lived, and was trained at the Curragh, Co. Kildare. The mare's grandsire was Desmond, who was the leading sire in Great Britain and Ireland in 1913 (the stallion whose offspring won the most prize money during the flat racing season). Frank Morgan's son Tom saddled Yahoo to second place in the 1989 Gold Cup behind Desert Orchid.

Danny Morgan.

Young Danny began his horse-racing apprenticeship with Basil Jarvis at Green Lodge Stables and the Grange, Newmarket, in 1924. The *Munster Express* reminisced in 1946 on Morgan being fitted for his first set of riding breeches:

> ... a little story of Danny's first introduction to the jockey's wardrobe. For his first riding breeches, Danny was measured in a Waterford house – Messrs Robertson Brothers, of 88, The Quay. And he was fitted by a Waterford tailor, Mr Daniel Hallahan, at present residing at Tycor Avenue. He tells me that Danny looked and felt as proud as Punch when he first 'took silk' just before he went over to serve his apprenticeship to B. Jarvis.

Jarvis was considered of 'cheerful nature', beginning his trainer career in 1909 upon becoming too heavy to compete as a jockey in flat races. His notable success included four winners at the Royal Ascot meeting of 1921, taking home the Gold Cup with Periosteum. Jarvis' only trained winner of a classic was Papyrus, winning the Epsom Derby in 1923.

Morgan subsequently switched from flat racing to National Hunt, riding mainly for Ivor Anthony. Anthony was one of three brothers who were jockeys (his younger brother Jack rode three separate winners of the Grand National and was Champion Jockey in 1912. He retired around 1924 due in part to an injury sustained in a fall at a meet in Ludlow aboard Tedney). It was a partnership that would lead to Cheltenham Gold Cup success in 1938 with Morse Code, the only horse to defeat Golden Miller at the festival. Other successes with Anthony included the Champion Hurdle in 1934 with Chenango and victory in the same race in 1947 with National Spirit.

Anthony's training style is noted in *Jumping: A Different Game* about the life and career of Gordon W. Richards, starting with Anthony speaking to Richards:

> 'This jumping game is very different from what you have been used to,' ... without another word, out came the stick as we rode down the village street and he hit me on the knees, hit me on the arms and hit me up the bottom, repeating as he did go, 'Bottom forward, hands down, a different game these horses. Good boy. Just keep practising and you'll be all right ...'
>
> ... Danny Morgan was approaching the end of his stint as stable jockey, but he was a tremendous role model for any aspiring young rider. His record speaks for itself.

Richards' career was ended after breaking his back in a fall at Perth Racecourse and he subsequently trained two winners of the Grand National: Lucius in 1978 and Hallo Dandy in 1984.

Morgan also has the distinction of having worn the colours of three different British monarchs, being successful for two of them (Edward VII and George VI). The

News & Star reported in November 1936 on his ride aboard Marconi, the first horse to run for King Edward VIII:

> Keen disappointment was occasioned in Waterford last Tuesday when it was found that *Marconi*, the first horse to run in the name and colours of King Edward VIII, and ridden by that popular young Waterford jockey, Danny Morgan, did not make turf history at Wolverhampton as was expected. He blundered when well-placed and finished a long way behind the leaders. Odds of 5–4 were laid on *Marconi*, although he had 16 rivals. He was lying second approaching the last hurdle but one. To the general dismay, he blundered on landing. He blundered again at the last hurdle and finished about tenth. *Marconi* has never won over hurdles. He has won two steeplechases. Major Barrett, his trainer, was very disappointed at the horse's failure.

Notable races in which Danny Morgan rode to victory include the Scottish Grand National (three times in total: 1931, 1935 and 1938), the Welsh Grand National in 1936, Grand Sefton in 1935 and the Champion Chase (also three times with victory in 1933, 1936 and 1938).

Alas, the National at Aintree would continue to prove elusive for the Morgan family, with the *News & Star* reporting in 1937 that:

> *Golden Miller*, the mount of Danny Morgan, the popular young Waterford jockey, had faded out of the picture long before the end, thus once again disappointing his hosts of admirers and supporters and a large body of Waterford enthusiasts who were hoping 'Danny' would at long last break a tradition in a great family of horsemen.

Unfortunately for Morgan, he was defeated by Royal Mail, trained by Ivor Anthony. Morgan's ride that day, Golden Miller, is the most successful Cheltenham Gold Cup-winning horse ever, winning the race five years in a row from 1932 to 1936. Five of Danny's uncles had ridden in the Grand National, with the closest coming to victory in the fabled race being William, who came second on Matthew in 1902 (behind Shannon Lass).

The first of Danny's winners of the Scottish Grand National in 1931 was reported by the *News & Star*:

> *Annandale*, the property of Lady Glenaff, which was ridden into third place in the Grand National at Aintree last month, won the Scottish Grand National on Saturday at odds of 6 to 1. The horse was ridden to victory by Danny Morgan, the youthful Waterford jockey …

Edward VIII.

Morgan replaced his brother Tommy for the race, who had ridden Annandale at Aintree but was recovering from injuries sustained at Sandown ten days prior to Danny's success. Tommy Morgan, in his third public race aged 14, rode Viaduct to victory at Epsom at odds of 25–1, finishing six lengths clear of second place.

For the 1938–39 season, Morgan rode over fifty winners in England, his best figures since he started racing, and was reported to be 'sailing to America on the "Queen Mary"' that May for a holiday after the season's successes. The British Champion Jockey for that campaign was Fred Rimell with sixty-one winners.

Perhaps the nearing of the end of Morgan's career as a jockey was recorded in the

Munster Express in April 1946, 'Waterford people were sorry that Danny Morgan had no mount in the Grand National. That was due to circumstances which Danny had no control. But in another big race at Liverpool – the Liverpool Hurdle – he, so to speak, got his own back by winning on King of the Jungle at a nice price for his supporters.' Missing out on one of the premier events of the National Hunt season must have been a blow.

Morgan followed in his uncle Frank's training footsteps by starting as a trainer in 1947. His greatest success came in 1959 with Roddy Owen claiming the Gold Cup at Cheltenham, twenty-one years after he won the race as the jockey aboard Morse Code. He became the first of five Gold Cup-winning jockeys to also go on to win the race as a trainer. Fortune favours the brave as Roddy Owen capitalised on the leader of the race Pas Seul falling at the last and in doing so impeding two of its closest pursuers. Trained at the Curragh, Bobby Beasley was the victorious jockey after Bunny Cox had contacted the owner of the horse to tell him to give Beasley the ride as he had done better on Roddy Owen previously.

Closer to home in Waterford, the *Irish Independent* noted in August 1961 that:

Evening racing came to Tramore in earnest yesterday when a crowd rivalling Tuesday's big attendance thronged the enclosures. It was a happy holiday crowd with a large percentage of County Waterford racegoers who gave vent to their satisfaction when *Tax Law*, trained by popular Waterford man, Danny Morgan, and owned by his wife, came storming up the hill a clear winner of the Stewards' Handicap Chase. It was Danny's father, incidentally, who owned the first winner at the Tramore meeting 50 years ago.

Morgan died in 1984, aged 72. An able horseman with an impressive career in National Hunt racing, Danny Morgan continued a fine tradition from that of his grand-uncle Joe Widger and his uncles, the Morgans, with his popularity among racegoers a clear indication of the admiration and esteem in which he was held.

Camogie in County Waterford, 1913–17

On Sunday, 24 August 1913, a camogie match between teams from Dungarvan and Waterford city took place in Dungarvan. The *Waterford News* detailed that, 'This may be said to be the inauguration of ladies' hurling in Waterford City and County, and doubtless, great interest will be centred in the match.' Already, a return game in the city was planned for the following month.

In previewing three hurling matches to take place at the Waterford Sportsfield on Sunday, 14 September 1913, the *Evening News* (Waterford) noted that, 'One of them will be a camogie contest between ladies from Dungarvan and Waterford. It will be the first match of the kind played in the city.' A few weeks previously, the teams had met in Dungarvan, where the hosts from the Old Borough were victorious. As the city team sought to get one over on their west Waterford counterparts, throw-in was planned for one o'clock.

We learn that due to the inclemency of the weather, the camogie match was postponed. But this didn't stop the game between the second team of Meaghers and a

Camogie team at rear of Waterford Courthouse, Waterford City, Ireland, 17 October 1915.

volunteer team from Kilkenny taking place, with the Marble County visitors winning 7–1 to 2–1. Nearly three weeks later, a camogie match would be played at the Sportsfield on Sunday, 5 October 1913, with the Barrack Street Brass and Reed Band providing music on the day. The Monday edition of the *Evening News* reported:

> In the Camogie match keen interest was taken, and though the game was slow the ladies responsible for good play at intervals were encouraged by cheer. There was no score for either side in the first half, but in the second Waterford with their backs to the sun registered a point and soon after a goal. Dungarvan really never looked dangerous but they can reckon some good players on the team. The game was only for twenty minutes each, and at the finish Waterford won by 1 goal 1 point to nil.

Further detail comes from the *Waterford News:*

> The sides were evenly balanced and started at a brisk pace. The homesters attacked strongly but the visitors' defence was equal to the assault and sent back play to midfield. The Old Borough ladies showed some clever hurling but were unable to pass the home backs. Both sides attacked in turn but without effect, and half-time came with no scoring done. On resuming the city team were the better side but the Dungarvan backs kept them from scoring. A free, about 40 yards out, gave the homesters their opportunity and a puck which Garrigan might envy sent the ball over the bar. Dungarvan got attempts to equalise but without result. The homesters pressed again and sent under the bar. The lead of a goal and a point gave the homesters great heart and they continued to have the advantage to the end but without increasing their score.

Two weeks later, the Déise dozen were scheduled to face their Kilkenny counterparts at St James's Park to raise funds for the Gaelic League, in a 'Camogie contest between the fair wielders of the ash from the Noreside city and their sister Gaels from Waterford'. These proceeds were to be directed towards the Dungarvan branch of the Gaelic League, which had hit some financial difficulties. Unfortunately, the Irish winter would play havoc with the staging of the game and crowd numbers due to torrential rain that Sunday morning.

In late November we learn of the development of the Clonea Camogie Club, who believed it would be 'easy to form a team out of the splendid material Providence has so bountifully blessed the parish with that would achieve a record in a few years equal to that of the famous Toomevara heroes'. The following month we learn of the development of a camogie team in Kilmacthomas. Meanwhile, the *Waterford News* reported that the teams in Dungarvan and Waterford city 'are able to field good teams, and should bestir themselves and treat us to some more of their clever performances'.

Dungarvan.

However, after Christmas, the momentum surrounding camogie in the county had stalled. Although several clubs had been formed, they were still far outstripped by hurling and football teams, with one local periodical saying that women should take up the game as 'for in most districts our girls have very little amusement of any kind'. Come spring, we see games in Piltown, Carrick-on-Suir, and later we see the development of a rivalry in west Waterford, when teams from Ballinamult and Dungarvan played in Ballinamult in May. On Sunday, 14 June 1914, as part of the Dungarvan Feis at Gaelic Field, a local side played a Cork camogie team. The homesters won 4–0.

The greatest hurdle to the development of camogie was not player numbers or facilities, but rather the Catholic Church, and perceptions of femininity. A letter in the *Munster Express* (dated 23 May 1914) read:

> I regret very much to publish on your widely-circulated paper, that some of the clergy are condemning our pure Irish game of hurling which has been taken up lately by the Irish colleens in Co. Kilkenny, especially in South Kilkenny. Irish boys can play hurling, football, handball, etc., and why should not their sisters have liberty to do likewise? What better physical training can they have for the muscle? I wonder would there be any objections to their playing hockey or any other foreign game, which are played by the 'well-to-do' ladies who are helping to anglicise our Irish girls? It will be seen on last week's issue of the Dublin 'Leader' (one of our best Irish Catholic papers) a report of a camogie challenge match between the lady students of the Cork University and the lady boarders of the Ursuline Convent, Thurles. The report of that match wound up: 'His Grace the Archbishop, with a

big number of clergy and laity, witnessed the game, and all were at once in pronouncing it a delightfully exciting display of the fine physical training and ardent national spirit of the girls of Munster.' The writer of this letter wonders why should Kilkenny, the principal caman wielders of Leinster (and all Ireland), – why should Kilkenny not follow suit? I am not fighting for the interest of the woman in every way, such as the suffragettes, as I prefer giving them a hurl to a vote.

The trend of schools and universities playing camogie was reflected in Waterford city, when during Feis Portlairge, a game was staged between the pupils of the Presentation and Ursuline schools at the Sportsfield on Sunday, 12 July 1914.

Over the summer of 1914, the most active Camogie Clubs in the south-east were Ahenny, Carrick-on-Suir, and Windgap. On 2 August, at Mahon Bridge, Kilmacthomas defeated Kilrossanty by 3 goals to 2, although the *Waterford News* reported, 'Early in the match suspicion was aroused as to the sex of one of the Kilmacthomas players and the suspicion grew stronger as brilliant feat after feat was performed by the suspect. At about five minutes to go one of the home side took the hat off the doubtful one and it was at once seen that the latter was wearing a wig. A rush was made for the wig, which when procured was held aloft by a Kilrossanty player amidst a scent of great excitement.'

As well as Kilmacthomas and Kilrossanty entering the camogie fray, by June 1915, there was a side representing Portlaw as well, joined by Kinsalebeg. On Sunday, 15 August, the final of a Camogie Tournament for clubs in County Waterford was staged in Dungarvan, with a team from Waterford city and Dungarvan playing the decider. The city side won 2–1. The winners received a set of gold Tara brooches. The following month, Portlaw Éire go Brath faced the Champion Waterford city team in Mooncoin, with Portlaw winning 5–3 to be deemed 'the Champions of Co. Waterford'. Finally, we see some players named in a match report, with the *Waterford News* recording:

> Miss Falconer, captain of the Éire go Brath; Miss Harrison, Waterford's captain; Miss Sutton, Waterford; Miss Maggy Kirwan, Portlaw; the Misses O'Neill, Dower, and Hayes and Coffey, Portlaw; Miss Walsh and Galvin, do., did splendid work in their respective spheres, and were loudly applauded.

The Waterford Club Camogie captain, Eily Sutton, would win a gold brooch at the Ladies' Hurling Puck Competition staged at Clonea on 10 October 1915 by sending the ball over 60 yards.

The area seems to have been a hotbed for camogie from 1914 to the spring of 1917, when there were teams from Ballyduff Upper, Carrick-on-Suir, Dungarvan, Kilmacthomas, Mooncoin and Waterford, but it appears to have petered out, certainly in relation to media attention, until the 1930s.

Matt O'Mahoney: Kilkenny Soccer Pioneer

Born in Mullinavat, meaning the 'Mill of the Stick', on 19 January 1913, Matthew Augustine O'Mahoney's sporting exploits were very different to most inhabitants of Kilkenny. In the year of the enactment of the Act of Union, creating the formation of the United Kingdom of Great Britain and Ireland, the population of Mullinavat stood at 158 and reached 531 in the census seventy years later. Tory Hill overshadows the townland and acts as a natural landmark for the town. Rather than hurling or boxing, for which the Marble County has had many representatives and numerous amounts of success, O'Mahoney's sport of choice was that of soccer. In the same year as his birth, the town entered a hurling team in the Junior Championship of Kilkenny for the first time, having previously preferred the other Gaelic game of Gaelic football. A regular Irish town in a county whose devotion was to one sport would surely have made O'Mahoney's decision all the harder and even more unique in the circumstances.

His career began in earnest with Liverpool in 1933; sadly, his move there coincided with a decline in the club's fortunes as they slid down the table, losing their best players and failing to attract adequate replacements. However, his time there saw limited playing opportunities, with spells at New Brighton and Hoylake taken in before moving to Southport the following season. From here on, his 'footballing' pedigree was on the rise, a change to First Division Wolverhampton Wanderers led to a £175 move to Bristol Rovers in 1935, where he became a fan favourite at half-back. His performances caught the attention of local rivals Bristol City, who offered a transfer fee of £750 for his services, which was rejected by the Rovers board. His time in Bristol saw him make over 100 appearances. The club's only major trophy during the interwar years was a Division 3 (South) Cup victory over Watford. The match was notable as the game was played at the neutral venue of the Old Den, as neither team agreed to a coin toss for home advantage. Also, the Rovers' record defeat, 12–0 to Luton, occurred in 1936.

International recognition soon followed, his first cap coming for Éire in 1938 against Czechoslovakia, which ended in a 2–2 draw. Five more caps followed while O'Mahoney also has the distinction of being a dual international, having also played for an IFA XI (Northern Ireland) against Scotland in the prestigious British Home Championships, losing 2–0. Furthermore, it is remarkable that just five days after the Scotland match, he swapped the IFA jersey for the FAI in a 3–2 victory over Poland at Dalymount Park.

Once more, O'Mahoney also became the first FAI international to travel by plane, for a home fixture against Switzerland in 1938. In the 1930s, the popular means of transport was ferry and train for international games. He arrived in Dublin just over an hour before kick-off, but in time to help in a 4–0 victory. Perhaps as a Kilkenny man, he can be seen as a soccer prodigy and an aviation pioneer for the county. In one respect, post-Irish independence, a statement of such sovereignty was demonstrated through its airspace, which had no limitations imposed under the Anglo-Irish treaty of 1921.

Such was Matt O'Mahoney's form at this time, a transfer to Ipswich Town (for £600) ensued. The team were elected to the Football League in 1938 ahead of Gillingham. A 1–1 draw against rivals Norwich City was the club's last competitive game before the outbreak of war. Sadly, the outbreak of the Second World War not only stymied his club but also his international career. The war years saw guest appearances (a regular occurrence during the period with no fixed leagues and games, so players had to seek playing time with other teams) for clubs such as both Bristol sides Rovers and City, Rochdale and Tranmere Rovers. Upon the cessation of hostilities in Europe, O'Mahoney was the first-choice centre-back for Ipswich and would go on to play ninety-seven games for the club.

His soccer career finished in 1949 with a brief spell as manager of Yarmouth Town. With that, it appears he had little interaction with the game until his death on 25 January 1992. Although he has little silverware to match that of the Kilkenny hurlers, perhaps his main achievement is in being a professional sportsperson and having played at an international level.

From 1985 to 2008, his home county had a League of Ireland side in EMFA, later Kilkenny City, and there is clearly a strong if small (particularly when compared with hurling) support base for soccer, which continues to seek a return to League of Ireland representation and maintains the grounds of Buckley Park as a sports facility. In the national league itself, players such as Gavin Holohan and Sean Maguire of Cork City and Dave Mulcahy of Bohemians, among others, hail from the county.

Well over a hundred years since his birth, and over thirty years since his death, there is surely a need for Matt O'Mahoney to be suitably remembered.

'Sleeping Draught': Michael Lacey, the Forgotten Contender

Michael Lacey was born at Grady's Yard, Johnstown in Waterford City on 21 June 1913. Named after his father (a labourer at McDonnell's Creamery who married a Mary Long), he would be known as either Mick or Matt to distinguish him from the patriarch of the family. By his early 20s, Lacey was married (on 23 June 1935) to a Mary O'Brien of 81 The Mall, who worked as a 'domestic servant'. Matt worked as a 'bill poster' and was noted as a well-known amateur boxer in Waterford as a southpaw with a 'savage punch' by most papers and commentators. His left was described as carrying a 'sleeping draught' that would put any opponent to drift. However, the *Irish Independent* noted that though he packed a considerable punch, if 'boxing is the gentle art of self-defence then Lacey … is not a boxer … but … has a punch, and if he hits his opponent the question of self-defence does not arise …' However, it was outside of the 'sweet science' that he came to national attention.

'A Credit to the People, City and Country': Lacey and the Rescue of Agnes Dunne, Tramore, June 1936

In June 1936, Lacey was swimming around eight o'clock out from the Strand in Tramore near what was then the 'new promenade'. While exercising he heard the screams of Agnes Dunne (aged 16, the daughter of Mr Tom Dunne, the prominent Secretary of the Waterford Branch of the ITGWU) of Morrisson's Road in the city, who had got into difficulty. She was quickly being carried out by the tide when Lacey reacted speedily and, as noted by the *Cork Examiner*, brought an exhausted

Dunne back to shore. The unconscious girl was then brought to McCoy's Riveria Café, where she received first aid and recovered. So treacherous was the rescue effort by Lacey, the local *Munster Express* recorded that 'the scene of the rescue is close to the spot where on the previous Tuesday evening Mr Michael Brett, Clonmel, met his death under tragic circumstances after he saved his little nephew's life'.

Clearly, Lacey's physical prowess and athletic ability had not only saved Agnes Dunne's life but also his own in her rescue. Nearly twelve months later, the Waterford man received the Royal Humane Society's Certificate from Waterford County Commissioner Mr S.J. Moynihan, who noted that the young boxer 'was a credit to the people, city and country' and noted that it wasn't the first time that Lacey had been a life saver.

'A Real Dark Horse in Heavyweight Circles': Lynn, Louis and the German Tralst

Lacey was being described as a 'real dark horse in heavyweight circles' with consecutive victories over the experienced Cork boxer L. Lynn in autumn 1937. As the Waterford Champion, Lacey fought and defeated the 1937–38 Irish Army Heavyweight Champion, Pte Kerry (Collins Barrack) on points at Tramore Boxing Club in 1938. The *Evening Herald* concluded that the result put 'the Waterford boxer amongst our leading heavyweights, and it is almost certain he will be included for the selection of an Irish team for America'.

The Central Council of the Irish Amateur Boxing Association (IABA) selected Lacey after trials against P. Gannon (Galway), whom he knocked out, and defeating Kerry again on a points decision. Originally, Lacey was to fill the position of substitute for J. McMullan of the Royal Ulster Constabulary, who subsequently had to cry off, and this meant the Johnstown man was primed to fight in Chicago. The Irish team travelled from Dublin to

Joe Louis.

Southampton, where they would embark on the Cunard White Star liner *Queen Mary* for New York. Upon reaching America, they would travel by plane to the Windy City. They were the guests of the Catholic Youth Association of America who arranged the ten-bout fight card, which saw Lacey named among boxers such as a young Joe Louis of a Chicago Youths selection. Lacey's opponent was to be Clarence Brown. In front of 3,000 spectators at Soldiers' Field on 13 July, Lacey–Brown was the deciding bout as the score stood at 5–4.

The Irish southpaw wasn't able to gain a draw for Ireland, with some papers saying it was a valiant defeat in a close fight decided on points, while others say he was battered in a brave performance. The following month, Lacey was facing the most in-form amateur boxer in Europe. His opponent, the Berlin Police Officer Tralst, had finished runner-up in the European Police Championships but, even more impressively, had defeated the Olympic Champion Nagy of Hungary. At just 22 years of age, he was considered to be Germany's best heavyweight prospect in years. Ireland dominated against the Berlin Police selection, winning 5–2 with Lacey's southpaw style causing Tralst major problems that ended with him being knocked out in the third round.

'Inadequate Training Facilities': Threatening to Retire?

At 25 years of age, Lacey's victory over Tralst looked like being a springboard to further success, but surprisingly it was to lead to him threatening retirement from the sport. This wasn't due to injury, but his sole reason as recorded in the *Munster Express* was 'to protest in a practical manner against the inadequate training facilities with which he had to contend'. In preparation for the bout, Lacey found the local training school was locked up and even if it was open, he would have found no sparring partners. Furthermore, he stated that 'this is not an isolated, but a typical instance, and with such training and co-operation I am expected to enter an international contest and win'. Though he would receive support from locals in Waterford, it appeared to be a black mark against Lacey by the IABA as he received fewer international honours for Ireland than such a talent deserved. The issue of training and facilities would dog the rest of his boxing career as even events in Waterford would begin to turn sour, but more of that later.

It seems Lacey didn't act on his threat of retirement as he continued to fight into August 1938 against the Ulster Champion C. McGlade (Central Hall, Belfast) and J. McMullan, who he had replaced on the Chicago trip. Lacey easily defeated McGlade in a one-sided affair, though lost to McMullan where the Waterford man's lack of training was apparent. There was still goodwill towards him from his native city, which would lead to an interesting development in boxing in Waterford.

Waterford City Boxing Club: Amateur Ethos and Professionalism in Conflict

A letter addressed to the editor of the *Waterford News* proposed to raise a training fund for the Johnstown southpaw by subscribing a pound a week, to avoid 'seeing its most promising boxing protégé of the decade fading out in decay and inaction'. These funds were then used for the establishment of the Waterford City Boxing Club at the Bridge Hotel on 22 September 1938. The meeting was presided over by Mayor James Aylward to create a body that would promote the development of the 'manly art locally'. A dual function of the club was to support the efforts of Lacey in guaranteeing to pay his expenses with a substantial Monster Tournament organised to raise funds. The proceeds would go directly to his training for his rematch with McMullan at Portobello Barracks.

By the following month it was rumoured that Lacey had come to the attention of the London boxing promoter Dan Sullivan (the man who brought Cobh's Jack Doyle to America) but the Waterford man rejected a tempting offer to turn professional as he was content in the amateur ranks. A hectic schedule saw him have bouts in Cork, Waterford and even Bristol. In the latter, he faced Colchester Police Officer A. Porter, then considered to be the best heavyweight in Europe. The English fighter was considered unbeatable for their November 1938 bout and with Lacey's preparations hampered by a heavy cold, the Waterford boxer was easily knocked out in the second round.

Going into 1939, Lacey was still held in high regard as a genuine contender for a national title, with his left considered a devastating weapon. His first fight of an expectant year was against J. Boyd of Belfast and of the contest, W.P.M of the *Independent* wrote, 'Lacey, the idol of Irish boxing enthusiasts in recent months,

Portobello Barracks, Dublin.

let his supporters down badly when he was beaten' in a one-sided contest. For no obvious reasons (that we are aware of through newspaper reports), he didn't enter the National Championships, but a comeback was scheduled for Tramore, where he would again face Boyd. It was hoped, under the guidance of trainer Garda J.W. 'Boy' Murphy, that Lacey would recapture the form and spark that had brought him to national attention.

The fight was switched to the Waterford Volunteer Hall for 9 June 1939, with his opponent now Pte Maher (Curragh) as Boyd had to pull out of the meeting due to illness. As a large crowd waited for the main event organised by the Waterford Boxing Club, it was announced by the MC, Sgt Spillane, that Lacey had failed to show up for the bout and he was automatically suspended. It was a backdated one-month suspension, with Lacey brought before a committee to explain his actions or, rather, inactions in this case. His complaint to the boxing club was that they had not arranged with his employer to get the required time off, and the failure to deliver on the promise of oils was the last straw for him. In consultation with his family, he decided 'to dress, go out for a walk and take no notice of anyone'.

Garda J.W. 'Boy' Murphy.

The club that had been formed to support his efforts had now turned hostile towards him. One committee member, a Mr Falconer, suggested that some of Lacey's advisors were getting in his ear about the club making substantial money off his efforts. Lacey in return highlighted his dissatisfaction with the training at the club, suggesting that juveniles and seniors should be accommodated on different nights. The most cutting remarks came from Captain J. O'Meara (Irish Volunteer Force), who believed Lacey 'should be suspended for two years, and the club will get on very well without him'.

Later Career and Life

Despite all the trouble in his hometown, Lacey was selected as a substitute for another Irish selection to Chicago, but he did not step in for Mourneabbey's P. Sullivan as he had for McMullan previously. Returning to Ireland, we know Lacey was in contention for an Irish team travelling to Warsaw, but his role was very much down the pecking order.

In August 1939, he married Mary Coughlan of Mall Lane at the cathedral in Waterford (yes, I know what you're thinking, a second marriage? On the marriage certificate from 1939, it notes that Lacey was a widower). The two worked together at McDonnell's Creamery. His boxing commitments would dwindle as the 1940s began and eventually peter out completely as the decade went on. He was disqualified in the 1940 National Championships against Fethard's Louis O'Donnell. Notable victories for the Waterford boxer included defeating North of England Champion J. Craig in Manchester (a powerful right doing the damage this time) and promising Windsor boxer J. Agnew at the National Stadium. The arrival of George Bennett on the national scene saw Lacey fall down the pecking order further.

There was more tragedy to follow for the boxer, in 1942, when his brother died on the way to attending 12 noon mass. It is around this time that McDonnell's Creamery, which specialised in the manufacture of margarine, closed temporarily, leading to him moving to England for work. He worked at their Essex operations until his own death in 1953, when he was killed by a jeep in London. The information relating to his marriages, time in England and death require further investigation.

Lacey packed a lot into his forty years, from being a life saver, bill porter, boxer, a husband twice and travelling across the Atlantic and Irish Sea. His crusade to see that training standards were improved was not only to boost his own chances in the ring but also the competitiveness of boxers from his native city and country. One wonders what could have been if his warnings and pleas had been heeded.

Check Mate: Austin Bourke, Chess and the Irish Weather

Patrick Martin Austin Bourke was born on 10 May 1913 in Dungarvan, Co. Waterford. His father was a stationmaster for the Great Southern & Western Railway. Bourke's mother Claire held a BA degree. Austin began his education locally and for a time at Ballyduff NS before attending Mount Sion CBS in Waterford city (this was due to the family moving to Ferrybank). The Bourkes were a talented family, Austin's brother Charles began his career with the Clyde Shipping Company, resigning to take up a position in the army and later employed as a traffic superintendent with Aer Lingus Teoranta. His younger brother John was one of Ireland's most recognised sculptors. Another brother named Hubert would become the head of the Meteorological Department at Shannon (it would appear to be a family obsessed by all things weather related). All the information gleaned for this piece are based on searches concerning Austin Bourke or the Irish Aistín de Búrca.

Austin Bourke.

Bourke's studies continued at University College Cork, where in 1933 he obtained first-class honours in mathematical science and was awarded the Peel Memorial Prize for being the outstanding student that year. Bourke studied at Imperial College London, and later completed an MSc (while also lecturing mathematics at UCC, 1935–38) at Cork. During his studies, Bourke was president of the students' union, editor of the college paper, lead player in the Drama Society, a noted hurler and also excelled at the game of chess. His expertise saw him contribute a column to the *Evening Echo* on the game. Such was his ability, he represented Ireland at the Warsaw Chess Olympiad in 1935.

The Dungarvan man's journey to Poland was not plain sailing. After the Irish Chess Union (ICU) had raised funds to send a selection to the tournament, he retrospectively noted in the publication *Chess in Ireland* in January 1960 that:

> When the composition of the Irish team was announced, I immediately sent an indignant telegram to the Irish Chess Union demanding representation for the provinces and challenging the entire team to personal combat! Luckily for me, no doubt, the Irish Chess Union did not take up this challenge, but they did invite me to come to Dublin to play a five-game challenge match against the promising young player, Oscar Quigley.

It appears that the then UCC postgraduate was acting on an *Irish Independent* article that was alluding to the composition of the team being largely Dublin-based. Bourke won the first two games with Quigley coming back to send their duel to a deciding fifth game, which Bourke won in 32 moves. Two days of arduous chess were followed by what would become a three-game trial against Tom Cox. Another victory (2–1) led Bourke to declare that he had fought his way on to the team. For his international competition, he entered under the name Aibhistín de Búrca. In Warsaw he took one point from seven games.

In May 1936, it was noted that the Waterford man was making his presence felt at the Irish Chess Championships, though it would be well over a decade before he would win the ultimate prize. Professionally, Bourke joined the newly established Metrological Service at the beginning of 1939. He was initially based at Foynes and Dublin Airport before being promoted. His passion for the original 'game of kings' saw the Mount Sion past pupil compete almost annually at the Oireachtas Championship; a tournament restricted to Irish-speaking chess players from 1942. He won the events' Corn Cú Uladh (made from Irish bog oak) in 1953, 1957 and 1959.

Eventually, Bourke became Irish Chess Champion in 1951 when the tournament was held in Cork for only the second time (the previous staging by the Lee was in 1947). The Dungarvan player finished a mere half a point ahead of Cork's Noel Mulcahy. In 1984, the *Waterford News & Star* noted:

Few people are aware that Waterford produced an Irish champion ... [which] was played at University College Cork, from the 16th to the 24th July. Eighteen competitors took part in an eight round Swiss. The title went to civil service champion Austin Bourke.

Such was his notoriety in the world of chess on these islands, Bourke had a write-up in the *British Chess Magazine* the same year as his national victory. He was the last Waterford man to be named in such a prestigious international chess publication until 1985, when Paul Kiely finished joint fifth at the Channel Island Tournament.

From 1948, Bourke served as the Assistant Director of the Met Service and during his tenure in the 1950s he developed a technique to forecast the occurrence of potato blight. Such was his success, in 1955, he was appointed to a twelve-month position as a special adviser to the Chilean government under a United Nations aid programme. Further international recognition came in 1958 when Bourke was appointed president of the Commission for Agricultural Meteorology of the World Meteorological Organisation, which he served in until 1962. Bourke was promoted to Director of Met Éireann in 1964. He served in this position until his retirement in 1978.

Austin Bourke was able to use his background in science and meteorology in analysing the Great Irish Famine by shifting focus from the history of the administration to the potato itself and the disease that impacted the rural economy of Ireland in the mid-nineteenth century. His early work on the subject developed into a thesis titled 'The potato, blight, weather and the Irish Famine', for which he was awarded a PhD in 1967. He would become the unchallenged authority on the epidemiology of *tophthora infestans*, the potato blight that caused so much damage in Ireland, and the research he conducted made him an 'agricultural meteorologist of world repute'.

In 1973, Bourke was awarded an honorary doctorate by the National University of Ireland in 'recognition of his outstanding contribution to Irish science in general'. Yet, Bourke would later disown and return this honour in 1984 in protest at US policies in Latin America when Ronald Reagan was conferred an honorary degree by the NUI on his visit to Ireland. Bourke explained his decision by using the following rhyme in a radio interview:

> Thinking thoughts I could not utter,
> I thought I heard a passing lady say,
> You can know the man who boozes,
> By the company he chooses,
> And with that the pig got up and walked away.

Clearly, his time in Chile informed the decision of a principled man standing for what he felt was right. That is no surprise really when you look at his protests to the ICU in 1935. He was later awarded the William F. Peterson Gold Medal for his work in the field of plant biometeorology. The 1980s saw him work with H.H. Lamb as part of an EU project on the meteorological aspects of potato blight in western Europe in the 1840s.

In 1993, a collection of his writings on the meteorological background of the Irish Famine was published by Lilliput Press and entitled *The Visitation of God? The Potato and the Great Irish Famine*, with the *Sunday Independent* noting 'the layman will remember the famous book on the potato famine by Mrs. Cecil Woodham-Smith. Austin Bourke's courteous criticism of part of her argument is typical of these essays, dedicated but far from obsessive investigations of a national trauma.'

On Tuesday, 1 August 1995, Bourke died suddenly. He was survived by his wife Clodagh, sons Adrian and Austin, daughter Iseult and several grandchildren. His obituary in the *Cork Examiner* noted that 'it is sad irony, or perhaps looked at another way, appropriately fitting that the death of Austin Bourke should take place in the sesquicentennial year of the Great Famine'. Bourke was clearly a man of many talents and his pursuit of chess was more than an appropriate illustration of the man as it is everything: art, science and sport. His contribution to Met Éireann, Irish history and chess are a lasting legacy.

Ronald Reagan.

35

Dungarvan's Denis Kelleher: An 'Unpredictable Irishman'

Denis Kelleher was born in Dungarvan, County Waterford, on 20 November 1918, but his childhood in Ireland was brief as his family left these shores for England in 1921. It was across the Irish Sea where Kelleher became a star of amateur soccer and was considered 'without doubt the finest inside forward of his era'. A piece by David Williams profiling Kelleher as part of a series on notable amateur soccer players in 1948 noted that he always 'maintained the facility for the unique'.

While at St Joseph's College in Croydon, Kelleher excelled at various sports such as cricket and tennis, but it was soccer where he really caught people's attention. In three seasons with the school, he scored the remarkable total of 333 goals. During these displays of his prodigious talent, Kelleher was spotted by former Barnet goalkeeper Harry Andrews, who recommended the Dungarvan boy to the Bees.

At 16 years old, Kelleher arrived at Underhill (the club's ground until its redevelopment as the Hive in 2013) in 1936 for his first game for Barnet, only to be refused entrance by the club's gateman, who thought this young schoolboy was merely chancing his arm. From this early blip in his sporting career, success followed rapidly. At age 17 he earned his first international cap for the Irish amateur team and twelve months later played an integral part in Barnet's London Senior Cup success over Leyton Orient at Highbury. He scored two of the goals in a 4–0 victory in front of 20,000 spectators.

His goal-scoring feats also brought Kelleher to the attention of the Middlesex Wanderers, who invited him to join them on their tour of Turkey in 1939. Its raison d'être as a touring side was precipitated due to financial matters. Their journey to Turkey was historic as they were the first British side to visit the country and they played Fenerbahçe in the process.

Sadly, throughout Europe such sporting endeavours were put on hold with the commencement of the Second World War. Kelleher joined the Royal Navy, becoming a lieutenant of a motor torpedo boat. During the war, he was captured at Tobruk by the Germans and held as a prisoner of war, first in Italy and subsequently Germany. He managed to escape from the camp in March 1944 by cutting through a wire fence. Kelleher and an RAF pilot named Stuart Campbell managed to evade capture by disguising themselves as Dutch workers (with only blue overcoats to cover their military uniforms), reaching Lübeck.

Even in such circumstances, Campbell and Kelleher had time to enjoy the local hostelries. From there they managed to reach Sweden by cargo ship and twenty-two days after their initial escape they reached England. Apparently, after arriving back at his parents' home after the ordeal, he greeted them merely by saying, 'Hi all, how's the war?' He was awarded an MBE for his escape.

Not only that, but only two days after his arrival in England he played for Barnet in a game against Grays Athletic, scoring two goals.

In 1946, his playing career almost came to an abrupt end after he sustained a nasty head injury, but he was able to play a part in Barnet's greatest success. That year he scored what was to be the winning goal in a 3–2 victory over Bishop Auckland in the FA Amateur Cup Final at Stamford Bridge with an attendance of 53,832. The opposition can be deemed the Arsenal of this guise of the FA Cup, being the most successful club in the history of the tournament as they have won it ten times as well as being runners-up on eight occasions.

The competition was set up in response to the legalisation of professionalism within football, with England's oldest club, Sheffield FC, suggesting that a separate competition be created for amateur clubs in 1892. It lasted until 1974, when it was replaced by the FA Trophy. While with Barnet, Kelleher reached another final with the club in 1948 but lost out to a Leytonstone side 1–0. The 1946 success still remains Barnet's only major piece of silverware in a golden age that encompassed two Athenian League titles, three London Senior Cups and a London Charity Cup. In a time of 'wine and roses' in the history of the club, Kelleher played in 358 games for the Bees and scored an impressive 286 goals.

He was the only Irishman from the southern state of the island (which became the Republic of Ireland in the same year) in the Great Britain Olympic soccer team in 1948. Not only were his sporting talents recognised, but his 'resonant tenor notes' were admired by many, including Dutch FA officials at a dinner in Amsterdam. In the same piece by David Williams, he said of Kelleher's character, 'There is something of the leprechaun in the impish twinkle of his eye.' This would appear to be an illustration of the meaning of the name Kelleher, an Anglicisation of O Ceileachair, meaning 'lover of company'.

Unlike the hullabaloo that surrounded the selection of the 2012 Great Britain team, in 1948 a trial game was held on 8 May under the gaze of Matt Busby (who subsequently led Manchester United to European Cup victory in 1968) in Blackpool. A special correspondent of the *Observer* was unimpressed by the players on display, but did record that 'D. Kelleher (Ireland) was the only player to put any real life into his play in the first half and played like a tired man afterwards'. In making the squad, he played in the first three games, scoring his only goal of the tournament in a 4–3 defeat of the Netherlands. The Great Britain side lost 3–1 in the semi-final to Yugoslavia.

Although Kelleher was raised in Ireland for a few brief years, he did later manage to play soccer on the island. He appeared once for Cliftonville in the Irish League in 1950. In the opening fixture of the season against Crusaders, much of the attention surrounded Kelleher, and he duly obliged with two goals in a 3–2 victory at Solitude. Around this time, he had been contacted by Bohemians of Dublin to play with them in the League of Ireland, but Cliftonville did not wish to release him to fulfil this offer.

His international exploits included eight caps for the Ireland amateur side, as already mentioned. His debut came at 17 years old against Scotland, in which he scored in a 2–1 win. Perhaps his greatest moment in the green of Ireland came when he scored the winner against England in 1949 at Carrow Road, where he also captained the side. In the same year, he orchestrated a 5–2 defeat of Scotland in Aberdeen's Pittodrie, with Ireland coming from two goals behind at half-time. In total, Kelleher, scored four goals for his country.

In March 1951, he was invited to join a touring Hendon side in Hong Kong and the Philippines for that May. However, there was doubt over his participation due to his medical studies. Kelleher qualified in 1952 from St Mary's (while there he met his future wife Anne, with whom he had six children) and became a general practitioner at Harold Wood. He continued as a GP until 1989, retiring aged 71. Unfortunately, the onset of Alzheimer's and Parkinson's disease were further cruel tests of a remarkable man, who passed away in 2004. In his obituary it is remarked that, 'He will be remembered by all who knew him for his humility, kindness, compassion, and, above all, his smile, which never left him, even in the later stages of his illness.'

A conversation with Barnet club archivist and fan John Adkins revealed the esteem in which Kelleher is held in the folklore of the north London club and that his career coincided with the pinnacle era of the amateur game in England. It's unfortunate to think that such a man whose life and sporting career were equally interesting is not further known or acknowledged in his own birthplace and in the country he represented with such distinction.

Probably the only time you'll read the words of novelist Cecelia Ahern in relation to soccer (other than in reference to her Old Trafford season ticket-holding father) is that Kelleher should be more than 'a vague face and a distant memory'. His story transcends, whether in relation to issues such as emigration, the Irish in Britain, war or Irish sporting history, and is as relevant to the people of Waterford today as it was weekly news to the Barnet faithful over sixty years ago.

"'Non-Political' Bosh …':
Gaelic Games Abandoned at the Sportsfield, 21 October 1923

On Sunday, 21 October 1923, the opening two matches of the Waterford City and District Hurling and Football League were to take place at the Waterford Sportsfield. The recently formed league sought to bring 'all teams together under one aegis, ensuring more interest and enthusiasm in hurling and football, and affording greater opportunities of interplay between various teams in the city and district'. The clubs included were Ballytruckle, Cloughernagh, De La Salle, Dunmore, Erin's Hope, Fenor, Gracedieu, Knockboy, T.F. Meaghers and the O'Rourkes. The scheduled fixtures were the Knockboy hurlers playing De La Salle at 2.30 p.m., followed by Dunmore and Gracedieu in Gaelic football at 3.45 p.m.

Prior to the gates being opened, four prominent members of the local Sinn Féin Club reached the venue, and approached players individually, requesting that there should be no games played while Republican prisoners were on hunger strike in prisons across Ireland. It appears that the players were undecided on whether to fulfil the fixtures as advertised, while the president of the local league, M. Flannelly, responded that he could not stop the matches, but if the players refused to play, he could not compel them to do so.

Before the games in Waterford city, we know that around 300 to 500 prisoners were on hunger strike in Mountjoy Prison. Those from Waterford and the surrounding area were Mylie Fanning, M.L. Small, Thomas Walsh, P. Cuddihy, Mick Sullivan, Tom O'Carroll, Tim Kehoe, Derry O'Mahony, Ned Walsh, Sean Purcell, John McGrath (Ballinamult), Jerry O'Donoghue (Crowhill, Cappoquin), Patrick Murphy (Windgap), Michael Hunt (Butlerstown), John Morrissey (Stradbally), Patrick Kiely (Foxcastle), Thomas Kiely (Youghal Road, Dungarvan) as well as Pax Whelan (Dungarvan), Mick Wylie (Parnell Street) and G. Waters.

Subsequently, after a dialogue between the captains of the two hurling teams, it was decided to postpone the match. This was followed by a meeting of the League Committee, where they reached the conclusion to postpone all matches, and 'that future action on the part of the League would be governed by what would transpire at Dublin, Kilkenny and other centres where matches were also down for decision'. A further statement from the local league was to 'impress on the public the fact that they were in no way responsible for what occurred; that they were not at all in favour of the postponement of the advertised programme, and that request was sprung upon them at the last moment'. The Waterford and District Hurling and Football League offered their apologies to the public, and a commitment that such an incidence would not occur again.

This was scant consolation to the crowd, estimated to be of 1,000 spectators, that had assembled at the Sportsfield to witness the games. The *Belfast Newsletter* recorded that later, 'On Sunday night a large procession marched through the streets of Waterford in protest against the imprisonment of the political prisoners, the Rosary being recited en route and also opposite the local infantry barracks. Huge red placards bearing the words, "All Ireland Hunger Strikes" appeared on the city hoardings and dead walls yesterday morning.'

A meeting of the Hurling and Football League was held on Tuesday, 23 October, presided over by Flannelly, who noted that 'matches were played all over Ireland on Sunday last' and it was unanimously decided by the assembled committee that games would go ahead. Regarding other sports, later that week, on Thursday, the Waterford Sportsfield hosted Shannon against Waterford in a rugby match, with the Limerick side running out 11–0 winners over their Suirside counterparts. The difficult political climate did not stop the Shannonsiders playing in Waterford for the first time in fourteen years. However, we learn that by early November, the Wexford County Board and Cork County Board in GAA either suspended or abandoned the playing of matches while the hunger strikes were ongoing.

Gaelic games played on Sunday, 28 October at the Waterford Sportsfield were Emmets (De La Salle) and Erin's Hope in Gaelic football, while Ballytruckle faced Thomas F. Meaghers in hurling. Emmets ran out 2–2 to 0–3 winners, and in 'one of the best-contested games witnessed in the Sportsfield for some time' Meaghers won by 2–2 to 2–1, the winning point coming from a 70 just a couple of minutes before the final whistle. Remarkably, referee T. King managed to officiate the game without having 'capable men as umpires'.

However, criticism comes from the *Waterford News* that, 'It would be well if Waterford sports men followed suit [in abandoning games]. To talk about the G.A.A. being a non-political organisation may be all very fine; but when Irishmen are starving this is no time to be prating "non-political" bosh.'

A Portrait of My Grandfather as a Young Man

Michael Manning entered the army with the address 41 Roanmore Terrace. He was aged 21 in 1925. His father James was a cattle driver, and his mother was Mary, originally from Tipperary. Michael was the third youngest of nine children. Although his father could 'read only', his mother was illiterate, a situation that was unfortunately more than normal in Ireland in the early twentieth century. Ireland had the highest rate of illiteracy in the British Isles prior to the Great War. In 1901, the country's illiteracy rate was 13.2 per cent, four times higher than Scotland and six times higher than England and Wales. Thankfully, it is a situation that has improved dramatically in the intervening 100 years.

The impact of this would be felt throughout his life. It was a journey filled sadly by entertaining folklore, of which little was recorded on paper. Thankfully, by the chance of circumstance, my grandfather was a child at the outbreak of hostilities in Flanders, and by birth and nationality avoided conscription near the culmination of that slaughter. However, Christmas 1917 was traumatic for many a family in Waterford City, as December saw the carnage of the Great War reach close to home off the shores of the Irish coast.

Michael's father James died on board the *Formby*. On 14 December 1917, the SS *Formby* sailed on her homeward voyage only to be torpedoed off the Wicklow coast by U-boat *U-62* with only one body recovered, that of the ship's stewardess Annie O'Callaghan. The tragedy was exacerbated and amplified by the sinking of its sister ship, the *Coningbeg*, by the same U-boat. The quays of Waterford were bleak with families waiting for news of the victims but it would be after Christmas before the eighty-three people (sixty-seven from Waterford) were confirmed lost at sea. These tragic events were evoked by Captain Redmond (son of Irish Parliamentary Party leader John) when questioning Sinn Féin's attitude to Germany in the by-election of March 1918, 'Our glorious and gallant Allies have sunk two Waterford ships outside the harbour'. The 'gallant Allies' phrase was a reference to the Proclamation of the Irish Republic.

Heartbroken, devastation, despair are words that don't adequately reflect the trauma that a death in such circumstances can induce. Perhaps it is best summed up by the author Marlon James' line that, 'The dream didn't leave, people just don't know a nightmare when they right in the middle of one.' Not only had nine children lost a father, but a young woman (then aged 40) a life partner. One cannot contemplate the agony. A message in a bottle that washed ashore in 1924 appeared to be a decree of a soul resigned to his fate; however, like any piece of a jigsaw with no instructions, we have merely speculation. The morsel which survived the seas read, 'We will never reach the Hook' and was signed 'Jack'.

The effect of losing your father at such a young age leaves a great impact on anyone person's life. (Family) legend has it that Michael was arrested after being caught out after curfew as a teenager but managed to escape his confines. Such rebelliousness was endemic on an island in which many sought to overthrow British rule and influence. However, it's more likely that this was an incidence of the recklessness of youth, if little else.

A career in the army may have been influenced by the strong British military presence in the city. The fledgling Free State in the mists of a fraternal conflict had a burgeoning army. The Curragh was a vibrant base as the Training Centre for Non-Commissioned Officers. New drills were implemented as not only state formation but identity affirmation of an Irish state. As always, sport was to play its part in these twin efforts.

For nearly thirty-five years a Waterford man's journey to Croke Park was like Moses in the desert searching for the promised land. September appearances akin to Marlon Brando accepting Academy Awards, rarer still. However, Private Michael Manning made it to Croke Park and in the 'hop, step and jump' (now known as the triple jump) claimed victory in the All-Army Championships on 17 September 1924. It was a spine-tingling moment to realise he had graced the hallow sod of Jones's Road (granted before the various relaying of pitches and redevelopments); he is a thread woven in the tapestry of an integral part of Irish society and culture.

Yet in a monthly update on the sports activities of the army in *An t-Oglac*, it commented, 'Why does Pte. Manning, A.M.C., Curragh Training Camp, refrain from competing at open athletic meetings. Manning's only open contest that we know of was the Irish National Championships at Croke Park, where he secured second place.' Perhaps he was like the old (if now outdated) phrase about Cork hurlers 'rising like mushrooms' for the big occasion. Only months after this titbit he claimed victory in the high jump and a respectable second place in the 120m hurdle.

While at the annual sports at Beresford Barracks, Curragh, he was to 'distinguish' himself in the 120 yards' hurdle, high jump and pole jump. Now, 'corporal' was the prefix to his name. At 36, he married Johanna Sullivan. By that time, he was a sergeant in the army of Éire. The rest of my grandfather's story is more familiar, like a fable by Aesop. He had four children with Johanna: Terry, Oliver (my father), Bennie and Elizabeth.

Sadly, my only connections with Michael were through stories and photographs. Learning more about his early life through the census, newspaper reports and his army file has opened up a story that has made him more vivid in my mind. With such sources becoming more readily available online, the recent past is accessible at just the click of a button. Unfortunately, there are still blanks, but everyone likes to think of themselves as a bit of a Sherlock Holmes. The decade of centenaries that commemorates the events that took place a hundred years ago, which impacted greatly on people and influenced the country we live in today, will allow us to delve more into the stories of our ancestors.

If this is as close as I can get to learn of Michael Manning as a young man, all I can say proudly is that this was part of the story of my grandfather.

Waterford Hockey Players Tour America, 1925

The Irish Ladies' hockey team that embarked on the SS *Baltic* for New York in 1925 numbered three women from Waterford: Miss Mabel Fudger (Belvedere, Newtown), Miss Isabel de Bromhead (Ardkeen) and Miss Irene McCullagh. They were selected for an Irish side that would tour the United States, facing local teams. The group from Connacht, Leinster and Ulster left Ireland on Friday night for Liverpool to make their transatlantic journey aboard the White Star liner, which departed from Merseyside on Sunday, 11 October. The remaining Munster contingent, made up of the Waterford players as well as Miss. E. Williams and Miss I. Cummins, boarded the *Baltic* at Cove.

We know of the Waterford contingent that Mabel Fudger was a daughter of Thomas William Fudger, who established a tea business in the city, with the family acting as agents for various firms until Irish importers took over the trade. Thomas was a native of Cork, and came to Waterford in 1888 to work for the Clyde Shipping Company. Named after her mother, Mabel Edith Fudger was born at South Parade on 26 August 1896, and the family were Wesleyan Methodists. Mabel's father had entered into a business partnership with her maternal grandfather, Christopher Lawrence, with them representing H. Tate & Sons (sugar manufacturers), London, as well as Appleton and Machin & Co.

Similarly, Irene McCullagh came from a wealthy background. Her father, John Charles McCullagh, was the managing director of McCullagh Ltd (Coal Importers). He was a member of the Waterford Chamber of Commerce, and represented that body on the board of Waterford Harbour. His sporting interests included being a member of the Waterford Boat Club and Waterford Lawn Tennis. Irene Kathleen McCullagh was born on 19 November 1902 at Richmond Terrace in Wexford. Just a couple of years later, the McCullaghs moved to Abbeylands (Waterford), and the family lived in Abbey House, Ferrybank until 1922. From the 1911 census, we know that the family were members of the Church of Ireland.

Our final Waterford representative on the trip Stateside was Isabel Agnes de Bromhead, who was 25 years old when she was selected for the touring team. Isabel was born in 1900 in Shefford, Bedfordshire. Her father Henry was a merchant (born Broomhead, he changed his name to de Bromhead), who moved to Shefford from Brighton in 1893 as a partner with Arthur Staunton Wade-Gery, solicitor. While there, Henry played cricket, was President of the Shefford Club of the Brass Band, and joined the local angling club. He married C.M.J. Fanning of Ardkeen in Waterford, and they moved to Ireland in 1906.

The travelling Irish hockey team would reach New York on 21 October, and their playing schedule consisted of:

Oct. 24 – vs U.S. 1923–24 Touring Team at Philadelphia; Oct. 28 – vs Vassar College, N.Y.; Oct. 31 – vs New York Asso.; Nov. 4 – vs Farnchester; Nov. 7 – vs Brynmawr College, Philadelphia; Nov. 10 – vs Philadelphia; Nov. 14 – vs Chicago or Madison; Nov. 23 – vs Wellesley College; Nov. 26 – vs Boston; Nov. 29 – vs United States; Dec. 1 – vs Baltimore; Dec. 3 – vs Richmond, Virginia. The team will embark for Europe on December 5.

The *Irish Independent* reported that, 'The team kept training steadily throughout the whole trip, as long as the balls held out: and after that they took to skipping, as long as the supply of rope – and the deck – held out.' After receiving a terrific reception in New York, they made their way to Philadelphia. It appears that the touring side reached America earlier than scheduled, as they played the Germantown Cricket Club XI there, winning 2–1.

Next up was the United States XI, who had toured Britain and Ireland the previous year. Both McCullagh (in goal) and Fudger were named in the starting XI. After their opening victory, they would continue to be referred to in the American press as 'the colleens in green', who received great hospitality from the American Association, which was making huge strides in developing hockey Stateside. We know that the Irish team played a New York team in the Big Apple on Saturday, 30 October. The Waterford trio were in the side that attained a convincing 9–1 win for the touring side.

The All-Ireland Ladies' hockey team defeated Brynmawr College 8–0, followed by a 3–2 victory over Philadelphia on 10 November. Another impressive performance for the Irish came on the 23rd, when they beat Wellesley 16–1 in Massachusetts.

Nearly a week later, the touring team defeated an all-American XI 2–1, with the *Belfast Newsletter* noting that the 'latter team was made up of the best players in the American Intercity Tournament which has just concluded'. This was considered by the members of the Irish side as the greatest victory. Of the tour, the *Irish Independent* highlighted that during their seven-week excursion, 'they spent five whole days in railway travel', while the greatest encouragement came from Irish-Americans in Chicago. We know that the team were presented to President Coolidge in the White House three days before their departure for home. Their final game came against Richmond, winning 7–1, with McKissack scoring the hundredth goal of the tour in this match.

It was a successful tour for the Irish team as they went undefeated across the United States. In total, they won all thirteen of their games, scored 102 goals, and conceded only eight goals. If Irene McCullagh was happy with her performances as netminder, her teammate Mabel Fudger was deemed the 'crack scorer', being the Irish side's top scorer with thirty-two goals.

They returned to Ireland on Monday, 14 December, arriving at Queenstown around four o'clock in the morning. The majority of the team disembarked there, but Miss McCullagh continued to Liverpool on the SS *Doric*. Both Fudger and de Bromhead reached Waterford that evening by motor car. Such was the attention directed to the successful tour, both de Bromhead and Fudger were interviewed by the *Waterford News*. Mabel Fudger stated:

> We had a most wonderful time and really I am sorry it is all over. In America we were entertained 'royally'; everywhere we went to banquets, theatres, supper parties, and when not playing hockey, our days and nights were one round of entertainment. From the moment we boarded ship on our way out to our arrival in Queenstown yesterday morning, it was all the most delightful time I have ever spent.

Of their latter lives, Mabel Fudger's sister Jennie also went on to represent Ireland in hockey. Sadly, Mabel was to die at the young age of 46 on 22 December 1942. She was recorded as a spinster, and working as an assistant to a commercial agent. For Irene McCullagh, we know little of her life after 1949 upon the death of her mother. We know that Irene was a resident at Grange Park, and was involved in umpiring and playing lawn tennis, and played for a South-East selection that defeated Munster in an interprovincial hockey match in early March 1945. The final member, Isabel de Bromhead, married Thomas Leonard, an engineer in Dunshaughlin, Co. Meath, on 9 February 1927. They would later live in Culmillen, Drumree, Co. Meath.

Waterford City: Munster Junior Cup Winners, 1928

Former Taoiseach and President of Ireland Éamon de Valera believed that, 'For Irishmen, there is no football game to match rugby and if all our young men played rugby not only would we beat England and Wales but France and the whole lot of them put together.' Like any journey, time and experience are needed for success to be achieved or a goal to be reached. The same could be said of Waterford City RFC and their maiden Munster Junior Cup success in 1928. Some of the notable games in the early twentieth century included a fixture on Easter Tuesday 1909 that saw Waterford defeated by Port Talbot of Wales 23–0 in a game of which one commentator said, 'The Taffeys were all over the best of the teams'.

In January 1915, University College Cork were the visitors to Grantstown to take on Waterford City RFC in what the *Munster Express* described as 'a well-contested game, which resulted in a victory for the visitors' by 16–3. Ten years later, the two clubs would meet again with Waterford (this time at the Sportsfield) the victors, scoring one try to none. The *Cork Examiner* reported, 'The ground was impossible for football, and as rain was falling heavily the attendance was small, though enthusiastic.' St Patrick's Day 1925 was witness to another rugby game at the Sportsfield, a friendly between Waterford and Cork City Bankers' rugby team, with the side from the Rebel County winning 24–0. The *Munster Express* report of the game detailed, 'The game was well contested, and not so one-sided as the score would indicate. The home team were the cleverer side, but the visitors were deserving of a score or two.'

At the Sportsfield in March 1926, a Waterford City selection beat the CYMS, who had only recently taken up the game, by one try to nil. In December 1926, Waterford City played Wexford in the Sportsfield and ran out easier winners on a scoreline of 41–0.

Early 1927 saw City organise games with a high calibre of opposition in the form of Dublin University and Dolphin of Cork. The game against the Cork side saw the club achieve a record gate receipt of £30 12s 3d, which saw Waterford City RFC's accounts show a credit balance of £22 13s 3d in September 1927. City defeated Dungarvan 9–6 in the Munster Junior Cup in December 1927, the latter club's first appearance in the competition.

The start of 1928 saw a game due to take place between Waterford and Dingle in Tramore postponed due to the ground being unplayable. In May 1928, Waterford City were victorious against Young Munster of Limerick (who won the Bateman Cup in the 1927–28 season, effectively the All-Ireland Championship of Irish Rugby) in the final of the Munster Junior Cup.

The annual meeting of the rugby club took place in August 1928 in Breen's hotel, The Bridge, with John D. Palmer presiding and a large crowd in attendance. The club's captain, P. Breen, detailed Waterford City's victory in the Munster Junior Cup and that throughout the season the side scored 140 points while conceding only 50. Furthermore, he stated:

> There was one gratifying thing ... that in every match they played, whether they won or whether they lost, they had always obtained splendid co-operation from every member of the club. All worked well together, and there was no pulling against one another ... [which] went a long way towards the attainment of the success which they had achieved.

However, preparation wasn't always plain sailing, as Breen commented that training had been 'pretty hopeless ... when one went on a Sunday morning to the practice ground to find only one or two men there'. Their Munster Junior Cup run saw the team travel to Kerry, Limerick (twice) and Cork. Such journeys added to the expense that players had to endure.

With silverware achieved, the future looked bright for the club and the subject of new club grounds were explored at the meeting. The chairman outlined the possibilities the club had:

> They had looked all around them from all ends of the city to the centre, but could not find no ground bar one. Mr Ryan's field at Ballinaneesagh. The field was admirable but would be more splendidly situated if it could only be transferred a mile nearer town ... But in Ballinaneesagh they would find they would have a very fair ground. It was hoped to effect an amalgamation between the Waterpark Club, the C.Y.M.S. Club and the Waterford Rugby Club ... [and] that it was up to them to do everything they could to promote sport and good-fellowship amongst the different clubs.

Two years after their first Munster Junior Cup, Waterford City added a second title. Later, Waterpark RFC became the second Waterford club to win the same competition in 1938 and would go level with City on two victories in 1974. One wonders though if the clubs had amalgamated and pooled their resources what could have been achieved by Waterford in the sport of rugby.

An inspirational saying in rugby is 'play for what it says on the front of your jersey, and everyone will remember what it says on the back'. This success from 1928 surely must be acknowledged as a remarkable achievement considering the logistical, financial and training problems that were encountered.

40

A Tale of Two Millionaires: Donaghy and Capelli, 1937–38

Many of Waterford's successes have come through those who sought fame and fortune elsewhere. The many waves of immigration and emigration down through the centuries would lead the *Waterford Standard* to opine in April 1937 that, 'It happens nowadays that one has to emigrate to succeed in this sad world'. It was a conclusion that was very much a reflection of the economic misery that engulfed Ireland as the Free State was reaching its teenage milestones. And as we can all relate, those teenage years were often arduous and difficult.

The *Standard*'s rather grim supposition was not the final paragraph concerning a story of failure, but rather an introduction to the tale of a Waterford native 'who started life as a "bucket and sponge" boy wiping prices from the boards of bookmakers, and is now a millionaire bookmaker.' Eugene Donaghy left Waterford as a young man, and took each and any job offer that was made to him in England. His early career saw him as a 'bucket and sponge' boy for several bookmakers.

From those modest beginnings, Donaghy was considered to be 'one of the most flourishing and popular on the American Turf, [and] is a millionaire who started to "make a book" on the racecourses in England and Ireland at the beginning of the [twentieth] century'. Having amassed a substantial fortune, Donaghy visited his birthplace just outside the city in 1937, took in a trip to Glengariff, and it was noted that 'the beauties of that romantic pleasure spot so captured his fancy that he is seriously thinking of buying a house there and settling down in the years of his retirement'. The story of a local boy 'done good' across the Atlantic, the life of Donaghy certainly added to the attraction of America as a land of opportunity compared to an Ireland hampered by protectionist policies and a rather futile economic war with its near neighbours across the Irish Sea.

However, around the same period as Donaghy was profiled in the *People*, we heard of a man who had connections in County Waterford, and whose father had come to

Ireland to improve his circumstances from his native Italy. So, as one Waterford millionaire was looking towards retirement, a year later, we learned of the death of South Africa-based millionaire Ernest A. Capelli, a successful racehorse owner, who had won the 1938 Durban July Handicap with Extinguisher II. That September, realising the end was near, Capelli asked for his Irish relatives to visit him in Cape Town, with his wish to be buried in County Waterford.

Capelli was born in Rathdown (Dublin) on 5 May 1882. His Italian father was a waiter, who apparently later worked in the copper mines in west Waterford, while his mother, Kate Keane (who lived at Knockmahon) was buried in west Waterford (she having died only five or six years before her son's demise). His mother was from the area, later moved to Dublin and opened a tobacconist shop, which was frequented by her future husband. Their son, Ernest, would make his fortune through a chain of Eastern hotels in places such as South Africa and Egypt.

The *Cork Examiner* said of Capelli's connection to the area, 'Many years ago when Bonmahon was a thriving mining centre the late Mr Capelli's father came from Italy to supervise the working of the mines as an expert. While there he met and married a member of a well-known Bonmahon family of which the late Mr ... Capelli was one of an issue of four children.' Capelli had grown up in the Stradbally area, and had left it around 1903, although he would holiday there each year, and stay with the Buckley family at Glebe, Bonmahon.

It was Capelli's final wish to buried beside his mother in Stradbally. His remains arrived in Waterford from Southampton via Fishguard, with the *Sunday Independent* recording that the remains were 'conveyed by motor lorry to the Infirmary mortuary, where they will remain until October 24 when the funeral will take place in Stradbally'. The preliminary arrangements had been made by the undertaker, John Thompson. It was believed that Capelli's remains had been brought 5,000 miles for burial, with very little attention directed to the burial in his maternal county. The *Irish Independent* concluded that 'the poignant event went almost unnoticed'.

Preparations were being made for a new monument to be erected in the Stradbally graveyard, with carnations being selected as the principal flower for the grave of the South African millionaire. Two lorries were needed to transport wreaths sent from South Africa, across Ireland and England, with one inscribed with, 'to the whitest man who ever lived'. Many of these wreaths were embellished with Capelli's racing colours of pink and purple.

We have the stories of two millionaires with strong Waterford connections. One made his wealth through the turf, while the other spent his in pursuit of glory on it. For all their riches, neither could resist the call of home.

41

Josie McNamara: Waterford's 'Queen of Sport'

Josephine 'Josie' McNamara was born in Newrath, and spent her early years in Kilmacow. The McNamara family (her father Aiden worked as a signalman for Córas Iompair Éireann) moved to St Carthage's Avenue in Waterford city in 1939. While within the confines of the Gentle County, McNamara was noted by the *Munster Express* as, 'Having spent her early formative years in an area steeped in hurling tradition it was hardly surprising that she played the fair-sex version of that game and developed a love for it …'. Josie's brother Aidan would become a noted hurler with the Mount Sion club before moving to Dublin, while her other brother John was a talented set designer of the Waterford Dramatic Society, and stage director of the 1959 Waterford Festival of Light Opera.

Josie's first competitive camogie match came on Easter Monday, 1945, when she lined out for St Carthage's, noting in conversation with the *News & Star*'s Adrian Flanagan that, 'in the De La Salle college field we played three matches. One in the morning, one in the afternoon and the other game in the evening and I remember playing St Otteran's, who were the Mercy Convent team.'

Soon her performances would see her selected for the County Waterford team that lost the All-Ireland final to Antrim in Cappoquin that September. They had defeated Tipperary at Cappoquin to win the Munster Championship on Sunday, 5 August 1945. McNamara later told the *News & Star*, 'I was the youngest on the team in 1945 and it was the end of the war when we played in the All-Ireland senior final … There were six of us from the city on the team.' They included Angela Spencer, Kitty O'Sullivan, Mary Kennedy, Nellie Long and Mamie O'Meara. However, they all played for St Colm Cill while McNamara lined out for St Carthage's.

It was the start of an intercounty career that would span twenty-three years, with McNamara's final appearance coming in the 1968 Munster final at Tramore, where Na Déise were beaten by Cork. Traditionally, west Waterford was a stronghold of camogie, with teams such as Brickey Rangers, Kilbrien and Ballinamult providing players to the county team. Sadly for camogie in Ireland's oldest city, McNamara returned to South Kilkenny. In early 1948, she was involved with the new Camogie Club established at Mullinavat, where she was elected to the position of captain. It was part of the revival of the sport in the Marble County, where a club championship was to be staged for the first time in fifteen years, with twelve teams entering the competition. Later that summer, McNamara played for Kilkenny in the Leinster Championship. On Sunday, 24 October 1948, she was part of the Mullinavat side that defeated Gowran 6–1 to 4–1 in the Kilkenny County final at Thomastown. The loss to the White and Blue was definitely to the benefit of Mullinavat and the Black and Amber.

Of the period, McNamara stated, 'I was living in Kilmacow for a while and I played with Slieverue and Mullinavat, and I played for Kilkenny in the 1948 and 1952 finals.' At intercounty level, the era was dominated by a Dublin team, who won eight All-Irelands in a row from 1948 to 1955. The best of the rest were Antrim, who won the O'Duffy Cup in 1946 and 1956, and were runners-up three times to the Dubs. In 1952, McNamara was on the losing Slieverue side that were defeated in the replay of the Kilkenny County Camogie Championship by a goal.

Thankfully, from a Waterford perspective, McNamara was elected as representative to the Munster Council at the 1958 Annual Convention of the Waterford County Camogie Board. The body numbered J. Coffey (Ballymacarbry) as chairman, Miss M. Nugent (Ballinamult) as vice chair, Miss S. Carroll as honorary treasurer, and Miss J. Kiely (Brickey Rangers) as honorary secretary, with Mr S. Curran as her assistant. It was expected that the Club Championship would involve twelve teams. That autumn, McNamara and May Nugent were selected for the Munster camogie team to play Ulster.

McNamara's club career saw her win County Championship medals with four different clubs: St Carthage's and Éire Óg in Waterford, as well as Mullinavat and Slieverue in Kilkenny. She recalled that she won at least three medals with Munster selections in interprovincial tournaments. While lining out for Slieverue, McNamara was selected to represent Leinster in interprovincial competition. She eventually transitioned from playing to refereeing camogie matches, and later coached the Kilmacow Camogie Club. However, there was still time left in Josie's playing career to make a mark at intercounty level.

One of the great days of Waterford Camogie, since their provincial breakthrough in 1945, was when they defeated reigning champions Tipperary 1–3 to 1–2 in the 1959 Munster final. Played in Cahir on 28 June, Tipperary later lodged an objection that would subsequently be overruled by the Munster Council to allow Waterford to play in the semi-final for the All-Ireland Championship. Playing at full-back, McNamara collected her second Munster title along with Biddy McGrath. The Munster and Leinster player had played midfield in 1945, full-back in 1959, and, as we will see for her last intercounty game, numbered among the forwards in 1968.

Locally, east Waterford would see the formation of one of its strongest Camogie Clubs in 1958, when the Gall Tír Camogie Club was established and would become one of the strongest exponents of the game in County Waterford. Inspired by the victory of the men's Gaelic football team in claiming the 1958 County Junior Football title, figures like Pat Doyle and Anne Dingley started their playing days by striking a ball against the wall of Martin Dingley's house. They initially played at Cheasty's Field, followed by Stubb's Field at Belle Lake, before becoming a fixture on the Gall Tír Football Field from the 1970s. Retrospectively, they would name McNamara among their charges and stalwarts.

McNamara refereed the 1959 All-Ireland Camogie semi-final between Dublin and Antrim at Casement Park in Belfast. Just a few weeks later at Gaelic Field she played on the Éire Óg side that defeated Brickey's 5–8 to 4 goals in the County Camogie Championship. The city side lined out as Peg Robinson, Josie McNamara, Ann Power, Marie Murphy, Nora Breen, Lillian Howlett, Geraldine Power, Deirdre Forrest, Rosaline Atcheson, Teresa Byrne, Ann Cleary and Marian Frisby.

A year later, McNamara was the match official for the Munster Camogie Final between Tipperary and Cork at the Cork Athletic Grounds. A report from the *Munster Express* in early May 1963 detailed that:

> It was stated at the annual general meeting of the Éire Óg Camogie Club on Saturday last that, owing to the rather poor support during the year under review, the Club was not in a very sound financial position. An appeal was made to the public for every possible support during the coming year.

Around the same time, McNamara had risen to the position of vice chair of the Waterford Camogie County Board. In preparation for the county side playing Clare at Tulla in the Munster Championship, the Gaultier Camogie Club offered to stage a concert at Rainbow Hall.

Early September 1963 saw Waterford win the McCalmont Cup, an interprovincial tournament, beating Kilkenny 4–2 to 2–2 at Ashgrove, Mooncoin. McNamara's last bow came in the 1968 Munster final, staged at McGrath Park in Tramore. Cork were winning at half-time, 2–2 to a single point, when McNamara was introduced (she had retired four years previously), with the *News & Star* reporting that:

> Her introduction was a revelation. The match up to then like a Sunday afternoon stroll, burst into life. Waterford started a tremendous fight for victory and with the craft of a veteran, Miss McNamara scored two goals, one in the last minute of normal time when she slipped the ball under the advancing Cork goalkeeper's legs, rounded her full and hit the ball into an empty net to level the match and force it into extra time.

Sadly, it was to be a third Munster final in a row that would end in defeat for Na Déise, with McNamara having a 30-yard free to draw the game, but it narrowly went wide.

At times, McNamara appeared to be a gun for hire, which she referred to by saying, 'I also was illegal a couple of times I played. I was a spectator at a serious match Waterford were playing in and somebody came over to me and gave me a hurley and I played and other people called me a "rented" Camogie player.' The decision to bring her camogie career to a close was due to her 'walking down Bunkers Hill to training down in Erin's Own one day. There were these two girls standing at either corner of the street. Without looking at me one said to the other "don't tell me that she is playing with that thing all the time" and at that stage I knew that there was more to life than Camogie.'

McNamara turned her attention towards sports such as tennis, badminton and table tennis. She was a member of the Árd na Greine tennis and table tennis club, and played with the Waterford Badminton Club at Lady Lane. With the latter, she won the Munster Singles Championship and the Doubles title with a Cork partner. Additionally, Josie McNamara could claim County Waterford and Munster titles in table tennis, a county title in lawn tennis, and while being a member of the De La Salle Squash Club she was a county champion in the indoor racquet sport (which she took up in 1973). She would remain the number one-ranked player in the county for nearly five years.

In 1976, Josie added pitch and putt to her sporting repertoire, and within a year of taking up the game, McNamara won all the Open titles in County Waterford. She commented of her early years in golf that, 'Either I'll beat the golf or it'll beat me.' In winter 1980, Josie won the Senior Alliance (Golf) outing at Courtown. McNamara's sporting achievements are remarkable in variety, longevity, hunger and determination, which saw her claim silverware from camogie to golf. She gave so much back to the sports she loved, was heavily involved in camogie, and was always noted for her organisation of golfing events in her later years.

The *Munster Express* of 8 September 1978 concluded that:

> Josie is one of the biggest 'characters' sport in Waterford has produced. She is her own woman, to coin a phrase, and that allied to her consistently jolly nature and the fact that she is ever willing to assist in the organisational side of things, makes her a highly-valued member of various clubs with which she is associated.

On Sunday, 30 January 2005, McNamara was elected Honorary President of the Munster Council at the Clarion Hotel in Limerick. It was recognition of her playing career, but also the esteem in which she was held in the camogie community. Figures like McNamara were the lifeblood of a sport that was treated as second class to men's games until relatively recently. Noted by the *Munster Express* as the 'queen of sport', she ranks as one of Waterford's greatest sportspersons. Josie passed away in 2018.

'Ideally Suited to the Irish Temperament': Waterford Fencing Club, 1948–73

The Saturday, 24 July 1948 edition of the *Waterford Standard* carried a letter from the Honorary Secretary of the Arts Fencing Club (Dublin), Edward C. Fanning, who was living at 37 St Alphonsus' Road. A native of Waterford, Fanning attended the College of Art in Dublin, and while in the capital, he became an ardent student of fencing. While there, Fanning was taught by Maître Daniel Sacile, who had an incredible record of being the Senior Foil French Champion for ten years, as well as the European title-holder for four years. Fanning's letter read:

> To the Editor, 'Waterford Standard',
> May I request the hospitality of your column to contact persons interested in the formation of a Fencing Club in Waterford.
>   Fencing is as yet a comparatively unknown sport in this country, but since the war years it had gained considerable popularity especially in Dublin where there are now eight Clubs in operation. Fencing also flourishes in Kilkenny (Ireland's oldest Club), Limerick, Curragh and Athlone. Waterford could add at least two or three clubs to that number in time.
>   Contrary to popular belief Fencing is not an expensive sport and compares favourably with Hurling, Football, etc. It is particularly suited to the Irish temperament and is a sport in which Éire could rival other nations, given a sufficient number of clubs. This fact was proved conclusively at the Irish Open Championships in Kilkenny when, against a large foreign entry Éire had three out of six in the final pool. A. O'Connor, then Irish Foils Champion, was 2nd to L. Froucht of France.
>   About 20 to 30 persons are needed to start a club, and I am sure that a number

of potential Fencing champions can be found in Waterford. To those thinking of taking up the sport I would like to say that persons of all ages are capable of making good fencers provided they train. Youth, height and reach are all assets but none are essential; the feeling for fencing is the great asset. If persons interested in starting a club would get in touch with me at the above address I will call a meeting and endeavour to get the club established before the beginning of the Fencing season in October.

Such was the response in numbers, the first meeting of the Waterford Fencing Club was held on Saturday, 21 August 1948 at the Imperial Hotel in the city. It was presided over by Mr T. Crotty, President of the Irish Amateur Fencing Federation, with exhibition matches staged by the Kilkenny Fencing Club in foil, sabre and épée. Explanation of the sport was provided during the matches. The meeting was open to all who were interested in learning more, or taking part in fencing. Crotty was a prominent figure in the business and social spheres of Kilkenny. A founder member of the Kilkenny club, Crotty was a member of the FCA, as well as numbering the local Chamber of Commerce, of which he would become secretary.

Under the guidance of Fanning, a few local enthusiasts were being schooled in the art of fencing in Waterford, with arrangements already being made for a French professional expert, who was being engaged by the IAFF, to come Suirside to provide further instruction. The Waterford Fencing Club officially came into existence at a general meeting staged on Thursday, 7 October 1948, and was immediately affiliated to the national Fencing Federation. The following officers were elected to run the Waterford club:

President: Mrs C.G. Patterson
Club Captain: Mr J. Power
Ladies' Captain: Mrs H.T. Perry
Hon. Secretary: Mr T. Fewer
Hon. Treasurer: Mr H.T. Perry

The hundreds of people who attended the demonstration by the Kilkenny club in the Imperial did not translate to members for the Waterford club. By late February 1949, the local group consisted of twenty members, but was largely unknown in the city by the River Suir. Part of the issue appeared to be over E.C. Fanning returning to Dublin. As outlined by 'Lunger' in the *Standard*:

The girls and boys practised with a will for about three months, when suddenly their instructor [Fanning] was recalled to Dublin. That would have been enough to damp the ardour of another club but not this one. They went to the club to practise two nights a week, revising what they had been taught and now, as a reward for their labours, they are to have a French fencing master to give weekly instruction. He has just arrived in Dublin and will shortly visit the many clubs scattered throughout the country.

It was hoped that the arrival of the French instructor would provide an extra incentive of glamour and exoticness that would attract more members to the fledgling club. However, promoting fencing by extolling the benefits of the exercise, which helped an individual's poise, and by pointing out it was not expensive, with the added benefit of foils and masks being provided by the club, failed to attract new members. Meanwhile, Fanning was chief occupational therapist with Dublin Corporation, and his efforts in fencing saw him represent Ireland against Scotland and Poland. A competitive swordsman, Fanning had the rather ignominious distinction of finishing runner-up in the Irish Senior Open Fencing Championships seven times, before returning to his hometown in the early 1960s. Even his greatest honour, of representing Ireland as a 'foilist' in the 1948 London Olympics, was cruelly taken away, when he had to forfeit his place as a punishment for giving a fencing demonstration without prior permission from the Irish Fencing Federation.

Eventually, by mid-April 1949, the 'fencing maître' was arranged by the Irish Fencing Federation and visited Waterford. Pierre Gainet had a wide experience of fencing with foil, épée and sabre, and it was hoped he would provide a level of expertise that would see the sport take off in Waterford. Meanwhile, the neighbouring Kilkenny Fencing Club was holding an international fencing tournament in the Mayfair Ballroom over the 1949 Easter weekend, which numbered entries from France, Holland, Sweden, the USA, England, Scotland and across Ireland. This marquee event by the pioneering club from the Marble County would only cost an admission of 1*s* to view.

Waterford continued to be left in the shade by the Athlone and Kilkenny clubs, while the addition of a club being established in Clonmel saw efforts in *Urbs Intacta* peter out. The Kilkenny Fencing Club was active in holding fundraisers, such as an annual dance at the Mayfair Ballroom in the 1950s, and having Mick Delahunty's band playing to draw in a revenue stream and promote the club as being on trend with the popular showbands of the era. A revival of fencing in Waterford started in late 1954 when a new club travelled to Clonmel for a friendly, which saw an invitation from Mr Danny O'Beirne for the Clonmel club to participate in a forthcoming tournament to be held in Waterford. The Waterford team numbered Misses M. Hopkins (Bank of Ireland), N. Sharkey (teacher), M. Coughlan and Messrs F. Lanigan, D. O'Beirne and Gerry Walsh (Power's).

The new club practised at the Crystal Dance Studio every Tuesday and Thursday, from 8 p.m. to 11.30 p.m., and its membership stood at twenty-five people, the majority of whom were women. Their instructor was Mary Coughlan (of the Bank of Ireland), who tutored Peg Neary, Alice Condon and Agnes Acton (PT instructor) in the art of the sport. The men's section was coached by Frank Lanigan (ACEC) and Danny O'Beirne, an engraver with Waterford Glass. They trained Walsh, Jim Phelan (who owned a confectionary shop), David Grant (described as the club's comedian), Paul Cassin, Alfie Brophy and J. Brazil. The annual subscription was 21s, while members were expected to purchase their own equipment. However, this club also eventually dwindled, while the Clonmel and Kilkenny clubs went from strength to strength.

In early 1963, there were reports in the local press that an archery and fencing club would be established in Waterford city. The duo behind the development were Eddie Fanning (Thomas' Hill) and Teddy Guilfoyle (Parnell Street). Fanning had been behind the initial effort in 1948 and was going to take charge of the fencing section. The *News & Star* reported that, 'There are a considerable number of people in Waterford and the surrounding areas interested in both archery and fencing, so any day now Urbs Intacta will be echoing to the clash of blades and the whizz of arrows.' The fencing club established a temporary headquarters at the Knights of Malta Hall on the Mayor's Walk, where the club would meet every Saturday at 8 p.m. Anyone interested in taking part was directed to get in touch with Tommy Guilfoyle at Patrick Street. For beginners, all that was needed was a pair of rubber-soled shoes.

Frank Lanigan, from the wages section of the ACEC, who had gained considerable experience in organising club events with his role with the Beekeepers' Association, staged a popular annual dinner dance for the fencing club. We know in autumn 1964 that the revived Waterford Fencing Club hosted a visiting English selection, which included two Olympic team members. Lanigan was seen as integral to the organisation of the exhibition, which the *News & Star* noted was 'well attended and spectators were thrilled with the superb swordsmanship'. The Yorkshire Fencing Association were visiting Waterford in 1964 in preparation for competing in the National Fencing Championships held in Cork that September. They were led by their coach and instructor, Paddy Power MBE, who was from Waterford, and had a career as a professional soccer referee and sports coach at York University. A Waterford–Yorkshire exhibition was held at St John's.

Originally from Morgan Street, Power had served as a sergeant major in the British Army, where he was a physical training instructor with soccer players and future managers Joe Mercer, Matt Busby and Joe Harvey. It was for his military service that he was awarded an MBE by King George VI. The most notable association football fixture he was involved in officiating was the 1954 FA Cup final at Wembley when West Brom beat Preston 3–2. That day, Power was a linesman. His passion for fencing saw two Yorkshire fencers under his guidance go to the Munich Olympics, while his son Anthony was involved in the team event. His work with the York Education Department included coaching running, while in his spare time, Power volunteered with the Samaritans from late evening until dawn. Sadly, Power suffered from depression and in March 1978 was found dead from gunshot wounds at his home in York.

On the crest of a wave, junior members of the local fencing club travelled to Dublin in February 1965 to compete in the Schoolboys' Championships of Ireland for the first time. Five of the six Waterford boys, N. Harding (Grange Lawn), P. Martin (Grange Park), B. McHatton (Grange), M. Hilliard (South Parade) and P.J. McCarthy (Catherine Street), reached the semi-finals of their sections, while T. Lyons (Cork Road) made it to the quarter-finals. Their schedule for the rest of the year was the Killanin Trophy (for schools) in April, the Irish Open Championships on Whit weekend, and the South of Ireland Open Championship to be staged during the Light Opera Festival. In the latter event, one of the best performers was Mrs Perry Fanning, who with three wins and four defeats placed sixth in the Ladies' Foil Final.

In January 1966 Eddie Fanning again took pen to paper, with the *News & Star* publishing his letter seeking new members:

> Fencing lessons can be had free of charge at the Waterford Fencing Club which meets every Thursday night at the Central Hall, The Quay. The club itself, although still numerically small, is rapidly gaining a reputation for itself in both Irish and English fencing circles. The members are always ready to welcome newcomers to their ranks, because they want to popularise a sport which is ideally suited to the Irish temperament.

That September, the South of Ireland Open was held at the Badminton Hall on Lady Lane, and was dominated by the Royal Military Academy Sandhurst's Lt Rodney Craig, who claimed three trophies in the épée, foil and all-weapons sections. Two years later, the Slough native competed in the Mexico Olympics and later the 1972 Games in Munich. Craig's greatest success came at the 1970 Commonwealth Games, where he won a silver in the sabre individual, and was part of the gold medal-winning English team in the same discipline. Another Olympian present at the competition was John Boucher-Hayes. After the competition, a tournament dinner was held at Dooley's Hotel.

Such events aided the development of the junior fencers coming through the Waterford club, and this was reflected in nine individuals from the group competing in the National Junior Championships at Salle Duffy in Dublin in February 1967. They were Aileen Kennington, Anne Kearney and Perry Fanning in the Ladies' Foil, while Richard Keane, Niall Harding, Vincent O'Hara, Peter McCarthy and Eddie Fanning Jr took part in the Men's Foil. Due to the increased demand, the Waterford Fencing Club began to meet on Mondays and Thursdays, as the sport enjoyed a popularity that it had never known in the city. All of this resulted in Waterford staging their third successive South of Ireland Championship in October 1967.

Furthermore, the greatest milestone that marked the Waterford Fencing Club as truly being a fixture on the Irish scene was when they defeated the illustrious Kilkenny club at the Franciscan Hall in the Noreside town in February 1968. It was a resounding 12–4 victory for the Waterford team, which numbered E. Fanning (capt.), B. Baston, R. Keane and N. Harding. Their opponents were T. Kearney (capt.), R. O'Carroll, M. Buggy and D. Hermann. The Kilkenny ladies' foil team gained a modicum of revenge by beating an inexperienced Waterford side, which saw Niamh Harding and Susan Hicks making their debuts for the club, led by Perry Fanning.

The next big event organised by the Waterford Fencing Club was a dance at the Strand Inn, in Dunmore East, on Saturday, 7 March 1970. Music was to be provided by the Comerfords, with entry costing 8s 1d. The club would hold numerous such dances in Dunmore over the coming months in an effort to raise funds for the club, which was burgeoning with talent. No doubt such dances helped with their efforts in organising the South of Ireland Open, which was staged for the seventh successive year in the city. An ESB strike on Saturday, 18 September 1971 saw the scoring apparatus that was usually powered by electricity converted to battery, while the dinner later that evening at Dooley's was by candlelight. The President of the Waterford Fencing Club at this time was Guy Perrem. Interestingly, there was a decline in the sport nationally, with fewer entrants competing in the tournament held at the Badminton Hall on Lady Lane.

Perrem was noted as a pioneer of fencing in Ireland. It was believed he introduced the sport to the island around 1932, when he was the French Junior Champion. Perrem later worked as area manager for Guinness in Waterford. The first golden age of the sport in Ireland, in the 1940s and '50s, was accelerated by the army, with clubs sprouting up across Dublin and in provincial towns such as Kilkenny. After the false dawns of 1948 and 1953, the second resurrection of the fencing club in 1963 turned out to be the longest continuous period of existence enjoyed by the group. It was hoped that the club would thrive for another decade when, in 1972, Irish Olympian Michael Ryan came to teach in Waterford and started a fencing club at the Regional Technical College. However, both the Waterford and RTC clubs saw a drop-off in membership in March 1973, with Eddie Fanning noting, 'We get a lot of teenagers interested in learning to fence here, but then they leave Waterford to work or to go to College and then we lose them. The absence of a full third level education in the city hits us.' Fanning and Ryan decided to come together to combine their efforts in tackling the issue of membership numbers.

Sadly, the high point that the Waterford club had enjoyed with nine juniors competing at the National Championship in 1967 and the club defeating the famed Kilkenny club in 1968 was as good as it got. As young people looked to the future, they saw that the economic and educational circumstances that pervaded Ireland's oldest city at this time would not form part of theirs. The south-east haemorrhaged young people, who have been leaving its confines for decades, if not centuries, and it is sad to reflect on the stories of Eddie Fanning and Paddy Power, who made careers elsewhere and returned to their native city to promote their passion of fencing, for their efforts to be undone by what had seen them leave decades before: a search by young people for opportunity and prosperity.

Colonel James Flynn: Irish Olympic Basketballer

James 'Jim' Flynn was born in Stradbally, Co. Waterford, in 1921. He went on to attend the CBS in nearby Dungarvan. Jim's father, Thomas, was a brick and stone layer. Thomas was ten years older than his wife Mary. Jim's brothers included Tomas Uls O Floinn, who worked as the Chief Inspector for the Department of Education, and Miceal Uas O Floinn, a national school teacher. The family were well known as the Flynns from The Square in Stradbally.

Military Career Overview: From Cadet to Colonel

James Flynn enlisted in the Irish Army as a private in 1940. He was made a cadet in 1942, and was commissioned four years later. The early years of his military career were spent in the Curragh, Co. Kildare. Flynn was subsequently appointed Officer Commanding 13th Infantry Battalion (North Cork), a position he held for nine years before being promoted to lieutenant colonel in 1968. This role saw him commanding the 4th Infantry Battalion and Collins Barracks in Cork. A year later, he was made Executive Officer of the Southern Command. Over ten years later, Flynn (after a period as Officer Commanding First Brigade in Cork) was promoted to colonel in 1980. The last years of his military career were based in Limerick as Officer Commanding Southern Command of the FCA.

During his time with the Irish Army, Flynn served on four trips overseas, which were in the Congo (1960 and 1962) and Cyprus (1967 and 1970). For his time in the Congo, Flynn was awarded the Distinguished Service Medal (Second Class) for outstanding 'leadership, resourcefulness, courage and prudence' during the early years of the conflict in the African country. Then a captain, Flynn served as Staff Officer with

C Company in the 33rd Battalion, which attempted a 1,400-mile rescue bid as they (sixty soldiers) patrolled for eleven days searching for three Europeans who had been kidnapped from a derailed train by hostile Balubas on 2 October at Niemba. The *Irish Press* noted that, 'Though they failed to trace the kidnapped persons, the long ordeal was an indication of the Irishmen's fitness and devotion to duty.'

C Company Patrolled 1,400 Miles in Congo Rescue Bid

Under Comdt Patrick Keogh, they tried to establish a UN post in Niemba, but 6 miles from the area they found that the railway line (as the group travelled from Albertville) had been pulled up by Balubas in the vicinity. They returned to Albertville and decided to reach Niemba to search for the missing Europeans by road. Encountering many roadblocks, they managed to ably navigate any aggression with the aid of a Swedish interpreter. Upon reaching Niemba, the Irish patrol discovered the streets of the town were littered with bodies, and it was essentially burnt to the ground. While there, they were visited by Lt Col R.W. Bunworth, who would return to Albertville with Comdt Keogh. Leaving fifteen men in Niemba, Captain Flynn led the rest of the patrol southward in search of the Europeans and encountered 'many roadblocks and Balubas armed with bows and arrows and elephant guns'.

Along the way, the men of C Company had to rebuild a bridge, but were surrounded by Balubas. Flynn attempted to talk with the tribesmen, but they were unwilling to let the Irish soldiers pass. They resorted to using a 10-ton truck and putting their foot down to disperse the Balubas that encircled them, then leading the convoy to safety. Meanwhile, at Niemba, a substantial number of Balubas had gathered near the Irish Army's post, leading to a doubling of sentries to keep watch while 'forming vehicles into a circle and illuminating the surrounding undergrowth with headlights'. The patrol led by Flynn continued their search through Manono, Pweto (a Swedish UN post), Baudouin and back to Albertville with the round trip coming to 1,400 miles. Sadly, they were unable to find the Europeans.

Flynn returned to Congo in 1962, this time serving in the 36th Battalion. Flynn wasn't awarded his DSM, designed by Oisin Kelly depicting Cú Chulainn on his chariot, until 1967, with the *Irish Independent* commenting:

A/Comdt. James Flynn, Art McMurrough Hill, Curragh Training Camp: Military Police: For courage, prudence and resourcefulness on a 1,000-mile patrol of unknown territory, in October, 1961, in pursuit of a Baluba war party. Despite obstacles of broken and burned bridges, impassable roads and rivers, armed and threatening Balubas, he brought his patrol safely back to base.

Cyprus 1970

Comdt Flynn was second in command to Lt Col Martin J. O'Brien of Curragh Camp Headquarters when Ireland sent its largest contingent to Cyprus in 1970. It comprised the 18th Infantry Group (which was 400 strong), made up of a Headquarters company, two infantry companies, an armed car unit and a heavy mortar troop. Flynn was the United Nations liaison officer with the Greek National Guard during the Turkish invasion of Cyprus.

Sportsman

Flynn was an excellent sportsman, having played senior Gaelic football for Kildare, Wexford and his native Waterford. The Stradbally man was an adept hurler, rugby player and soccer player to boot. His most unusual distinction was being a member of the Irish basketball team that participated at the 1948 London Olympics.

The sport was introduced to the Irish Army by Sergeant Major Doogan in 1920. This was primarily to supplement training programmes for boxers, but grew increasingly popular as a pursuit in its own right. As the game was in rude health in the Curragh over twenty years later, a club was formed at University College Dublin.

The development of basketball on the island was cultivated by the formation of the Amateur Basketball Association of Ireland (ABAI) in 1945. Previously, the sport had been confined to members of the Irish Army, and the aim of the ABAI was to promote the sport to civilians. The Irish version of the game used a bigger and heavier ball compared with that adopted internationally. The army had been using a rulebook from 1936, so the version of the game played in Ireland had not kept in train with the latest rule changes. For example, Waterford sports historian Tom Hunt notes, 'International basketball disallowed physical contact; Irish basketball was intensely physical, closer to an indoor version of Gaelic football than to international basketball.'

The same year as the first Olympiad after the war, Flynn scored 11 points for the Curragh as they were defeated by Eastern Command in the semi-finals of the Army Basketball Championships at Portobello Barracks with a scoreline of 32–30. A similarly impressive performance from Lt Flynn was witnessed in the Leinster semi-finals, as he led Kildare to beat Louth 33–8, scoring 20 points himself. The *Irish Independent* described him as 'deadly accurate' at left forward. Extra time was required in Kildare's win over Dublin in the provincial final as the Lilywhites won 28–26, with Flynn again leading the scoring charts with 10 points. Thus, the first-ever Leinster Basketball Championship could number the County Waterford man among the trailblazing, winning Kildare side.

On 23 May 1948, Flynn was part of the Leinster side that was victorious in the All-Ireland Basketball Final, which saw them defeat holders Connacht 46–39, with Flynn contributing 6 points. On the back of such performances, Flynn was selected for the Irish Olympic team managed by W.C. Allgood, coached by Comdt D.F. MCormack and trained by Sgt C. Cleary. Hunt notes that, 'Lt James Flynn was completing an officer's course and travelled separately to London.' It was hoped that an Irish team taking part in the competition would provide experience and promotion of basketball at the highest level, which Irish basketball could build on. This aim was dispelled from quite early on.

In their four matches the Irish team were clearly overwhelmed by opposition that were adept in the intricacies of the game. The team finished in twenty-third and last place over all. They had been drawn in Group D with Cuba, France, Iran and Mexico. They played Mexico first, losing 71–9, although Flynn was one of his side's point scorers. This was followed by a 49–22 defeat to Iran, with Cuba then beating the Irish, 88–25. As qualification from the group was a mathematical impossibility, the coaches decided that all members of the fourteen-man panel would get game time, and in the final match Ireland were defeated by group runners-up France, 73–14, to finish bottom of the section, without a win and with a score difference of minus 211.

The only consolation was that both Mexico and France made it to the semi-finals. Both were defeated by the all-conquering United States, with France claiming silver, while Mexico missed out on bronze by losing to Brazil in the play-off tie.

Ireland's woes at the Harringay Arena didn't improve. They lost to Great Britain (46–21) and Switzerland (55–12) to finish bottom of the pile. As of the most recent Olympics in Tokyo, 1948 remains the only time that Irish basketball had a representative side at the Olympic Games.

In later years, Flynn was a driving force behind the Fermoy Rowing Club. Flynn had a remarkable career in the Defence Forces and, upon his retirement in 1982, the *Evening Echo* noted that the Stradbally man's 'greatest claim to fame was his membership of the Irish Basketball team at the London Olympics in 1948'. Family connections continued with the defence forces, as his daughter Marie was a second lieutenant upon her father's retirement, while David (Jim's son) was serving in the navy. Flynn's sporting endeavours were equally as remarkable, playing inter-county Gaelic football for three counties, and being a point-scoring pioneer in Irish basketball. One wonders what could have been if the Irish Army had had an updated rulebook all those years ago; some would say the sport has been playing catch-up ever since.

There is no doubt that Jim Flynn served his country admirably, be it in conflict zones or on the basketball court.

44

Waterford FC in Iceland, May–June 1953

The 26 May 1953 saw a party of twenty-two made up of fifteen players and seven officials of Waterford Association Football Club depart Dublin Airport on a KLM plane at 8.30 p.m. for Reykjavik, Iceland. A notable absentee was Jack Fitzgerald, the side's star player, who was in hospital after having cartilage removed from his knee, an injury he sustained in the club's last official game of the season against Shamrock Rovers. While recuperating in Waterford Hospital, he was to miss out on the two-week tour of Iceland. He was replaced by R. Dwyer of Shelbourne for the tour. The *Waterford Standard* highlighted that the, 'Association code is Iceland's only ball game and, with the enthusiasm attaching to exclusiveness, it is played everywhere and by everybody physically capable of it. The standard is very high, with the emphasis on team work rather than individual brilliance.'

There were two players from Manchester United travelling with the team, Harry McShane and Ed McIlvenny. The latter had been offered a player-coach role with Waterford for the following season, and it was expected that he would decide on the offer after the tour. His teammate McShane was a Scottish winger who played for United from 1950–54 and was the father of the actor Ian McShane, star of *Lovejoy* (1986–94) and *Deadwood* (2004–06). McIlvenny had graced the world stage by playing at the 1950 FIFA World Cup, with the Scottish-born wing-half captaining the United States in their famous 1–0 victory over England at the tournament.

To add to the excitement of the trip, the players all sported new blue club blazers. The mood of the group was captured in the quote of Club Chairman Michael McEvoy to the *Irish Independent*, 'We are more than a football team, we are a big happy family.' The trip was viewed as a just reward for the local players, who were amateurs. The club was also able to count on two Scottish professionals, goalkeeper Wingate and inside forward McQuade, who had re-signed with Waterford for another campaign.

Waterford were the first Irish soccer team to tour Iceland, a country that had defeated club teams such as Brentford and Queen's Park Rangers. The club were initially scheduled to play four games, but upon their departure from Ireland still didn't know the opposition they would face nor the grounds in which the fixtures would be staged. It was estimated that the trip would cost the Icelandic Football Association around £2,000, with Waterford having to reciprocate nearly the same figure when an Icelandic team was to visit Ireland the forthcoming August. The trip received national attention from the printed press as well as the radio. The programme *Sports Stadium* on Radio Éireann included interviews by Phillip Greene with Michael McEvoy, Jim McNamara, Michael Doyle and Tommy Fitzgerald.

Waterford's first game against Valur FC on 27 May was watched by a crowd of 4,000 people, with gate receipts around £1,000 in what was a thriller. The Reykjavik club were originally formed as part of the local YMCA and, by the time they played the Kilcohan club, had won their national championship eleven times. The Blues lost 2–1 with them taking the lead through 'a nice piece of approach work by McQuade gave McIlvenny a chance to send across a perfect centre which Dwyer headed past the helpless Valur goalkeeper'. The *Waterford Standard* concluded of the game that Waterford 'had laid the foundations of their popularity with the fans, and this was to make them a big attraction in all their succeeding games'.

In their next game, Waterford drew with KR Club, the 1952 Icelandic Champions. KR is the oldest club in Iceland, established in 1899, and had won the league fourteen times by 1953, including the inaugural championship in 1912. The Blues led 3–1 at half-time. The *Irish Press* described the ground in Reykjavik as 'gravel and was wet' as the home side took the lead after ten minutes from a goalkeeping error. Waterford equalised seven minutes later through Tommy Fitzgerald, with his brother Denny putting them in front after twenty-eight minutes. By the half-hour mark, Waterford scored a third through Halpin. The draw was deemed to be a fitting result.

The club's first win on Icelandic soil came in its third game there against a select XI made up of the clubs Fram and Vikingur FC. Fram were also nicknamed the Blues, with thirteen league titles as of the Irish club's trip to Iceland. This included six in a row from 1913 to 1918. Vikingur were less illustrious but they had won the Icelandic League in 1920 and 1924. Waterford won the game 5–2 (with the score 2–2 at half-time) in front of a 4,000-strong crowd. The Blues had now won one game, drawn another and had one defeat so far on their tour of the island. The club were to pick up a new fan along their trip: Professor Patrick Henry, who was a UCD graduate studying the Icelandic language, and became the club's 'constant guide and interpreter … and was the only one able to argue out the issue with excitable Icelanders in their own language during the course of the games'.

Waterford were defeated by Akranes 5–4, with Dwyer scoring two goals in the first half. This was followed by one each from McIlvenny and McQuade in the second. The west Iceland club were to be the team of the 1950s in their native land, winning the domestic league five times from 1951 to 1958. Their manager at the time was Ríkharður Jónsson, who held the distinction of being the record goal scorer for his country with seventeen until it was broken by former Chelsea and Barcelona player Eidur Gudjohnsen in 2007.

The club would complete their tour with a fifth game against a select team made up of Reykjavik clubs. The Blues won the tie 4–1. They were to make their return journey to Ireland, firstly via boat on the SS *Gullfoss* to Scotland. They reached Glasgow, where the plan was to travel to Belfast via boat. This was changed to the group being spilt into two, with half travelling to Dublin Airport from Edinburgh via plane, with the rest doing the same from Glasgow. They then made their way from Dublin to Waterford via rail.

Upon returning to Ireland after their successful tour, Waterford Chairman Michael McEvoy commented to the *Cork Examiner* that the climate was similar to Ireland except that at this time of year Iceland enjoyed twenty-four hours of daylight. This led to the players wearing sunglasses to protect their eyes against 'a brilliant 3am sun' when coming back from some early morning entertainments. McEvoy noted the absence of green fields and trees, and commented that grass around monuments in cities would be kept in a greenhouse in the winter and returned to its location by the following spring. The Icelandic cities were smokeless, as electricity was used for nearly all purposes.

The travelling side adapted to these conditions and a lighter ball to lose only two of their five matches, and that 'a selection of five Icelandic teams they played beat Sweden in a full international game last year'. The Blues were gifted a miniature flagstaff with the Icelandic flag and a replica of a football with the image of a Viking ship on it. Mr Toms, a director of the Waterford club, stated that 'the people of Iceland are the most-friendly we ever met and everyone was most anxious to make our stay as pleasant as possible'.

In several articles published in the local papers on the tour, Toms detailed how they had met Waterford-born John Butler, born and reared in John Street. Butler had left his native city thirty-two years earlier, living in New York with his family. Butler was in Iceland as supervisor of Icelandic personnel at the US Airbase at Keflavik, around 30 miles from the capital of Reykjavik. Another Waterford exile who was met on the trip by the team was Flt Sgt Jack Murphy.

The trip was noted for several evenings of singing from players as the Irish and Icelandic mixed company. There were visits to the National Park of Iceland where the old parliament used to meet and to the heights overlooking the valley where the

Declaration of Independence of the Republic of Iceland was made in 1944. They were accompanied by Professor Eirir Olafar Sveinsson, a professor of Icelandic History at the University of Iceland, who highlighted the significance of such historic locations to the team.

Waterford's tour of Iceland pre-dates the creation of the European Cup in 1955, which was later rebranded the Champions League in 1992. This makes the trip even more remarkable and shows not only how football is a common language among nations, but also the joy of supporting your local team, be it at the regional sports centre or in Reykjavik. The reports of the spectacle of the games, the personalities and characters involved, and the sheer novelty of travel by planes and boats captures an age that seems radically different to the world we live in today. It's hard to see players from Manchester United lining out with the club in the twenty-first century. Hopefully, it won't be too long until there are such travels in Europe again for Waterford soccer supporters.

Mutiny on a Boundary: The Blyth Affair, Waterford, 1954

Alexander Joseph Blyth was the Organising Secretary of the Waterford Cricket Club in August 1954. The Darlington native had served as a commercial representative with a number of English firms and had moved to the south-east of Ireland that July. Prominent members of the local community such as aldermen and councillors sought to revive the game in Ireland's oldest city. Letters from Blyth to local papers the *Munster Express* and the *Waterford News* appealed for members, financial assistance and a request that a landowner or farmer would provide a playing field for the club. The club's secretary, who resided at 10 O'Connell Street, just off the city's Quayside, aimed to form a social club and was particularly anxious that it attract young members from the ages of 10 to 17. An appeal was made for other clubs and schools in the city to come forward to form a league programme. Blyth wanted local businesses, especially factories, to come forward to form an interfactory league in the area.

Waterford Cricket Club, Est. 1954

The main fundraising effort to support the Waterford Junior XI was a weekly football pools that cost 3*d* to enter, with subscriptions requested to be sent to Blyth at his home address. On Friday, 10 September 1954, a meeting was held at the Adelphi Hotel to launch a senior club in the city. Addressing the gathered crowd, Blyth said that 'the club hoped to hold out the hand of friendship to the G.A.A.', while requesting that that organisation would pledge its approval to all forms of sport. The movement for the revival of cricket in Waterford received support from the City Manager, Liam Raftis, a veteran of the 1916 Easter Rising. Raftis promised to help with acquiring a pitch for the senior team, while provisions had been put in place for a practice ground at the People's Park. The City Manager's opinion on this was:

All our youngsters may not be physically fit or inclined to play hurling and I did not see any reason why those people could not avail of any amenities which the Corporation could provide. Their fathers pay rates as well as the fathers of those advocates of the G.A.A. Anybody who knows my views in the past will understand that I have not deviated from the national attitude but I have come to realise that if any unity is to be achieved we must be more tolerant than we were when it was necessary to unite everyone into a compact body to expel the British.

It appeared that the project was developing at a healthy rate and there was even enthusiasm that the city could attract famous teams for matches.

Importantly, key officers of the new Waterford club were appointed, with J. Butler as chairman; Blyth as secretary; A. Brophy to the position of treasurer and Teddy O'Regan as captain. The members of the local team were already pencilled in to face a side at Lismore in west Waterford. Butler, who chaired the meeting, noted that the fledgling club had been offered Kilcohan Park (the home of League of Ireland side Waterford FC at the time) for a lease of £35 a year but due to lack of funds could not take up the offer. The effort to secure playing facilities led to the club requesting the use of 1½ acres of land belonging to the Waterford Mental Hospital. That institution's board voted ten to six in refusing this arrangement as proposed in a letter by Blyth. The most hostile reaction came from Mr J. Kirwan (Bonmahon), who stated that 'foreign games are not appreciated in this country' and that 'we should get rid of the sassenachs [English] and shoneens'.

The club, which boasted eighteen senior and thirty-three junior members, still remained without adequate playing facilities. Blyth noted his disappointment at the mental hospital board's decision and felt that Kirwan's outburst had been unfair and unrelated to how the use of the land by the cricket club could affect the operations of the hospital. Blyth commented, 'By all means let them get priority, but the [Gaelic Athletic] Association should hold out the hand of co-operation to all other sports and get the Irish games played internationally.' In his statement to the *News*, the club's organising secretary made it known that they had secured the use of grounds (with a rent of 2/6) next to a new housing scheme at Ballytruckle.

Invitation from Blyth to the Duke of Edinburgh

The first game on the new club's grounds was to be the last of the season between the Waterford senior side and a team from Dunmore East. However, by mid-October the gains made would be lost and the Waterford Junior Cricket Club extinct. This was largely due to the fall-out in relation to Blyth writing an invitation to the Duke of Edinburgh to become a patron of the Waterford Cricket Club. The secretary had done this unofficially and without the committee members' knowledge or input. This was partially due to Blyth extending the invitation in August (the letter was dated the 14th), prior to the first official meeting of the newly formed club and appointed committee on 22 September 1954. The Durham man had sent similar requests to the President of the Olympic Council, Zan Zarisise, Sir Donald Bradman and several of the Republic of Ireland's national leaders, such as Sean T. O'Kelly, Éamon de Valera, Oscar Traynor and General Mulcahy.

In a statement to the *Munster Express*, Blyth wrote that, 'I did not realise at the time that my request was inadvisable from a diplomatic point of view, but I assert that it was made in good faith to the Duke as a sportsman ...'. He went on to apologise to 'the citizens of Waterford' for his unauthorised actions, which had

Queen Elizabeth II and Prince Philip, Duke of Edinburgh. Coronation portrait, June 1953, London, England.

placed them in 'an embarrassing situation'. The statement concluded that in future Blyth's activities would be confined and duties to be carried out as directed by the club. To rub salt into Blyth's wounds, a response from the duke written by Lt Gen. Sir Frederick Browning detailed, 'His Royal Highness is loath to add to these responsibilities, because even now, he has not had time to take personal interest he would wish in those things with which he is already connected.'

The response to Blyth's actions was the resignation of four committee members and the future of the club was plunged into much uncertainty. The final nail in the coffin of the venture were the strange and somewhat unsubstantiated events that led to the 29-year-old Honorary Secretary having to flee Waterford and go into hiding in London.

'A Hornets' Nest': Blyth Flees for London

The English *Sunday Chronicle* reported that the man who had attempted to start a cricket club in Waterford and failed had been threatened with his life by the Irish Republican Army. The *Chronicle* quotes Blyth as saying that the issues that arose in relation to the Duke of Edinburgh debacle 'snowballed into a national issue' that apparently received national press and radio attention. Blyth took little notice of the coverage but received a phone call from someone who told him to get out of Ireland immediately. Referring to the turn of events, Blyth stated, 'I didn't realise what a hornets' nest I would stir up. To invite the Duke was not, of course, a diplomatic move. I will not go back to Éire. My friends tell me I must take these I.R.A. threats seriously.'

However, the members of Waterford Corporation found the story to be rather humorous treating these threats more like a practical joke on the unwitting Blyth. Also, a statement on behalf of the IRA made in Dublin, signed by Adjutant General D. Mac Diarmada, stated:

> Attempts are being made in certain circles to create the impression that the Irish Republican Army has had some connection with the following incidents:
> Alleged threatening of an individual in Waterford.
> Armed assault on newspaper delivery man in Kerry.
> Disarming of a member of the F.C.A. in Clare.
> Responsibility for any of these occurrences is emphatically repudiated by the I.R.A., whose sole enemy is the British army of occupation in Ireland.

In response to the allegations made by the Darlington native, the Waterford Mental Hospital Board passed a resolution stating they were satisfied with the explanation provided by the IRA that the paramilitary organisation was in no way responsible for Blyth's return to England.

The increased interest in cricket was part of a growing trend in Ireland of people taking up what were deemed 'British sports' such as cricket, hockey and rugby to the detriment of handball and hurling. This would lead the *Waterford News* to opine that this could be seen as a signal of 'the unquenchable spirit of the nation [with the increased pursuit of sports such as soccer and cricket as ... indications of a dimming of the fires of freedom itself'. Even with the fallout of the Blyth affair, interest in cricket continued to develop rather than be hampered by the event.

If anything, the story shows that there was still a strong suspicion of any British influences in the south of Ireland, particularly the reactions that were noted in the meetings of the Waterford Mental Hospital Board that begs the question: were some of the members governing that very institution in need of some of its services for their vehement hostility to an English man trying to apparently (from their viewpoint) corrupt Irish youths with the Great British pastime? Thankfully, times have changed but the person who made that threat to Alexander Blyth all those years ago, whether with malicious intent in mind or dark humour, had overstepped the boundary.

Top left: Don Bradman, c.1930. John Howard concludes, 'That since his [Bradman] death some observers have been critical of aspects of his character and conduct, notably in the lead-up to World Series Cricket, cannot diminish his achievement as the world's greatest batsman of his and, probably, all time. Discomforted as he was by fame, no other sporting hero had contributed so much to the Australian public's pride and sense of nationhood.'

Bottom left: General Richard Mulcahy. Ronan Fanning concludes, 'Few of the countries that, like Ireland, achieved independence in the aftermath of the First World War have since enjoyed an uninterrupted history of stable parliamentary democracy. The army crisis of March 1924 was the moment when that record was most obviously at risk. That the crisis was surmounted, that an army crisis did not in fact turn into an army mutiny, and that the stability of Irish parliamentary democracy was thereby assured, is arguably the largest achievement of Richard Mulcahy. But he paid a heavy price for doing things 'his own way': never again was he to occupy so pre-eminent a place in the corridors of power. For the irony was that the same factors that enabled him to sustain the larger democracy – his temporising and conciliation in calming the army, and his ruthlessness in suppressing the more wanton forms of republican violence in 1922–3 – so corroded his personal democratic credentials that he was deemed unsuitable for appointment as Taoiseach in 1948. And therein lies a further irony, for his other great contribution to the vitality of Irish democracy was as the architect of Ireland's first coalition government, in which he himself was denied the first place. Coalition governments had hitherto seemed taboo, a taboo that still found expression in the coalitions of 1948–51 and 1954–7 instead being christened 'interparty governments'. Mulcahy shattered the taboo and in so doing – another irony – tore the first hole in the straitjacket of post-treaty party politics by enabling enemies in the civil war to sit side by side around the same cabinet table. His role, as the leader of the largest opposition party, was indispensable to the creation of a climate in which coalition could flourish, a climate that became the norm in Irish politics in the decades after his death.'

Waterford and District Table Soccer League, 1957–60

The *Munster Express* published a letter (dated 15 April 1957) from the Honorary Secretary of the Waterford and District Table Soccer League, James Duggan. The local table soccer official, living at Rockenham, wrote:

> We are non-political and non-sectarian. If any reader would be interested in joining the above League next season (September starts season), please get in touch with me ... or write, stating age if under 21 years, and enclosing a stamped addressed envelope. We would like to have all intending members registered before the 1st August ready for the kick-off. All enquiries will be answered promptly.

The fledgling Table Soccer League was being dominated by ex-St Joseph's and Glenard player Billy Browne. Browne had previously played in the Irish League, but his career was cut short due to injury. The game was being promoted as 'for strategists who are past the playing stage and also for a lot of those who are still active'. A few weeks later, Browne would depart for England.

The Waterford and District Table Soccer League had been members of the World Table Soccer Association since 1953. Founded in the 1953–54 season, the Waterford League had eight members, staging three competitions, which were closely fought between Sean Brown and S. Power. Annually, the body would stage the Shield, League and Cup, however, membership had fluctuated over the years. For the 1957–58 season, the League Committee saw Leo P. Dunne as President; S. Casey as Chairman; S. Brown succeeded Duggan in the role of secretary; and Seamus Upton serving as treasurer.

The Secretary of the Dublin Table Soccer League was Thaddeus A. Cantwell, whose father, Daniel, was a Freeman of Waterford city. Cantwell contacted the local press, wishing to promote table soccer and form cordial relations with the Waterford body. However, both bodies differed in their playing of the game. The *Munster* noted that:

Waterford and District Table Soccer League, 1957–60

Waterford is 'Subbuteo,' as distinct from our Dublin friends, but the principle is the same. The players mounted on plastic bases are propelled by a simple flick of the finger and the blurb says 'enables them to produce the body swerves and ball control of Association Footballers.' That 'simple flick' is of course the secret and separates the men from the boys in this interesting game.

Cantwell hoped that Subbuteo would make its way to the capital shortly, but in the meantime wished to develop some organisational affiliation. It doesn't appear that this hand of co-operation was explored further.

We know that in March 1958 the Waterford and District Table Soccer League's Shield was won by League Secretary Joe Duggan. He defeated S. Casey 3–1 in the final. Furthermore, Duggan received the Adolph Cup on behalf of the Waterford League. This was awarded to organisations for outstanding records by the Table Soccer Players' Association. It had only been awarded on a handful of occasions.

Later that year, local player Stephen Power secured a place on the Irish team to compete at the Silver Cup tournament in England. Power had reached the final of the Irish Championship in Dublin on Whit Sunday, but was defeated by the reigning champion, M. Fennell of the Three Castles (Dublin) Club. The Waterford man had already won several tournaments in England. In the first round, he defeated clubmate Seamus Upton, 2–1. This was followed by victories over G. Flanagan (Cliftonville) and M. McHugh to reach the decider. The *Munster* recorded that, 'In a very hard fought final, against Power, Fennell retained his title. The Waterfordman looked all set to wrest the Championship when he scored twice in the opening minutes but the Dublin player gradually got on top and eventually won by five goals to two.' A good year for Power locally saw him match Sean Brown's 1953–54 record by winning the Cup and League trophies.

However, by the winter of 1959, it looked like the local table soccer league was slowly being subsumed by the burgeoning Waterford Supporters' Club. The last hurrah for the game in Ireland's oldest city was the staging of the Irish Table Soccer Association's Cup competition on Whit Monday, 1960. Sixteen players from Belfast, Dublin and Waterford took part and Dublin's C. Grace won. In existence less than a decade, the Waterford and District Table Soccer League drifted into oblivion.

Subbuteo 'table soccer' pieces.

Suirsiders, Sliotars and the Silver Screen: Hollywood and the 1957 All-Ireland Hurling Final

A report in the *Cork Examiner* in August 1957 noted that production of a film to be entitled *Rooney* was to commence on 20 September. Based on a book by Catherine Cookson (her fourth novel), the story details the life of Dublin bin-man James Rooney and his sporting exploits in the world of Gaelic games: 'set in Dublin ... a shy dustman who is the reluctant hero. A tower of strength on the hurling field, he is also a bachelor whom many a Dublin landlady has tried to snare as a husband.' The protagonist was to be played by English actor John Gregson, formerly of the Royal Navy, who made his name in film in the comedy *Genevieve* (1953), *Three Cases of Murder* (1955) with Orson Welles and *The Battle of River Plate* in 1956. In the same year as the latter film, he was voted the eighth biggest film star in Britain.

The role of Rooney's grandfather was performed by Dublin-born Barry Fitzgerald, an Academy Award-winning actor for his supporting role in 1944's *Going My Way*. The tagline for the film was 'Not since *The Quiet Man* has Barry Fitzgerald played Cupid to the hearts of Irish lovers'. The John Wayne and Maureen O'Hara classic had been a success five years earlier, and it's clear to see the parallels between both stories of love, Ireland and sport, though the only reference to the 'Clash of the Ash' in *Quiet Man* was the line, 'Sure don't you know the Mayo hurlers haven't been beaten west of the Shannon in the last 20 years'. Maybe their modern-day Gaelic footballing counterparts could use some of the talents that made this fictional team such a success. They do say film can allow us to fantasise! Once more, the *Examiner* described the role for Fitzgerald as 'one suited to his talents – that of a crotchety grandfather'.

Gregson's love interest in the film was Muriel Pavlow, whose career started as a child actress with John Gielgud and the Shakespeare Memorial Theatre, with noted roles on the big screen in films such as *Doctor in the House* (1954) and *Reach for the Sky* (1956). The story develops further, as the *Examiner* outlined:

> Rooney gives her [Pavlow] a necklace which has been salvaged from rubbish … the trouble becomes serious because the necklace is in fact a valuable one which has been reported as having been stolen. Rooney, playing in the final of the All-Ireland Hurling Championship, learns that she has been arrested. He rushes around after the game to the police station and realises that he is in love with her.

Hollywood had its story and its stars in place, now Croke Park and the game of Cú Chulainn was to provide the backdrop. The participants of that year's All-Ireland final were to play the role of extras, whether they were willing or not.

The 1957 Hurling Championship saw Waterford defeat Limerick in the semi-final of the Munster Championship in front of 14,589 spectators, with a score of 4–12 to 5–5. In the provincial final, Na Déise faced Cork in Thurles, where a crowd of 39,254 saw the 'white and blue' victorious, winning 1–11 to 1–6. Galway were easily defeated in the All-Ireland semi-final, placing Waterford on a collision course with neighbours Kilkenny in the decider for the Liam McCarthy Cup. The Waterford side numbered Austin Flynn, Martin Óg Morrissey, Seamus Power, Philly Grimes, Mick Flannelly, Tom Cheasty, Larry Guinan and Frankie Walsh.

The film's production team had to approach the sides about whose colours Gregson would wear in his role as a Dublin hurler. Jamie O'Keeffe details, 'Waterford declined the approach but Kilkenny County Secretary Paddy Grace obliged the camera crew and actor.' Pat Fanning told of how it was the Gentle County's first appearance in the final since 1948 and they did not want further pressure or distraction provided by Gregson and filming. On 1 September, a crowd of 70,594 at Croke Park witnessed the two sides line up

Barry Fitzgerald, 1945. Patrick Geoghegan highlights, 'Fitzgerald was the first Irish person to win an Oscar and on 8 February 1960 he was awarded a star on the Hollywood Walk of Fame.'

behind the Artane Boys Band, however, the 'Black and Amber' had sixteen men marching, John Gregson being the extra man.

The *Kilkenny People* records:

OUR SIXTEENTH MAN: - Mr John Gregson, was at a reception to the Kilkenny team ... he was talking to Paddy Buggy and the lads ... Mr. Gregson told me that he was quite thrilled with his experience at marching around Croke Park. When he heard Father Maher addressing the team in the dressing room prior to the match telling the boys to go out and win Mr Gregson added: 'I felt like going out to win with the boys also' ... He jokingly remarked to Paddy Buggy: 'What are you going to do without me next year'.

Buggy was subsequently elected President of the GAA in 1981, having served in administrative roles for his club, Slieverue, Kilkenny County Board and the Leinster Council.

Of the game itself, Julian Walton notes that, 'It was one of the great hurling matches of all time: leading by six points ten minutes before full time, Waterford were the losers by one point when the final whistle blew.' Kilkenny were victorious on a scoreline of 4–10 to 3–12. The hero for the Cats was their captain, Mickey Kelly of Bennettsbridge, who scored the winning point from 50 yards. The *Irish Times* described the shot as 'so sweetly hit that it sailed dead straight over Roche's [the Waterford goalkeeper's] reach'. Footage from the game was used in the film, and players from both counties received £5 for their collaboration.

The *Irish Independent* detailed that there was additional shooting as a 'six-hour marathon hurling match was played on Saturday at Croke Park for Rank Organisation with thirty players from Kilkenny and Waterford, many of whom had played in the All-Ireland final. Filming of the game lasted from 9am to 3pm.' The film's director, George Pollock, stated, 'That point just suited us, because the same thing happens in the book of the film with a last-minute point winning the match, but this time John Gregson had to score the point, and though he worked hard at it, he is still no Mickey Kelly.'

The difficulty of the shot is further elaborated by the film's star, Gregson, who commented that hurling is 'demoralising because all these other fellows can play it but I can't'. It would appear the efforts of Dublin hurler Dessie Ferguson in coaching Gregson the skills of the game were in vain. One can imagine it was even a longer day of shooting for the actor than it was for the natural hurlers. Yet, the Waterford hurlers would rewrite the script in the 1959 final, defeating Kilkenny after a replay. Even more dramatic than *Rooney*, Na Déise needed a replay to overcome Kilkenny, with Frankie Walsh captaining the side. One wonders if Gregson was the lucky charm in the 1957 final for the Cats.

A smaller part in the film of Tom Reilly was filled by Godfrey Quigley, who in his latter career acted as Captain Grogan in the Stanley Kubrick epic *Barry Lyndon* (1975), which was partially filmed in Waterford with exterior shots of Waterford Castle and Little Island. But Hollywood and Waterford hurling were not finished with their affair in 1957. In 1963, the final was again between Kilkenny and Waterford, with glamour provided by the presence of Prince Albert and Princess Grace of Monaco. However, the star of *Rear Window* and *To Catch a Thief* would be less nostalgic, once stating, 'I avoid looking back. I prefer good memories to regrets.'

Who knew that a film about a Dublin hurler played by an Englishman wearing 'Black and Amber' would become an important record in the history of Gaelic games and the golden age of Waterford hurling. Everyone knows Hollywood can never resist a sequel, so watch this space on the sporting field and the silver screen.

Sea Lions and Walruses: Baseball in Tramore and Waterford City, 1958–66

A Boys' American Baseball Club was formed in Tramore in the summer of 1958. As the world was becoming more globalised, the impact of American culture on Ireland could be seen in previous summers on Tramore Strand by six boys playing a modified game of baseball called 'One Old Cat'. One of the parents of that group of youngsters was Tyresoles manager Clive Butterworth, who put his experience of having previously worked in the United States for a baseball team to good use and formed the baseball club, which practised at Graun Park. That early group membered Simon Butterworth (Clive's son), Edward Deevy, Arthur Hyde, Paschal Kelly, David and Gregory Kenny, Liam Morrissey, Patrick O'Brien and Michael O'Connor.

From Tramore Strand to Tramore Racecourse: Local League to National Championship, 1959–61

A year later, the club had enough youngsters made up of local residents to form two junior teams. Further momentum was built when former Waterford FC and Irish international soccer player Billy Barry (and top salesman with Butterworth's Tyresoles) aided Butterworth in coaching the youths. Butterworth's Sea Lions and Barry's Walruses staged their final game of the 1960 season at Graun Park, where a fifth inning was required, with Barry's charges claiming victory 9–8. Of the winning hit, the *Munster Express* reported 'a blooper hit by Pat O'Brien, and a fielding bobble by the Sea Lions counted the winning run, when pandemonium broke out on the Walrus bench, which the umpire was unable and unwilling to control'.

By July 1961, player numbers increased to forty youths, who now practised on a field with a baseball diamond laid out on it provided by the Tramore Racecourse Committee. The local league had turned into a national championship when the *News & Star* from 21 July 1961 reported that 'the Walruses and the Sea Lions ... have just commenced a series of seven games to decide the Irish Baseball Championship'. Such momentum led to Bill Barry seeking to develop a team based in Waterford City, as he was already bringing youngsters from the city to Tramore for games. Commenting on the progress of baseball in the south-east, Butterworth said, 'I don't know where we are going with this business. It started as a frivolous effort to amuse and occupy a few children with something new, but it grew and grew and last year [1960] when Bill [Barry] and many more boys came in, I began to wonder if I should not take it seriously.'

Greyhound Tracks and Cricket Clubs: Waterford Baseball and US Air Force Connections

Later that July, Butterworth and Barry brought thirty-six boys to Shelbourne Park to watch a softball exhibition among members of the US Air Force in aid of the Irish UNICEF Committee. The festivities saw the Lord Mayor of Dublin, Robert Briscoe, in attendance and a recorded message from Danny Kaye broadcast via the speakers at the greyhound track. While there they met Master Sergeant John Gay, Assistant Director of Athletics with the American Third Air Force in Europe, who was intrigued by the baseball activities in Tramore. It proved a fruitful day as the Tramore club returned with enough equipment for three teams after being given the Americans' cast-offs after the game. Such gear was put to good use when the Tramore Sea Lions and Waterford Walruses competed in the first public game of baseball between two Irish teams under Championship rules on Saturday, 2 September 1961. The Tramore side were victorious, winning 14–12, with Mickey O'Brien hitting two home runs. Tramore's quartet of pitchers to Waterford's pair of Denis O'Brien and Pat Ryan proved to be the difference going into the extra inning that not even the excellent fielding of Tony Condon could overturn.

The following season saw the fledgling Waterford city outfit obtain the use of a full-sized diamond field located by Skibbereen way, aided by the support of CIE's Paddy Higgis, who had played the game on a semi-professional basis in his younger days in the United States. July 1962 saw Master Sergeant Gay visit Tramore to hold a baseball demonstration for twenty-six players and he later had tea at Tramore House. Subsequently, the baseball boys took on their adult cricketing counterparts of Tramore Cricket Club in a game of baseball, losing by a single run. No mean feat in a game of boys versus men.

Baseball Beats the Ban at Gaelic Field? Brize Norton Broncos vs Alconbury Spartans, Walsh Park, 8 September 1962

Perhaps the most impressive event of the period was a baseball exhibition that took place on 8 September 1962 at Walsh Park between the Brize Norton Broncos and Alconbury Spartans as part of the Waterford International Festival of Light Opera. The teams were made up of American servicemen in England, with the players staying at the Tower Hotel. The American Ambassador to Ireland, Matthew McCloskey, made the ceremonial first pitch in the game, which was in aid of the United Nations Children's Fund. The Broncos beat the Spartans 5–2, with 28-year-old Charlie Kines hitting a home run in the first inning. The *Munster Express* carried the wry headline of 'Cicero Nearly Hits Homer in Gaelic Field', referring to the Broncos' Cicero Lofton providing the perfect opportunity for a Roman statesman to whack a Greek philosopher by Slievekeale. As we know, Waterford hurling supporters are a stoic lot!

Although there was a charitable context to this exhibition of a foreign game at Walsh Park, which was appreciated, there was opposition to its staging due to the infamous 'ban' on foreign sports stipulated in the codes of the GAA. The *News & Star's* Gaelic games correspondent Déiseach commented that such disapproval 'revealed regrettable ignorance' of both the rules and values of the GAA. It was a positive event in raising funds for charity but also allowed the Americans to enjoy Irish hospitality and a much-needed break from 'the "cold" impersonal attitude of the phlegmatic Britishers

Advert.

among whom they have lived for nigh on two years'. Essentially, the Americans were aiding a good cause and in return, we were giving them a break from England for a few days. Where was the harm in that? It must be noted that the British Ambassador to Ireland was also in attendance at Walsh Park, so it wasn't a complete break.

Waterford Baseball Club, 1963–66

The development of the Waterford Baseball Club in May 1963 saw its practices taking place at Poleberry on a field made available by the Erin's Own Hurling and Football Club. On 31 August, the Waterford Championship decider saw the Tramore Saints beat the Waterford Pirates 10–4. In driving rain, the star play of the final was from Joe Hodge, whose catch and composure to throw to first base and get the onrushing batter out exemplified the athleticism and presence of mind needed to excel at America's pastime. However, the development of the sport was hampered when Clive Butterworth moved to Dublin for work commitments in 1964. Yet, the first baseball match between two Irish cities took place on 5 September that year, between Waterford and Dublin. The game, sponsored by the Waterford Light Opera Festival Committee, saw the Déise victorious with a score of 5 runs to 3. Joe Hodge at bat and John Stokes pitching were key to Waterford claiming an historic victory.

An Irish Baseball Association was formed in 1965 with games taking place between Waterford and a Dublin Home Farm side. However, there was little baseball activity in the south-east after 1966. Billy Barry had continued holding practices at Grantstown, but things petered out when Clive's son Simon left Ireland in 1967 to study in the United States and the deterioration of Clive's health saw two of the central figures in baseball in Tramore depart the scene. Simon Butterworth suggests that a lack of adult volunteers coupled with participation levels not reaching a critical mass to be self-sufficient to develop the game further were issues that hampered baseball in both Waterford and Dublin.

The French-American historian Jacques Barzun surmised that, 'Whoever wants to know the heart and mind of America had better learn baseball' and the story of the game in Waterford illustrates the greatest lesson from childhood summers ... friendship. For those young men who excelled at America's pastime it was as much about spending time with companions as it was for the love of the game.

49

The Brown Bomber at the Arch in Tallow

The Brown Bomber, Joseph Louis Barrow, more commonly known as Joe Louis, was the longest-reigning champion of any heavyweight in history. He was the World Champion from 1937 to 1949, during which he fought twenty-seven championship fights and was victorious in twenty-five consecutive defences. It would be fair to say that after the US President and the glamour of Hollywood, he was the most famous American in the world. In total, he fought sixty-nine times, fifty-two of which he won by knock-out, and suffered three defeats, two of which were KOs. His last fight was on 26 October 1951 at Madison Square Garden, when he was sent to the canvas in the eighth round by Rocky Marciano. His sporting prowess wasn't only demonstrated in the ring; in 1952, he became the first African American to take part at a PGA Tour golf event when he was invited to play as an amateur in the San Diego Open.

Certainly well past his athletic peak, he was touring Ireland in 1966, and it was hoped during his four-day visit that he would take part in a number of exhibition matches. His visit to Ireland was being funded by Associated Ballrooms Ltd and the schedule was for Louis to appear at the Arcadia in Cahir, the Arch Ballroom in Tallow, and the Majestic Mallow. The *Irish Press* in late September noted that Louis was 'coming mainly as a cabaret artist, but it is hoped to erect boxing rings in the three ballrooms for exhibition bouts against suitable opponents'. The former champ arrived in Dublin on 4 October. At 52 years of age and weighing 16st, it was remarked by many that the years had weighed lightly on him, and he noted to the press that boxing was the only sport that gave African Americans a chance. However, if things had been different, he may have been a violinist or trumpeter. Wanting to be the next Louis Armstrong, he was given a dollar by his mother, who wanted him to take violin lessons. The young Louis spent it on boxing lessons in a gymnasium instead.

The aim of Louis' visits to Ireland with Kerry strongman 'Butty Sugrue' was to find a boxer who could compete to become the Heavyweight Champion of the

World. One boxer brought to his attention was a Sean O'Regan from Killarney in County Kerry. The Alabama fighter made his way to the Arch in Tallow on Friday, 7 October. A brief note of his appearance there was in the *Dungarvan Leader* on 15 October 1966:

> **Joe Louis at the Arch:** Joe Louis, one of the all-time greats of world heavyweight boxing made an appearance at a dance in the Arch Ballroom, Tallow on Friday night. The 52 years old ex-heavyweight champion was in Ireland looking for a future heavyweight hope with the Killorglin, Co. Kerry barn strong man 'Butty Sugrue'.

And that was it for the fanfare greeted to the great champion from years past. More detail on that night comes retrospectively from the *Avondhu*, which noted that the Q&A session was kept in order by radio disc jockey Larry Gogan. Local legend suggests that Tallow native Paulie Harty approached Louis on the street and remarked, 'I want to shake the hand that shook the world', possibly mistaking Louis for Cassius Clay. There is film footage of the Fitzgerald family, the proprietors of the Arch, having tea with Louis, who was relaxing at their home.

The passing of time has seen the Arch become the Tallow Community Centre and the story of Louis' visit to west Waterford may have faded but forms parts of the wonderful tapestry of a village that had an evening with one of the very great sporting figures.

Waterford Ladies' Soccer League, 1967–70

The Waterford Football Club Supporters Club provided an ample contribution to the city's League of Ireland representative that often far outweighed its small stature, where member numbers were often described as 'a bit of a joke'. However, over the course of the 1966–67 season, the Supporters Club was transformed as the *Munster Express* noted that, 'Practically overnight, the membership began to rocket, especially with the big influx of ladies.' Many believed this to be a result of the success of Waterford FC winning its first League of Ireland title in the 1965–66 season combined with the 1966 FIFA World Cup in England, which had brought the game, with added glamour, to a new audience via television. A sport that had been played in the city and county for decades was getting a welcome new look.

The flood of new members joining the fan group led to an increase in the creation of committees of the supporters club, which had been established to raise funds for the Blues' coffers. The most notable development was the thriving Ladies' Soccer League, which was made up of over thirty teams. The local league received national attention when journalist Bill O'Herlihy covered the fledgling competition for *Newsbeat* on 19 April 1967. The new league played a modified version of soccer with games lasting twenty minutes a side, the ability to make two substitutes at any time and the requirement to wear rubber shoes, as O'Herlihy noted, for those who played the game 'just for kicks'.

From the outset, Benfica were the dominant side, as they went unbeaten in the opening rounds of the local league. Benfica went on to represent Waterford against a Cork Celtic selection at Turner's Cross on 28 May 1967. Nearly two weeks prior to the match in Cork, the Waterford club had two busloads of supporters booked to travel to the city on the River Lee. It is interesting to note (as well as signalling the prevailing values or attitudes of the era) that in the *Newsbeat* report, O'Herlihy asked the league's organiser Pat Sheridan about whether the participants' interest and commitment to the competition would waver if they were to 'go steady with boyfriends'. He said this was welcomed by the supporters club committee, which noted that many players already had boyfriends and hoped that they would all 'go steady' as it brought more spectators to games and increased the revenue streams, which was the endeavour's main aim. One would assume O'Herlihy didn't ask the same question of the male Waterford and District Junior League players, but then again it highlights how novel a development the Waterford Women's League was and the societal difficulties it faced.

Furthermore, some critics of the Women's Soccer League cited an apparent 'ecclesiastical ban on ladies' soccer', which was a complete nonsense. The *Munster Express* were ardent supporters of the Ladies' Soccer League, sponsoring the cup and congratulating the supporters club on 'providing such grand entertainment and recreation' for the young women of the city. As the competition neared its final stages in June 1967, seven of the eight quarter-finalists (a three-team round robin was needed to decide the final member of the octet) were Bilberry Rovers, Beavers, Benfica, Boston United, Rivals, Greenbeats and Fluffyball Rovers. The play-off teams for the final spot were Bective Rangers, Checkmates and Crystal Rovers but the final stages to crown the winners of the inaugural Munster Express Cup were made the more difficult by a shortage of pitches.

Bilberry Rovers: First Ladies' Soccer Champions, 1967

The surprise pairing in the final saw Bilberry Rovers and Greenbeats play out a scoreless draw in the decider at Ozier Park on Saturday, 8 July 1967. The replay the following Sunday was cancelled due to torrential rain. To increase the anticipation for the result of the debut showpiece, the *Munster* highlighted, 'You know, winning this game guarantees the players a place in Soccer history. They will become the first Ladies' Soccer Champions, not only in Waterford, but probably in the whole of Ireland.' When the replay was eventually staged, the winners were Bilberry Rovers by one goal to nil, and Esther Keoghan became the first captain to lift the cup. Tom Molly donated a trophy to be awarded to the highest scorer in the competition, which was to be shared in 1967 between Sarah Molly (Greenbeats) and Kay O'Sullivan (Rivals), who finished with eight goals each.

On Saturday, 2 March 1968, the Waterford Ladies' Soccer League Committee held a public meeting at the municipal library to discuss their plans for the season ahead. The league took on a much more formal guise as it recorded fourteen teams competing, which were: Benfica, Fluffyball Rovers, Boston United, Bilberry Rovers, Greenbeats, Checkmates, Tramore Celtic, Waterford Celtic, Juventus, Female Blues, Millers, Denny's Blues, Blue Defenders and Beavers.

Running over the course of the summer in 1968, the final saw the Waterford Glass team defeat Greenbeats 1–0 at Tycor Park on Sunday, 8 September 1968. The Infant League held a dinner dance in spring 1969, at which Kay O'Sullivan was presented with the Molloy Trophy. O'Sullivan had finished the previous season as the league top scorer.

Waterford Ladies 10–0 Hooped Dollies (Shamrock Rovers), Tycor Park, Sunday, 7 July 1968

Another notable development in ladies' soccer was the first representative game staged by Dublin's Shamrock Rovers and a Waterford selection at Tycor Park on Sunday, 7 July 1968. It was considered the first of a series of intercounty games and saw the Suir selection number:

K. Howlett (Benfica), P. O'Neill (Chelsea), B. Sheehan (Bilberry Rovers), M. Quinlan (Beavers), W. Manning (Greenbeats), A. Ormond (Waterford Glass), E. Keoghan (Bilberry Rovers), A. Ryan (Checkmates) and L. Power (Tramore). The reserves were N. Coady (Greenbeats), M. Douglas (Greenbeats), M. McIhenny (Checkmates), I. O'Toole (Hearts) and A. Quinn (Defenders).

The Waterford selection would prove far too strong for the Rovers side known as the 'Hooped Dollies' as the home side won 10-nil. The Blues getting a result over Shamrock Rovers representation is always welcome on Suirside and this result must be a record-winning margin in any pairing between Waterford and Rovers, be it in senior men's, women's or juvenile competitions or challenge matches.

Divisions?: Ladies' Soccer League Expansion and Decline, 1969–72

Again, the league continued to adapt as competitors were spilt into two divisions for 1969. The League Division 1 for the Munster Express Cup was made up of Benfica, Beavers, Bilberry Rovers, Greenbeats and Tycor United. The Second Division saw Chelsea, Tramore, Female Blues, Denny's, Juventus and Benfica 'B' compete for the Frank Davis Cup. However, by 1971 the running of the Ladies' Soccer League was considered doubtful and appeared to be in great jeopardy. Furthermore, in the early 1970s, Benfica and Waterford Glass played regularly in the All-Ireland Ladies' Soccer Championships. Sadly, by the winter of 1972, Benfica, managed by Joe O'Callaghan, were the sole ladies' soccer club in Waterford.

Rebirth: Waterford Ladies' Soccer League, 1982

Nearly ten years later, in the winter of 1981, the Ladies' Football Association of Ireland had a letter published by its PR officer B Finnerty looking to hear from 'anyone who is involved with ladies' soccer at individual, club, company, town or county level'. The following spring saw a Waterford Ladies' Soccer League re-established in the county.

So what was the cause of the Waterford Ladies' League dwindling from thirty teams in 1967 to just one club in the form of Benfica almost five years later? One could argue the success of Waterford FC in the League of Ireland overshadowed the development of the women's game in the city as the club went on to win six league titles in eight seasons (1965–66 to 1972–73) as it took the attention of the supporters' club away from what was an innovative and important development in Ireland at that time. The structure and foundations were not solid enough either as players juggled jobs, marriages and families, which left less time for the playing of soccer.

One wonders what inspirational figures Esther Keoghan, Sarah Molloy or Kay O'Sullivan could have been for youths in the city if things had gone differently. Their efforts certainly deserve more recognition than is currently enjoyed in Waterford, but hopefully, as the promotion of women's sport (belatedly) continues to go from strength to strength, when in future we look back at Waterford soccer in the 1960s and '70s, the names Shamie Coad, Alfie Hale and Johnny Matthews aren't the only ones that will come to mind.

'Sell a Dummy':
Louis Fulloné, Failed Waterford Trialist, and Diego Maradona

Fairs Cup finalists Leeds United began a tour of Ireland in August 1967 against Waterford at Kilcohan. The game was a testimonial for local player Peter Fitzgerald. The former Waterford Bohemians player was at the end of a playing career that saw him feature for Sparta Rotterdam in the 1959–60 European Cup campaign. The following season saw him sign for the Elland Road club and he was selected in the starting eleven for Don Revie's first match in charge. Returning to his hometown club in the League of Ireland in 1963, he went on to win the club's first League of Ireland title in 1965–66.

The game would serve as preparation for the league seasons ahead of both teams. The Blues' campaign in the League of Ireland Shield tournament was to start in earnest two weeks after Fitzgerald's testimonial. Waterford could call on two new faces to their line-up, Martin Ferguson and the South American Louis Fulloné (spelt without the accent over the 'e' in the Irish press). The game itself saw Martin Ferguson make his debut as the new player-manager. The 26-year-old Scot had played previously for Partick Thistle, Barnsley and Doncaster Rovers. He had been capped at junior level for Scotland. If the name seems familiar, Martin is the brother of former Manchester United manager Alex Ferguson. His managerial career was nowhere near as illustrious as his brother's at Pittodrie and Old Trafford. Ferguson was in charge of the Blues until being relieved of his duties in February 1968, the story of which deserves an article in its own right.

Waterford's other debutant in Ferguson's first game in charge was Louis Fulloné, his full name being Luis Oscar Fulloné Arce. He was born in La Plata, Argentina, on 4 April 1939 and his youth career was spent with Estudiantes de La Plata (four-time

'Sell a Dummy': Louis Fulloné, Failed Waterford Trialist, and Diego Maradona

Copa Libertadores winners and of Carlos Bilardo and Juan Sebastián Veron fame). Fulloné's professional career took him to Independiente Medellín of Colombia in 1962. The club's great rivals are Atlético Nacional, who in the 1980s were linked to a Medellín cartel led by Pablo Escobar as a way of laundering his proceeds from the drugs trade. Fulloné left South America in 1963 to ply his trade in Spain, joining Real Oviedo. Prior to the Argentine's arrival, the Asturian club had achieved its best-ever La Liga finish of third place in 1962–63. At one stage of the season, they were level on points with Real Madrid at the top.

However, some confusion surrounds Fulloné's playing career from his time at Oviedo until arriving in Ireland. In a time before information could be quickly processed and verified, much was based on word of mouth. In a preview to the game against Leeds, the *Evening Echo* detailed that Fulloné had played with French First Division side Rouen for the 1966–67 season. Over the course of the month of August, Fulloné was recorded by the Irish media as being 23 years old but ended the month aged 26. A week is a long time in football, but I don't think too many have aged three years in four weeks. The 5ft 11in or 6ft 1in Argentine had also played a spell the previous season with Albion Rovers and was noted by the *Waterford News & Star* as being 'acknowledged to be a "good un"'. Fulloné was considered adept as a wing-half or inside forward. He was on a month's trial with the club and lined out for the 1966 League of Ireland Champions at inside left.

A full-strength Lilywhites side defeated the Blues 4–2 in front of a 7,000-strong crowd, with Irish international Johnny Giles scoring the opener on the twenty-five-minute mark. The *Irish Press* said Don Revie's men had the 'power and precision to rip Waterford's defence apart in an entertaining first half'. The Yorkshire club's second goal came from the penalty spot (dispatched by Giles) on thirty-five minutes, when Billy Bremner was floored by Fulloné. Such was his performance, he was replaced by Mick Lynch at half-time. Of the Argentine's forty-five-minute showing, the *Evening Echo* described him as showing 'some clever touches, but seems to be a completely left-footed player'. The local *News & Star* was less sparing in its assessment, with 'Fullone proved something of an upset, certainly more to his own players than to the opposition.'

Waterford were 3–0 down at the interval but put in a spirited performance in the second half, with Lynch scoring a free kick and John O'Neill scoring five minutes from time as Leeds eased the pace. The *Evening Herald* reported that, 'The Argentinian forward Luis Fullone was unable to do himself full justice after a hectic weekend's travelling Glasgow-Manchester-London and back before coming to Ireland, and he retired at half-time.' Fulloné had been travelling for nearly two full days before lining out against one of the best sides in England and Europe.

He would not have to wait long to try for a reprieve as Waterford faced a Limerick side at Kilcohan Park in what was described as another 'loosener-upper'. It was a Limerick side that could boast new signings such as centre-half Paddy Kearns, who had won the League of Ireland with Drumcondra in 1965, and Irish international Andy McEvoy from Blackburn Rovers (although he was absent for the exhibition against Waterford). The only newcomer to the Waterford XI was a young wing-half named Ritchie Power, who had twice gained youth international honours against England and Northern Ireland the previous year. Power would go on to have a remarkable squash career and in 1979 became the first man outside of either Belfast or Dublin to win the national title.

The game finished in a 2–2 draw, with the Blues coming from behind through two John O'Neill goals in the last fifteen minutes. It was to be the last time that Fulloné would play in Kilcohan. In the *Irish Press* of 15 August it was reported by Tom O'Shea that he had left Waterford after two trial games. Club Secretary Michael Bolger remarked that 'he did not suit our requirements'. The *Munster Express* elaborated further in a match report of a game low on quality that:

> Louis Fulloné got his second chance with Waterford in this game. The result is that Waterford have told him that they do not require his services and he will leave this week. He gave the crowd a lot of amusement on Sunday last and showed some fine Soccer moves, but I doubt if he would be any addition to our forces. He can hold a ball, sell a dummy, and give a well-directed short pass. But that is the end of it. He is essentially a one-legged player and he showed little likeness for following up. Possibly if Waterford could afford the luxury of holding him until he was adapted to the Blues' style of play, he might be a valuable addition, but Waterford can't afford that kind of generosity, can they?

And what became of Louis Fulloné? He moved to England and became known as Oscar Arce. He and his brother Hector joined Aston Villa in around 1967–68 but neither would play a game for the first team. In 1969, both players were released by the club, with Hector returning to Argentina. Upon retiring from playing he went into coaching, and we know that in the late 1970s he was a youth team coach at Millwall. Around 1978 to 1979 he was on the staff of Sheffield United and was noted as playing an important role in the attempt to sign a young Diego Maradona for the Blades. After missing out on El Diego, the Argentine midfielder Alejandro Sabella signed for the Bramall Lane club for a fee of £160,000 from River Plate. He would go on to play for Leeds and returned to Argentina with Estudiantes in 1982.

Acre (or Fulloné) was apparently becoming an adept figure in the transfer market and played a role in probably one of the most successful transfers from South American to English soccer, with World Cup winners Ricardo Villa and Ossie Ardiles joining Tottenham Hotspur in 1978. Under the guidance of Keith Burkinshaw the two would win an FA Cup with Spurs in 1981, with Villa scoring a remarkable winner against Manchester City in a replay.

'Sell a Dummy': Louis Fulloné, Failed Waterford Trialist, and Diego Maradona

For Acre, the 1980s began managing FC Sion in Switzerland before spending the majority of the rest his career on the African continent. He would win league titles in the Ivory Coast, Libya, Morocco and Tunisia. The former Oviedo player's greatest achievement was winning consecutive African Champions League honours with two different clubs: ASEC Mimosas and Raja Casablanca. In 2001, he took over as manager of the Burkina Faso national team but resigned before the African Cup of Nations in Mali due to his wife's ill health. He went on to manage nine more club teams before retiring in 2010. In May 2017, Acre died aged 78.

The story of Luis Oscar Fulloné Acre still has many gaps but serves as another example of the transient and nomadic existence of a professional footballer, be it starting at La Plata or Pittodrie. One wonders what could have been if more patience was provided by a League of Ireland team that would go on to win five more titles up to 1972. Perhaps with Acre's time in Morocco, it's best to finish with the sentiment, 'We'll always have Kilcohan'.

Andy McEvoy.

Poles Apart: Piotr Suski, Włodzimierz Lubański and the League of Ireland

The League of Ireland had been dominated by Dublin clubs since its establishment in 1921 to the 1940s. Dundalk became the first team from outside the capital to win the league in 1933. The 1940s saw a side from the south's second city, Cork, in Cork United, win five titles in six seasons before folding in 1948. The subsequent two decades saw a return to the status quo, with the metropolitan clubs of Dublin (Drumcondra, St Patrick's Athletic, Shamrock Rovers and Shelbourne) achieving league title success on fifteen occasions from 1946–47 to 1964–65. Provincial clubs such as Cork, Dundalk and Waterford in the south-east of Ireland had to be resourceful and find different methods of recruiting players to compete, let alone achieve silverware.

Sligo Rovers in the west of Ireland had an impressive fundraising campaign throughout the season, holding dances and raffles to generate money to support the club, whereas Waterford recruited players from England to contend with the Dublin teams. This led to the club winning the League of Ireland title in 1966, three in a row from 1968 to 1970 and again in 1972. Yet, the old adage of 'if you stay still in football, you fall behind' clearly was on the minds of those who governed the club. Waterford looked for other ways to stay ahead of its competitors in trying to maintain the success of what was clearly the golden era of the club; this was to look to eastern Europe and Poland. The first player they recruited was a central midfielder by the name of Suski, a former Polish international. However, the Blues had their sights on striker Włodek Lubański of Górnik Zabrze. He had come seventh in the 1972 Ballon d'Or claimed by Franz Beckenbauer, was a player of international calibre, renown and in his prime. The Irish domestic game had never seen a player of his ilk grace its playing fields.

Poles Apart: Piotr Suski, Włodzimierz Lubański and the League of Ireland

The then Director of Waterford FC, Frank Davis (based in Dublin), said of the signing of Suski from Łódź and the pursuit of Lubański that 'the fact that we have had to go to Poland for players is an indication that all is not well with the state of football here [the Republic of Ireland]'. Davis noted that the fourteen-team League of Ireland was too large for a population the size of the Republic of Ireland, with not enough players to go around for each club. Previously, provincial clubs such as Waterford had sought players from England to compete and hoped casting their net further afield could yield dividends on the pitch. Davis noted, 'The Dublin clubs just have not tried in this respect and that is why in recent seasons they have won nothing.' Another advantage to a Pole signing for a League of Ireland club was that the competition took place during the Polish off-season.

Włodek Lubański.

Lubański, then in his early 30s, had spent his entire senior career to that point at Górnik Zabrze, winning six Polish Championships with the club as well as six Polish Cups. He was the league's top scorer for four seasons in a row from 1966 to 1969. In European competition, Lubański led the line as the club reached the quarter-finals of the European Cup in 1968 and were runners-up to Manchester City in the final of the Cup Winners' Cup in 1970. The latter is still the best performance by a Polish club in European competition. As the top scorer with seven goals in Górnik's journey to the final, Lubański came to the attention of Real Madrid in a rumoured $1 million deal, but this was apparently rejected by the Central Committee of the Polish United Workers' Party.

Waterford's pursuit of Lubański in what would have been 'the biggest soccer coup in Irish football history' in December 1972 was rumoured by the media to be hampered by a restriction placed on Polish players under 30 years of age leaving the country by the Polish FA. However, no such ban was in place, which Davis acknowledged. The Dutch giants Ajax of Amsterdam and Feyenoord were also in pursuit of the Polish international striker. The stumbling block for the Dutch sides appeared to be in failing to agree that Lubański could remain an amateur and be allowed to return to his homeland to play for the national team. This was an arrangement that the League of Ireland club were willing to fulfil. Although Feyenoord manager Gus Brox stated that there was 'no possibility' of the Polish star playing in 'Holland in the near future', they had enquired about the availability of the striker and were rumoured to have offered £58,000 for his services. Ajax were believed to have offered £60,000 (with 25 per cent going to the player himself). Yet, the League of Ireland club hoped to get the attacker on loan for a couple of months, with the *Irish Press* recording that they 'have been in touch with the player by phone'.

The signing of Piotr Suski was completed midway through the 1972–73 season. Although he was in hospital in Poland at the time, Seamus Martin of the *Sunday Independent* asserted that, 'Blues fans need have no worries at all, because most of the Polish soccer playing fraternity are in hospital as well'. At the end of the Polish domestic season, players were obligated to go to 'special sanatoria for a rest and a programme to build up the energy expended over the season'.

Suski was to play for the club as an amateur. He was born in Łódź in 1942, joined the academy of LKS Łódź and made his first team debut in 1959 aged 17. In his first season, he won the Polish National Championship, beating Legia Warsaw to the title on the final day. Between 1961 and 1967 he won nineteen caps for the Polish national team, the most notable coming against Brazil at the Maracanã in 1966. Suski's club team gradually declined and in 1969 were relegated to the Second Division, although they returned to the top tier in 1971.

The Pole eventually arrived in Ireland in February 1973 and the *Munster Express* noted that 'he has hardly a word of English' but suggested that 'he must have been appalled at the size of the pitch and the uncompromising tackling. In Poland, pitches are state-owned, subsidies and facilities are far superior to anything to be found in the League of Ireland.' He played an important role in the club winning its sixth league title, forming a great understanding with Tommy McConville in midfield. Local journalist Matt Keane notes of Suski, 'He had a lovely sense of balance and was capable of spraying the ball around the park with ease, and his work ethic was superb, although he made things look very easy, which of course is a sign of a very good player.' Jimmy McGeough provided the steel to complement Suski's ball-playing skills.

The summer of 1973 would see the League of Ireland Champions embark on a tour of the United States. Suski was going to return to Poland instead of travelling to America, but was expected to return to Kilcohan the next season. Sadly, the success of Suski was to last just that one season as he never did return to the south-east of Ireland. Instead, he took up a coaching position with his local team in Poland. His lone League of Ireland winner's medal is also the last time that the club has won the premier competition of Irish domestic soccer.

Lubański never did join the Blues in the League of Ireland. After 234 games and 155 goals for Górnik he joined Lokeren in Belgium, playing seven seasons before spending a campaign with Valenciennes in France, two seasons at Stade Quimper and playing one game for Belgian side Mechelen in 1985. He remains the Poland national team's second all-time top goal scorer with forty-eight in seventy-five matches. The Robert Lewandowski of his era did play against the Republic of Ireland national team, scoring on visits to Dalymount Park in 1964 and 1968. His record against the Boys in Green was just as impressive in his native land, scoring three times in two games in 1968 and 1973.

Yet, Waterford's pursuit of Polish players didn't end with Suski or Lubański. The *Evening Herald* reported in October 1976 that, 'Waterford director Frank Davis [...] the FAI president, is at present in Warsaw negotiating for the possible transfer to the Munster club of one of the biggest names in Polish football ... Deyna.' Kazimierz Deyna played for Legia Warsaw and was a member of the Polish team that achieved bronze at the Montreal Olympics in 1976. It appeared that the Blues were pleased with the Suski experiment and hoped to go one better than their endeavours for the services of Lubański with Deyna.

Davis was unable to obtain the signature of the Legia player, who played 304 games for the club, scoring ninety-four goals. His international record was just as impressive, as he received 102 caps and scored forty-five goals. At the Munich Olympics in 1972 he would help his nation claim the gold medal, finishing as the competition's top scorer with nine goals. However, the communist authorities would not permit him to play for a foreign team during the height of his powers. He did eventually join Manchester City in 1978 before moving to the USA to play for San Diego Sockers. Deyna even had a brush with Hollywood with a role in John Huston's 1981 film *Escape to Victory*, which starred Sylvester Stallone, Pelé and Bobby Moore. Tragically, he died in a car crash aged 41 in 1989.

As often is the case in soccer, the sense of what could have been tends to fade with the passing years. The hype and anticipation of capturing the signings of Lubański and Deyna for Waterford are like reels of film that fail to make the final director's cut of a movie. However, Suski's spell by the banks of the River Suir formed a part of the tale of a club that has gone through thin and thinner, with years in the second tier of Irish soccer and on the brink of collapse on more than one occasion. Investment from Lee Power, also Chairman of Swindon Town, in 2016 has propelled the club back to the Premier League by recruiting players from Estonia, Latvia and Belgium. Sounds familiar, doesn't it! Perhaps the glory days are just around the corner for the south-east club, and maybe they will finally land that international-quality striker. There's no harm in dreaming.

Celtic Squash Club: A 'Great Waterford Nursery'

All great clubs in any sport owe their origins to visionaries and those with commitment and a strong work ethic, whether it be Joan Gamper and Barcelona in 1899, Brother Walfred and Glasgow Celtic in 1888 or the establishment of the GAA in 1884 as foundation stones. In that vein, the starting point of the history of the Celtic Squash Club is down to Bobby Phelan in 1974.

Phelan, the proprietor of Celtic Squash Club and Norris' Bar on Barrack Street, was described as 'one of the pioneers of squash in the city' by the *Munster Express* in October 1980, having served as President of the Munster Squash Association. In starting the club, Phelan was 'a leading figure in making Celtic one of the strongest clubs in Ireland'. During the golden age of the sport in Waterford, the club could call upon players such as Richie Power and Jack Laffan as its representatives, both going on to international honours.

The early 1970s in which Celtic SC was formed saw a boom in the sport of squash, with more than 7,000 players and ninety courts across the island of Ireland in 1972. Also, the success of Jonah Barrington on the international stage (winning the British Open, then deemed the World Championships) six times between 1967 and 1973 heightened interest and participation in the sport. Barrington was born in Morwenstow in Cornwall to Irish parents from Wexford. He was educated at Trinity College Dublin.

Core to the stream of talent playing for Celtic was the role of Michael Moss from Belfast. Originally, a head of biology at a Christian Brothers school in his hometown, he switched to a career in professional sport as a squash, karate and swimming coach and held positions with the Squash Ireland Company in Limerick and Celtic Squash Club in Waterford. In 1976, he was appointed manager of the then newly built Tralee Sports Complex, which cost £400,000. However, it was not all plain sailing for the club from its inception.

Controversy arose in November 1976 when a Celtic SC request for its Dublin-based players (Richie Power, Val Flanagan and Jack Laffan) to represent their home team in a Leinster team tournament was rejected. A similar problem had been posed the previous year for the All-Ireland Championships, although the players had been allowed to play for Celtic.

Phelan believed that the ruling was unfair on the club, commenting to the *Irish Times*, 'if Leinster had accepted our entry in the league this situation would not have developed' and likened the situation to, 'if the English County Championship were prepared to accept an entry from a Dublin team who had ... the services of our two Dublin-based players ... surely Leinster can accept us'. In reviewing the situation, the Leinster committee deemed that the Celtic Squash Club was 'too preoccupied with winning, and not sufficiently concerned with the spirit of participation'. Due to their geographical location in the southern province of Munster, the Waterford club were impeded rather than allowed to join the highly competitive Leinster League. The latter boasted several of the best players on the island, and the Celtic players wanted to measure their skills against the highest calibre of opponents possible.

The club was not only a production line of talent but also devoured silverware a plenty. From 1974 to 1986, Celtic Squash Club claimed twelve Munster Senior Team Championships in a row. It was a feat that the Kerry Gaelic footballers or Kilkenny hurlers would love to boast in their respective provinces and sports. The twelfth of those came after finishing top of the pool on 40 points ahead of De La Salle and Limerick Lawn Tennis Club without conceding a single game.

An important member in the early years of the club was Fred Greene, who worked in the refrigeration industry and who first served as club secretary before becoming its president in 1980. He sought to continue to foster young players in the sport to challenge the older, more established members. In 1979, one of the latter, Richie Power, became the first player from the Republic of Ireland to win the Irish Close Squash Championship (which had been dominated by Northern players until that point) after switching his attention from League of Ireland soccer with Waterford to squash. He credited his success to Robin Dawson, Sars Smith, Fintan O'Brien and Michael Bolger, 'who introduced squash to Waterford'. In a personality profile for the *Munster Express*, Power stated, 'These men were never too busy to coach up and coming young players and devoted a great deal of time and energy to the game.' Additionally, the facilities of three full courts, a meeting room/clubhouse, changing rooms, and table tennis and pool room were praised as being instrumental in the club's growth and success.

In 1982, Harry O'Neill was named Chairman of the Celtic Squash Club and played a key role in the organising of the Milton Bradley Team Squash Tournament, then considered a 'prestigious' competition with entrants from all over Ireland taking part. The inaugural competition saw the hosts Celtic lose the intermediate final to Collins of Cork but achieve victory over the same opposition in the junior section of the competition.

The following year saw sides enter from Fitzwilliam, Belvedere, Mount Pleasant and two from Dermot Ryan's Eurocentre, all from Dublin. Orchard, from Cork, with Kilkenny, New Ross and Limerick also represented. In addition, the rivalry between local sides Celtic Squash and De La Salle continued to brew, the latter with the strong selection of Munster-capped Willie Cuddihy, Nicky Kavanagh and Tommy Cummins deemed as favourites. By 1983, players from Australia, England, New Zealand and Scotland took part, with a prize of a £250 cheque for the winner, while the runner-up received £200.

Once more the emphasis on developing youth was promoted by O'Neill, who had previously served as President of the South East Squash Association and selector of the junior international team. In addition, as a former pupil of Mount Sion, he was an example of the links between the club and the school on Barrack Street that has played an important role in its membership. In 1979, three Mount Sion pupils and Celtic Squash players were selected to represent Waterford schools: Denis Kelly, John Phelan and Peter Kavanagh.

The mixture of growing interest in the sport combined with diligence in promoting the coaching of young players paid dividends in 1981. For the first time, the All-Ireland Championship (then sponsored by Guinness Mahon) was claimed by a team other than from Belfast and Dublin. It was also the first time a side achieved full points; Celtic Squash had achieved the ultimate prize with 80 points out of a possible 80. The players who were a part of the success were Richie Power, Jim Skelton, John Phelan and Sean Twomley.

Around this time, a notable player to come through Celtic SC was Peadar Kavanagh. After six years working in Waterford Glass, he devoted his attentions purely to the pursuit of squash, joining Squash Ireland. His first World Championships came at age 18 in Singapore in 1982. Six years later, he was ranked number six on the Irish team and lived with that side's number one, Willie Hosey, in Clontarf. Another player who received acclaim in the 1980s was John Ryan, a printer at Atlantic Print in Waterford, who took the notable scalp of international John Young in the 1988 Munster Open.

Celtic Squash's success continued well in to the latter half of the 1980s. In the 1987 Munster Club Championships they had a record five teams participating, with two gaining victory. One of the successful sides was the seniors, earning a fourteenth Munster title in a row with the familiar names of internationals Peadar Kavanagh and Richie Power with John Ryan, Willie Clancy, Richard Kennedy and Jack Laffan. It was that group of players who aimed to win a third All-Ireland in succession, having won the competition outright in 1985 and 1986. That third victory in 1987 was not only their third in a row, but also the club's sixth in thirteen years. It was earned by defeating Sutton (Dublin) by three games to two. An interesting side story was the return of John Phelan to take part in the finals after taking up what was described as a lucrative coaching position in Germany. In the same year, the Junior Ladies claimed the Munster Championship and Ladies Novices in the Waterford League.

Such a run of victories was not the preserve of the men's team. More success connected to Celtic Squash was that of Sinead O'Connor, who achieved six Munster titles in succession in the Munster Junior Close in the under-19 girls section in 1989.

The growth of the sport in Ireland and Waterford mirrors that of the interest of one of the great personalities of the city, James 'Skinny' Fanning. A native of Morrison's Road, educated at nearby Mount Sion, he worked in Dawson's Pawnbrokers until volunteering in the Irish Army during the Second World War. Upon retiring from active service, he undertook a career in the bar trade and was a familiar face to punters at McLoughlin's, Downes (another centre of squash excellence) and Celtic Squash Club. The first Army Squash Championships took place in 1938 and would lead Fanning to develop a love for the sport, in which he was noted as an excellent coach (particularly with the Dunhill Squash Club).

The 1990s saw a decline in the sport nationally, but it has been in resurgence in recent years. The period saw Celtic SC as a facility for pay as you play, rather than cultivating players for future success. The closure of De La Salle Squash Club renewed the fortunes of the Barrack Street group. One of the most recent players of note produced by the club is Kevin Knox. In 2011, he won his third Munster Championship (2007, 2010 and 2011) in his fifth final in as many years. The year 2016 saw Kevin claim his eighth club title. He was also part of the five-man team that won Celtic SC (made up of players formerly of the De La Salle Club and its Dungarvan counterpart) its last All-Ireland Club Championship in 2005 (defeating Fitzwilliam), which also included Ray Crowley, Paul Freyne and Anthony Lyons.

Later that year, the five represented Ireland in the European Championships staged at Paderborn in Germany, achieving a top ten finish. They would go on to win four Munster titles in a row, reaching two more All-Ireland finals in which they were narrowly defeated (on both occasions by Fitzwilliam, in 2006 and 2007).

A noteworthy member of the side that lost those two showpieces was former Ireland No. 1 Arthur Gaskin, after representing Celtic SC in the Munster League. A native of Dublin (and member of Sutton), he moved to Carlow aged 12. While there, the occurrence of his local tennis club resurfacing their court led to the beginning of his love affair with the game of squash. He turned professional at 19, settling in New Jersey and balancing playing with coaching youths. In subsequent years, he has attained ninety-six caps for Ireland, achieving a career high ranking of sixtieth in the world in 2009. You can stay up to date with Arthur, who now resides in Ipswich, England, on the blog SportsShoes.com.

A club with such an illustrious history, combined with the efforts of its members, deserves more merit and attention than they receive. Hopefully, it won't be too long until Celtic SC claim an eighth All-Ireland and produce players of the calibre of yesteryear. A great nursey of sporting talent in Waterford has been reborn.

Alma Delahunty: Ruánmhór Rúnaí (1981–85)

On 22 March 1977, the newly formed Roanmore Camogie Club held their first general meeting, which saw Una Power elected chairwoman. A teenager, 13-year-old Alma Delahunty, was appointed secretary, and would be aided by an assistant in Siobhan Kennedy. The PRO role was filled by Maria Roche, and the treasurer was Margaret Sinnott. The committee were joined by Valerie Sheridan and Madeline Hayes. Previously, the club's under-14 team had reached the Waterford County final, but missed out on silverware as they were beaten 1–0 in the final. It is fair to say that was probably one of the lowest-scoring games in juvenile Gaelic games history. However, hoping to go one better, the club had a notice in the *Munster Express* (dated 8 April 1977), which read:

> Are you between the ages of 12 and 16 and interested in joining a Camogie Club? If so, why not join the newly-formed Roanmore Club and give your name to Alma Delahunty, 17, Ashe Road …

The equivalent of a social media post, the notice in the local paper was an attempt to engage a youth in Waterford city who were growing up in housing estates that had no facilities and, if anything, fed antisocial behaviour, which was often times developing out of sheer boredom and monotony. It was to provide a service to girls and young women, who for decades had been conditioned to act as vessels, with their great work to be done as a home-maker and raising a family in the traditions of Roman Catholicism. That a teenager like Alma Delahunty had to take on the mantle in helping setting up a club that would provide females an opportunity of playing camogie is an indictment of the society of the 1970s.

It was inevitable that a love for Gaelic games was fostered in the lives of Alma and her brother Kieran, as the Delahunty family had strong connections with South

Alma Delahunty: Ruánmhór Rúnaí (1981–85)

Kilkenny GAA. Alma's father, John, hailed from Kilkenny, and at 22 years of age moved to Waterford to work for the Ironfounders, where he was employed until his retirement in 1988. While in Waterford city, John Delahunty was a member of the Gaedeal Óg Hurling and Football Club, and was vice captain of that club's hurling team. The club played in the Waterford Junior Hurling Championship in 1947, and were on the brink of extinction more than ten years later. However, they managed to beat Ballygunner in the semi-final of the Infirmary Cup, which placed them as contenders for the County title in 1958. However, this club eventually dissipated, with some members forming under-age teams under the name of Ballybricken. John was also part of the Foundry side that competed in the Factory Hurling League, which included players such as Eddie Carew and Mick Dunne.

In 1979, the Roanmore Camogie Club had developed into co-ordinating under-14 and under-16 teams, which were captained by Deborah Kelly and Valerie Sheridan respectively. The aim was for the Roanmore Club to develop an under-18 team to vie for County honours. The Camogie Club was making great strides in a city that, to say the least, had neglected the sport for some years. Nearly ten years earlier, a hurling and football club bearing the name Roanmore was established, and the development of the Camogie Club would appear to be entrained with this entity. Though, sadly, it would appear to engulf the endeavours of the Camogie Club.

Such were the efforts of Delahunty in cultivating this Camogie Club, from scratch, that at the 1980 AGM of the Roanmore GAA, club history was made with her being the first woman elected to the club's Executive Council. Delahunty took over the newly created position of assistant secretary, and provided support to Club Secretary Noel Browne. Upon her election, Delahunty was living at Kingsmeadow, and this notable development for the era received much attention in the local press. Not only was she one of the few females involved in an administrative capacity in Gaelic games, at just 16 years old she was surely one of the youngest in the country. A year later, Browne would not seek re-election as secretary (but was subsequently elected to the position of treasurer), and was replaced by Alma Delahunty, who became the first female secretary in the history of the young Roanmore Hurling and Football Club. An early fundraising effort in her new role was a forthcoming victory dance to be held on 14 February 1981, with music provided by Take Three.

Six weeks later, Delahunty was part of the Roanmore Club's delegation at the County Board and Eastern Board meetings, where she was joined by Eamonn Power, Mick Murphy, John Cotter and Eddie Roche. The following year, she was present at the County Convention, as the progressive club were making waves in the Gentle County. At the 1982 AGM, Delahunty was able to note that the club had won two hurling championship titles (under-21 and minor), and had acquired their own playing field over the course of the previous twelve months. She deemed this to be Roanmore's most important development, as the land at the Cleaboy would be a new dimension in the club's history, brought about by unceasing work from the organisation's committee and volunteers.

Shortly after delivering her annual report for the Roanmore Club, Delahunty was elected at an Eastern Board meeting to the position of under-21 delegate to represent this body at the forthcoming National Congress of the Gaelic Athletic Association. It was a busy period for Delahunty and Roanmore, as in late February 1982 work had begun on fencing off the playing field at the Cleaboy, while plans had been drawn up for dressing rooms, a hall and an entrance to the facility. In an effort to raise funds for such developments, the club had instituted a '600' confined draw, which had been a huge success in helping finance the club's new grounds.

In previewing the Waterford delegation to the GAA Congress, which numbered Pat Fanning, Nicholas McGrath, and John A. Murphy, the *Evening Herald* noted that, 'One of the delegation is Roanmore's energetic female Secretary – Alma Delahunty'. The 18-year-old had made huge strides in an organisation that had predominantly been male and conservative in its outlook since its foundation in 1884. Nearly 100 years later, at the 1982 National Congress, Delahunty was one of three women delegates in attendance, the others being Margaret Buggle and Mary Weld, both from County Kildare. An example of the attitude (and blatant sexism) these women faced surfaces in Cork's *Evening Echo*, which noted of the Waterford delegation numbering 'for the first time ever – a petite member of the fair sex, 18-year-old Alma Delahunty who is secretary of the very progressive Roanmore Club in Waterford City'. It provided no coverage of her efforts in sports administration, which she had been involved in since her early secondary school days.

One of the strengths that Delahunty brought to her roles with the Roanmore Club, and the Eastern Board, was a strong emphasis on planning and preparation. Well over two months before the club's annual general meeting (as no specific date had been finalised), she pointed out that it was time for members to start thinking of motions to put forward, which should be directed to her, or any committee member as there was 'no use coming along on the night and having a load of points in mind which we just might not have time to discuss. Give them in now and we can put them on the agenda.'

Such organisation, and emphasis on detail, was key to the foundations being laid for the club's future success. In praising the work of the Cleaboy development, Delahunty was quick to note those who were aloof when it came to fulfilling their chores at the club's facilities. She concluded that 'a great deal had been accomplished by so few', with their drive enabling the club to make the Cleaboy 'a home of their own'. Further milestones for the club in 1982 included an under-21 County title in hurling, while the minor hurlers and footballers, as well as the under-21 football side reaching the Eastern finals. These efforts signalled that Roanmore was a coming force in both hurling and football in Waterford city, and it was hoped this would translate to senior success in the coming years.

Alma Delahunty: Ruánmhór Rúnaí (1981–85)

Having been only fifteen years in existence and obtaining their own grounds at the Cleaboy, the great milestone was marked by an official opening on Thursday, 31 May 1984. The facility was named after one of the club's founding members, Sonny Murphy, by bearing the moniker Pairc Ui Murchu. The club had spent £34,000 on the facilities to that point, while another £20,000 was required to complete the development. The club devised a plan, seeking a £100 contribution from prospective donors, and in return the contributor would receive a specially framed and illuminated club scroll. This fundraising effort was launched in January 1984 by the Mayor of Waterford, Dick Jones, who highlighted that the club were doing a tremendous job for the youth of the city. Also present was the President of the GAA, Paddy Buggy, who deemed the young Roanmore Club to be on par with the outstanding senior clubs in Waterford city.

The club now catered for 300 boys and adults from the Cork Road, Kingsmeadow, Roanmore, Hillview and surrounding areas. The club had capitalised on the change of population from rural areas to urban centres, which saw it receive support from the Waterford County Board, Waterford Corporation and even the Bishop of Waterford and Lismore, Dr Michael Russell, who believed Roanmore was providing a great service for the youths living in housing estates in the city. On the personal front, Alma Delahunty became engaged to her Roanmore colleague Noel Browne in February 1984.

The club's AGM in 1985 was to be Delahunty's last as secretary, and she opened the proceedings by saying:

> As we gather here to-night we can look back on 1984 – the Centenary Year of the Association, with a certain amount of pride. The main reason for this of course was the official opening of Pairc O Murchu on May 31st last. It was a proud historic occasion, the culmination of months of hard work and years of fundraising. The evening and the subsequent Banquet in the Ardree Hotel will always be remembered by everyone who had the privilege to be present.

However, Delahunty wasn't an individual to rest on her, or indeed the club's laurels. It was a testament to her, in a male-dominated environment, and only in her early 20s, in praising the club's fundraising efforts and the work of trainer Cyril O'Regan, that she also directed criticism towards the senior players, who had beaten city rivals Mount Sion for the first time at that level. However, she believed if they were to claim a first County title that:

> Different attitudes are called for by a lot of our players if we are to make a major impact in the coming year. Commitment must be the order of the day and while the club in the past has endeavoured to help out every team in the pursuit of ultimate success, some players were found lacking when the crunch arrived. With our Field

available from the beginning of the new season, I feel confident that matters will improve, and we can carry that elusive 'first' in senior hurling, and perhaps capture a few more titles into the bargain.

After giving her final annual report, club President Fr Farrell thanked Delahunty for the tremendous work she had done in her three and a half years as Secretary of Roanmore. Farrell believed she had taken on a role that not many women would relish, and her success could be seen by the esteem in which she was held by club members. At the club's dinner dance staged at the Ardree in March 1985, Delahunty received a special award for her services to the club during her tenure as secretary.

Later that year, in October 1985, Delahunty and Noel Browne were married at Ballybricken, with the ceremony performed by Roanmore Club President Fr Farrell. Just a few years later, in September 1988, the couple welcomed the birth of their son Shane at Airmount Nursing Home. As Alma departed the local GAA scene, her brother Kieran would go on to win two County titles with Roanmore, in 1989 and 1990, as well as representing Waterford at Inter-County level. Her son Shane went on to win numerous medals at underage level on the fields that her and her husband Noel had played such a huge part in acquiring and developing.

In early 2022, Colin Regan believed that the GAA, with a membership of 700,000 people, was 'an entity founded by men and moulded within a patriarchal system', which had seen its female members experience 'a lack of representation or perspective at leadership levels, sexism, stereotyping, condescension, and a lack of respect'. This is reflected in the association's twenty-nine national committees, with a total number of members of 304, which are filled by 232 men and 72 women. Only two committees at that time had more women than men – the Scór na nÓg and the Health and Well-Being Committee.

Nearly forty years after Alma Delahunty attended the GAA Congress, Tracey Kennedy became the first woman to hold the position of chair of the neighbouring Cork County Board in 2017. It is a testament to the former Roanmore Club Secretary that she attained a position that belied her young age, but also one feels that so much progress within the GAA locally and nationally was lost with the departure of Delahunty from the administrative side of the sport. She was a rarity in a sport that has always been slow to progress, her efforts were to the benefit of Roanmore, and if the Waterford County Board were keen to progress as quickly they would have done more to have her play a part in administrating the game Suirside.

What we see from her story and that of Roanmore is the power of community, and how it can serve as a social fulcrum, and provide opportunities and engagement that civic society is often all too slow to register. Alma was a pioneer in the story of Gaelic games in Waterford, and she serves not only as a role model to women, but to us all in her energy and dedication that laid the foundations of the Roanmore Club.

Samba in the South-East: A Brazilian in the League of Ireland

In January 1986, Waterford United signed Sebastiao Elias de Freitas Filho, a 26-year-old Brazilian from French Ligue 2 side, Chaumont. He played under the moniker of 'Tião Brasil' and was signed by Blues manager Alfie Hale on a month's trial upon the recommendation of then Millwall manager George Graham. Hale was already a club legend in his second spell as manager. He was part of the Waterford side that won six League of Ireland titles in the late 1960s and early '70s, and had been capped fourteen times by the Republic of Ireland national team. It was hoped that the first Brazilian to ply his trade in the League of Ireland would help recapture those glory days and even showcase some of that Samba flair that saw one of the greatest teams from his native country win the FIFA World Cup in 1970. Who was to know that just a month and three senior games later it would all be over?

De Freitas Filho was born in Rio de Janeiro in 1959. The *Munster Express* detailed that he was of 'south American Indian and Portuguese descent' and had been playing football from age 9. After a successful amateur career, Brasil turned professional in 1980 and played for Atletico Rio Negro in the First Division of the Amazone League for three seasons. During his time with *the* Galo da Praça da Saudade (Rooster of the Praça da Saudade) they won the Campeonato in 1982. He captained the Manaus-based club before moving to Chaumont in the north-east of France for the 1983–84 season.

In a letter to Waterford prior to his arrival he listed his qualities as 'courage, skill, leadership, good overall vision of the game and confidence'. Brasil's unveiling at a press conference led the correspondent of the *Munster Express* to write, 'No blushing violet this lad, who looks like something out of "The Magnificent Seven".' During his time at Waterford, the club were in talks with Bord na gCon (the Greyhound Board) over rent rates for Kilcohan Park. The financial troubles that engulfed United were lessened with the help of Hoffman's Lager, TNT-IPEC and Cherry's Brewery, whose sponsorship aided bringing the Brazilian to the club for a month's trial.

Waterford United faced league leaders Galway United, who were on an impressive nineteen-game unbeaten run. Jimmy Meagan of the *Irish Press* believed Waterford's task was 'tantamount to stopping a spring tide in full spate'. Hale commented on Brasil that, 'I watched him play in training and he was very impressive.' The new recruit was modest in stating that he could play in all positions across the pitch, bar in goal.

The largest crowd at Kilcohan that season were witness to the Tribesmen maintaining their unbeaten run and their championship aspirations with a final score of 2–2. Philip Reid's match report contained the following:

> … how very close Waterford came to earning a shock win. It was a real team performance […] they were nearly thanking for a cherished win the player with the longest name in Irish soccer […] The coloured attacker made his debut for the Blues as a substitute to the sound of James Last's 'Duke of Samba' and he did a jig of pure delight shortly afterwards as he shot Waterford into a 2–1 lead against the bemused Westerners […] Bennett, a half-time substitute, laid off a nice ball to Brazil from Reid's corner and the 26-year-old fired home a great shot from 16-yards.

George Graham.

His new manager's reflections, as noted in the *Cork Examiner*, were that Tião Brasil 'has tremendous skill and scored a very good goal when we introduced him in the second half. Conditions didn't suit him and he still has to adjust to League of Ireland football but he is a fine player.'

The Brazilian's qualities were further demonstrated in a reserve game against Shelbourne, scoring two goals in a 6–1 victory over the Tolka Park club. A teammate, Jimmy Donnelly described how Brasil had brought sweets to throw to the fans upon scoring (a custom in Brazil) but with such a sparse crowd the sweets were divided among the players on the pitch. The Blues' next league game was away to St Patrick's Athletic at Richmond Park. The Inchicore club were favourites for a victory to boost their push for a UEFA Cup birth. Brasil made his first start for the club and commenced the move that led to Waterford's first goal. Yet, he 'found conditions very much to his distaste … he did little of note' and was replaced by Vinny McCarthy after fifty-six minutes. The game finished in a 2–2 draw and led the *Munster Express* to decree, 'Realistically, Waterford Utd's chances of League honours faded at the halfway stage of the competition, especially as nobody seems to be able to stop the relentless progress of the two leading contenders, Shamrock Rovers and Galway United. So, the big prize at stake now is the FAI Cup.'

Waterford again faced Galway United in Kilcohan, this time in the fourth round of the cup. In a surprise result, Waterford defeated the title chasers by two goals to one, in a match that saw gate receipts of £6,060. Mick Bennett and Jimmy Donnelly gave the home fans 'a taste of the "rare ould times"'. However, it was recorded in the *Evening Herald* that, 'Tiao Brazil … ruled himself out of the match when he skipped the team talk after learning that he was to start on the bench.' These actions created a hurdle to any extension of his month's trial with the club.

The Kilcohan side's next opponents were league leaders Shamrock Rovers, two points ahead of Galway but having played one game more. Alfie Hale had the flu going into the game and sought to clarify the future of Tião Brasil before the Sunday fixture. To resolve the situation, Waterford United recruited a student from the Waterford Regional Technical College to act as an interpreter, with the *Herald* wryly asserting that he 'has some smooth talking to do if he wants to complete his trial period'.

A week later, the *Herald* outlined, 'Waterford, meanwhile, have lost only once in a dozen games. They scuppered the Cup hopes of Galway and undermined the Hoops' Championship charge in the past fortnight … Tiao Brazil [sic] has been released.' Waterford would finish the league campaign in fifth place (Shamrock Rovers were crowned Champions, finishing two points ahead of Galway) but qualified for the UEFA Cup Winners' Cup after being defeated by Rovers 2–0 at Dalymount Park in the FAI Cup final.

Brasil told the Waterford FC programme, *The Blue View*, that he was 'an idol of the Irish. It was impossible to even get out on the street without children screaming my name, "Tião, Tião, Tião". In the Irish pubs, the people sang Gaelic songs in my honour.' Not short on hyperbole, Brasil was certainly an eccentric character, which partially explains the nomadic journeyman nature of his soccer career. In the same article, he noted how his Catholic beliefs were entwined with the people of southern Ireland. However, he did not go as far to say that the admiration Waterford supporters showed towards him was akin to the devotion to Christ himself. Even if he didn't find a career in Ireland's oldest city, he did find love, having a girlfriend named Marion.

After his brief spell by the River Suir, Brasil returned to France and played for Red Star 93 of Paris. This was followed by Olympiakos Nicosia of Cyprus before he subsequently returned to his native land. Now known as DJ Tião Brasil, he can be spotted on the Copacabana displaying his soccer skills and selling CDs of his reggae mixes. Certainly, he is far more comfortable in his surroundings than on a rainy night in Inchicore. In 2014, he ran for election for Councilman as a Democratic Labour Party candidate, receiving 111 votes (noted as 0.00 per cent of the total vote). The Partido Democrático Trabalhista, or PDT, were founded in 1979 and number 1,250,777 in their membership. A centre-left organisation, the PDT was the first party of former Brazilian President Dilma Rousseff. Brasil declared his occupation as broadcaster/radio and television commentator as well as disc jockey.

Perhaps Brasil's spirit was more in keeping with reggae rhythm than the samba beat we all associate with Brazilian soccer. Instead of becoming a legend in the annals of the Irish game, he has done as much for the cause of socialism in his homeland as he had done for Waterford in the League of Ireland.

Jason Phelan (BMX Rider): Déise Daredevil

One of the iconic names of BMX riding in Europe is Waterford native Jason Phelan. The sport of bike motocross was developed in the United States in the early 1970s, and the increase in popularity of the sport is credited to the 1971 documentary *On Any Sunday*. It would cross the Atlantic by the early 1980s, just in time for the arrival of a precocious daredevil in Port Láirge.

Born in Waterford in 1986, Phelan has gone on a career path that many on Suirside only thought was possible for people in the United States, like Evel Knievel. Growing up in the Gentle County, Phelan spent his free time riding bikes, skateboarding and, in his own words, 'doing other crazy Jackass-style stuff' with his brothers. These not-so-gentle pastimes were further developed at his grandfather's farm, which had a motocross track on the land. Jason honed his skills by building dirt jumps, and when he wasn't practising drops and bumps, he would explore Ireland's oldest city, searching for abandoned buildings and locations where he could build ramps. It was his older brother who got him into BMX when Jason was around 12 years old. Phelan appreciated that his bike could take him anywhere, and this has led him to dream big in his pursuits.

Finding BMX to be the most exciting, Jason entered an amateur contest, and came to the attention of sponsors. Such was his ambition, Phelan moved to Liverpool in 2005, where he obtained sponsorship and opportunities that were not available to him in the south-east of Ireland. His travels would see him perform at BMX contests in Europe, North America and Asia, with his most notable excursion being a first-class trip to China with sports brand giant Nike. Speaking of contests, Phelan stated during his 'THIS IS ME' interview that 'Having that one minute where you just have to go mad. Sometimes you want to try a trick, it literally takes you a year before you get your nerve to fully try that, and it's just all little challenges you have to face while BMXing.'

In 2008, Phelan joined the bike manufacturer WeThePeople (WTP), a company he had looked up to for their innovative manufacturing, and spent seven years riding for them. During that time, he completed a BA in Television and Film at Liverpool John Moores University. We see Phelan's creative side on full display for his first magazine cover, which he described as a privilege. Of the cover image, Jason believes it to be one of the best photos he has ever taken. The complexity of the image does not convey the simple effort and effect of having his friends throw paint at him. Two years after joining WTP, Phelan came third at the Asian X Games, which still stands as a remarkable achievement within Irish sport. There was probably more coverage devoted to Phelan's efforts at the championships in China and India than there was in Waterford and Ireland.

Even with such success (which has led to Phelan being described as 'one of today's true BMX riding machines'), his fearless efforts haven't been reached without some pain or crashes along the way. In 2013, Phelan broke two ribs and suffered a concussion when he attempted to do a backflip off a self-built rail. Never one to let mental barriers get in his way, twelve months after the injury, Phelan achieved the trick. This was followed by doing a 'backflip barspin' out of the rail, which was captured and witnessed as a live Facebook video. The effort saw Phelan become the first and so far only person to do a grind to 'backflip barspin', and the video has been viewed over 4 million times. Not only was Phelan an adrenaline junkie, but quite clearly thrived under pressure.

When speaking to young riders today, Phelan posits that the only limitation in their pursuits is their imagination. In 2012, Phelan collaborated with COPA90 in a video that crossed football with BMX. Having achieved some remarkable stunts and flips on land, Phelan achieved one of his life's ambitions by riding among some deep-sea diving boats. Commenting on fear to Katie Roche (reporting for Red Bull), Phelan stated, 'The way I ride, especially when I'm filming, Mr Fear pops out quite frequently. Sometimes after I've landed, I have to lie on the ground and chill out and let my body wind down. The feeling is too good a lot of the time, and it's because I have survived something potentially very dangerous. This is why I do what I do, to me, it's not BMX, it's life.'

Inevitably, becoming one of the most noteworthy figures on the BMX scene worldwide has seen Phelan release multiple signature bike frames over the years, such as when he was riding for WeThePeople, with the frame named 'the Irish'. This was partly in response to being introduced as 'Jason Phelan from England' for years, which bugged the Waterford man no end. Speaking to Red Bull, Jason highlighted that, 'I'm really proud of being an Irish rider, so I called my frame The Irish.' When on GT Bikes, he developed a line of bikes for beginner or intermediate BMXers. A friend who he had grown up with, Daniel Leonard, designed Phelan's stickers.

Around 2018, Phelan became a commercial diver, feeling the new career allowed him to focus on his own ideas for BMX, and to explore stunt work opportunities. Phelan has worked for ABCO Marine in County Antrim, as an air diver for SJH Offshore in Stockholm, DCN Diving, Shearwater Marine Services in the United Kingdom, as well as Blackwater Divers. In October 2022, Phelan qualified with the British Stunt Register as a stunt performer. Looking back, Phelan believes the advice he would give to his younger self would be, 'Jay, just keep doing what you're doing, and enjoy it.'

One thing's for sure, Jason Phelan from Waterford has enjoyed a remarkable journey, be it on two wheels to under the seas; a unique figure, who we're sure will continue to do unconventional things. If the English try to claim you, you must be a success!

Grace Doyle:
'The Stoke and Love of Surfing'

Grace Doyle has understood the beauty and the power of the sea from a young age. Her family lived in Hillview in the city before relocating to Tramore when she was 12 years old. They were a family who loved the sea, and her eldest brother Paul introduced them to surfing. Her early schooling came at the Mercy, before going to Holy Cross and Stella Maris in Tramore.

She was part of the Waterford team who won the All-Ireland title at the National Junior Lifesaving Championships at Donegal in 2003. They were coached by the Tramore pair of Kate Molloy and Paul Doyle. Over the two-day competition in Donegal, the Waterford side won sixteen golds, two silvers and four bronze medals for individual and relay events. The various trials took place in the pool and sea, which saw the contestants rescue potential 'casualties' in swim, rescue board, surf ski, flag and relay races.

This success contributed to the development of the Waterford Surf Lifesaving Club in July 2005. The aim of the group was to improve sea rescue services along the Waterford coast. They were affiliated early on to Irish Water Safety, and after a few months could boast thirty-five members. Subsequently, the Juniors won the Denis Gunney Cup at the National Junior Lifesaving Championships at Brittas Bay in County Wicklow. The *Munster Express*' Jamie O'Keeffe highlighted that:

> Waterford has enjoyed enormous success in this up and coming sport in Ireland. As already mentioned, the WSLSC junior team recently won the nationals for the fourth year in a row, while the seniors took home the Irish title in both 1999 and 2001. The Waterford senior girls' squad have previously won the President's Trophy, while team members have also represented Ireland on the international stage, including at European and World Championship level.

The sport of surf lifesaving/rescue combines swimming, surfing, kayaking and running. Having such a support group helped Doyle in her selection for the Ireland team competing at the 2007 European Youth Surf Rescue Championships in France. That September, Doyle came sixth in the Female Open Sea Swim, which comprised fifty international competitors.

The following summer would be a hectic one for Doyle. After completing her Leaving Certificate in June, she was selected to represent Ireland at the World Surf Lifesaving Championships in Germany. These endeavours were combined with her membership of Waterford Crystal Swimming Club and surfing with T-Bay Surf Club in Tramore. After the World Championships, Grace competed at the European Championships at the Haag in Holland. Out of thirty-seven swimmers, Doyle won silver in the open Sea Swim, as well as bronze as part of the team in a rescue event. In September 2008, she started her studies in Physical Education and Maths at the University of Limerick.

Two years later, Doyle was part of the Irish team that travelled to Alexandria in Egypt to compete at the World Surf Lifesaving Championships. Over the years, Doyle has come to the fore in surfing competitions. In conversation with Dermot Keyes, Grace stated that, 'Surfing is such a hard sport to learn and there are so many frustrating moments in the first few years when learning to surf that I've always wished I'd started at a younger age.'

The sport would take on added significance for Doyle upon the passing of her father. She said that, 'The focus was more on using surfing to help me cope, have a focus and free the mind. My dad loved the ocean and always brought us surfing, so I guess I felt somewhat connected in that way, too.'

Doyle was one of four Tramore surfers who qualified to represent Ireland at the 2018 World Surfing Games in Japan. This competition was eagerly anticipated, as surfing would be included at the 2020 Olympic Games in Tokyo.

In 2019, Doyle was in an advert for the Volkswagen Tiguan in which she attempts to catch a wave along the Copper Coast. Grace combined this with her teaching and role as a surfing instructor. Such sponsorship would support her in her endeavours concerning surfing. Around this time, Doyle took a career break from teaching. However, she commented to Keyes that, 'I feel I started surfing too late to have been a contender for the World Surf League qualifying tour, which also requires a lot of money to be able to enter and travel to all of the different locations.'

Doyle is a team rider for Billabong Women's, Quiver Surfboards, BeyondSurf, Etnies shoes and SurfEars. In an article for *Surfgirl*, Doyle wrote:

A few years back, I applied for, and hastily accepted, a home school teaching gig at one of the best surf resorts in the world – Kandui Resort. My brother had tagged me into the Facebook ad for the job, and I couldn't believe the opportunity I had been given. What started out as a self-discovery and teaching venture, which would hopefully involve lots of surfing, very quickly turned into an incredible experience that went far beyond all of that. I have been so lucky to home school the owner Ray's three beautiful kids on their beautiful island where they live, play and surf. I get to immerse myself in the grommets' lives and enjoy teaching for what it's meant to be – the excitement, magic, freedom and fun of learning and discovering. And all the while, I'm also able to share the stoke and love of surfing with these incredible little humans.

The sea has afforded Doyle so many opportunities, and although she feels her late arrival to surfing has been an impediment, it has allowed her to live a life far from the shore of Tramore Bay. Far from being a story to be confined to history, she is the future of a sport that is now competed at the Olympics, and she will be acknowledged by future generations as the individual who showed them that possibilities, like attempting to catch waves, are endless.

Evan Power: The Future of Irish Polo

Irish polo has been in the doldrums since figures like Tommy Beresford, Sebastian Dawnay and Richard Le Poer departed the professional scene nearly thirty years ago. The future rests on the shoulders of Waterford's Evan Power, who entered the professional polo ranks in 2020 with Spain's Polo Valley. What has driven his pursuit are the words of his grandfather, Jimmy Keane, who has spoken about the decline of the sport, which Evan is admirably trying to arrest. Jimmy was the Master of Horse for the late Major Hugh Dawnay (the father of Sebastian) as the pair travelled the world as part of an incredibly successful polo team. Supported by patrons John Cooper and Louisa Watt, Power has become a fixture on the competitive scene through his playing ability and endeavours.

Power moved to England in the summer of 2019, where he was based at Windsor for the season. Upon his return to Waterford, he was frequently at Stradbally with Lord Richard Le Poer, tuning up ponies for the 2020 season. His time in England, with Louisa Watt's Brown Rudnick team, saw them win both the Berkshire Cup and Roehampton Trophy, the latter of which is considered one of the most renowned, in a tournament at the Ham Polo Club. When the polo season comes to a close, Power rides out from Joseph O'Brien's yard at Coolmore Stud.

Evan has spoken about the difference between Irish and English polo, where the former focuses on running after the ball, while the latter is about hitting the ball. He believes it's all about knowing where your opponent is positioned.

Subsequently, Power has played for the Farrington Polo Club (2020), Berkshire Polo Club (2021), and in Pakistan. For 2022, he lined out for Bel Polo team, the same year as he represented Ireland for the first time, in a match versus England. The following year, Evan was playing for the Guards Polo Club.

The Windsor-based club is closely associated with the British Royal Family. The biggest date in the Guards' calendar is the Hurlingham Polo Association's

International Day, which is held at the end of July and has previously attracted crowds of over 30,000 spectators. The association is at the forefront of supporting young people in the sport of polo, and this is a massive recognition of the ability of Waterford's Evan Power.

The future looks bright for a sport that we have read about being popular in the city and county well over 100 years ago. Power has the support of the Gentle County behind him, and carries Irish hopes on his shoulders as he learns the sport that has already led him to see much of the world. As we come to the end of this book, we finish with a story that is just at its beginning.

Epilogue

This book is far from an exhaustive history of sport in Waterford. The aim was very much to gather a collection of stories from across the county that demonstrated the sheer variety of sports that have been played in the Gentle County, and the importance it has in bringing people together within communities. It is a social history with sport as the theme, but people very much at its core. As the St Paul's scribe David Toms composed, 'You the water-mouthed/talk on/taking with you in your way/the stories that will not wash/bleeding sounds into sentences/stories into mind.'

Where I live, in Waterford city, it is surrounded by sporting stories. From the traditions of Ballybricken Fair and bull-baiting, there is also the revival of hurling in the nineteenth century, which is cultivated today by schools such as De La Salle and Mount Sion. There were pubs owned by sporting heroes such as Fad Browne, John Keane and Alfie Hale all lined along Barrack Street. There is the successful Celtic Squash Club at Norris' Corner, which looks on to a street that can boast figures such as the hurler Keane and soccer player Davy Walsh as its illustrious inhabitants. On Doyle Street is the home of one of the city's most favoured sons, Paddy Coad. All of which you can pass on a twenty-minute walk. This is not to elevate this particular place because it is where I live, but rather to illustrate that every village and town has such stories; they are there to be explored.

Hopefully, this collection of stories and biographies will inspire others to look at their locality and explore the sporting traditions that characterise their area. One of the great pleasures of researching this work was to encounter stories that connected Waterford with international events, organisations and influential global figures. As the Ulster poet John Stevenson wryly asserted of the way the Irish tell stories, 'I hev', says I, a gret respeck/For you and for your breed/And onything I cud says/I'd do, I wud indeed.' These stories are not the preserve of any one person, and the greatest impact of social media is the ability to share and exchange such information. Fundamentally, they come from respect and admiration.

We see various customs and traditions, from bull-baiting in Ballybricken to roller hockey during Lent, have disappeared in tandem with how Irish society has evolved throughout the years. One could assume that spectators and patrons of bull-baiting and roller hockey did not anticipate that their respective sports and pastimes would decline and disappear in the intervening centuries and decades. It echoes the words of Oscar Wilde, 'Never more will I play/ With the soaring and gay/ But cruel in its fall –/The mean old cricket ball.' Sport can be fickle, with many a game decided by the spin of a ball. No words can capture those moments better than actually witnessing the events.

You can see as the book progresses that the socio-demographics of the people involved change, from lords and wealthy merchants to female participants, or even people pursuing sport as a professional career, which demonstrates the various cultural shifts and trends in society and sport. The strength and popularity of any leisure pursuit is only ever as strong as the material wealth in which that generation endures. It comes down to time and money. Changes to workers' rights, such as the working week, probably had the most significant effect on the variety of sports being played and enjoyed in any era.

We live in a country that is very much obsessed with land – which for a variety of reasons we won't get into, because it would be a thesis in itself – and we see facilities provided due often to one individual's passion. This has a cumulative effect, from clubs being formed and competitions being arranged, to the opportunity for glory. We can see this commemorated in one of the island's most famous sporting ballads, 'A Ballad of Master McGrath', which captures the magic of victory. 'The hare she led on with a wonderful view/And swift as the wind o'er the green field she flew/But he jumped on her back and he held up his paw/'Three cheers for old Ireland,' says Master McGrath.' And such pride can be felt on a street, in a village or town.

Hopefully, any reader will be inspired by the stories of competitions and characters that are dotted around Waterford. I think 'tis clear to see that there is a strong affection there by these sporting people and the love for their area. They simply loved their county. To paraphrase the legendary Christy Ring, our better sporting successes and histories are yet to come.

Acknowledgements

Firstly, this book would not have come about without the generosity and support from Nicola Guy and the team at The History Press. Thanks for their patience and help throughout the process.

I can never thank my family enough for the support and love they show me on a regular basis. And this book is for each one of them. Thanks to my father, Ollie, for telling me stories of Waterford from the weird to the wacky, which has influenced my own research. I'll always remember those trips to matches, where years later, I now know there is no place better in the world than to be walking with your dad on a sunny day to Páirc Uí Chaoimh or Semple Stadium. To my mother, or I should say mam (she hates being called mother), Miriam, thank you for being the greatest role model I could have. Every day, you show resilience and perseverance in any challenge, but do so always with kindness and a smile. Thanks for showing me that I should look at things always with a smile and a laugh. And finally, to my *bestest* buddy in the world, my brother Olin, thank you for being the greatest sounding board in the history of mankind. I hope this work captures all our conversations during the period of writing it, as they were inspired by your character and work ethic. I'm forever grateful to have your support.

Thanks are also due to Dr Shane Browne, Robert Collins, David Cunningham, Bart Gozdur, Mick Guidera, Gillian Kennedy, Gavin King, Maria-Assunta Lawton, Richard Lucas, Michael Murphy (I omitted Michael's name mistakenly in a previous work, so double thanks here), Therese Myslinski, Dean O'Brien, Ger O'Brien, Donnchadh Ó Ceallacháin, Emma Pettit, Tommy and Aisling Phelan, Brandon Power, David Robson, Thomas Sampson, Jackie Sandford, Robert Sheehy, Eoin Walsh and Áine Whelan. Thanks for listening to me during the research and writing, and for not telling me to shut up. Special thanks to Shane, Bart and Áine for reading the text and giving me their thoughts on it. Thanks to Gillian for the weekly cinema and ice cream chat!

This book has been helped by the energy and inspiration of Dara and Grace Cunningham and Lily Guidera. They show tremendous energy and personality every day, and I find myself to be extremely fortunate to have them in my life. Continue having craic, lads!

I also want to acknowledge my debt of gratitude to Larry Breen (Federation of Local Historical Societies), Éanna Buckley (Cork City), James & Kie Carew (*Póg Mo Goal*), Barry Chambers (CricketEurope), Andrew Doherty (*Waterford Harbour: Tides & Tales*), John Fitzgerald (Irish American Baseball Society), Pat Flynn (Waterford GAA), Bob Gibhu (*A Little Bit of Irish Basketball History*), Mick Jordan (Handball), James O'Donoghue (Cobh Ramblers), Jamie O'Keeffe (*Munster* Express), Brianna O'Regan (*Waterford Camogie*), Clíona Purcell (*Waterford Treasures*), Joanne Rothwell (Waterford City & County Archive), Mary Frances Ryan (*Waterford News & Star*), Jonny Stapleton (irish-boxing.com) and Shea Tomkins (*Ireland's Own*). Thanks are also due to Simon Butterworth, David Carroll and Kevin Knox. I promise I will catch up with e-mails.

A special thanks is reserved for Kevin O'Brien, whom I first spoke to about the idea of this book a few years ago. Thanks, Kev, for being my favourite footballer, for making a great cup of coffee and for just being a thoroughly sound human being. I can finally start drinking more coffee now this project is finished.

Much appreciation is directed towards John Cullen for his kindness, support and encouragement for all my endeavours. John is a brilliant mentor, and I am incredibly lucky to have a figure with such positivity and humour to guide me. I'd like to acknowledge my study crew of Maeve Crowe, Keith Farrell, Melissa McLawrence, Vera Murphy, Shane O'Connor and Ngozi Thelma Olurebi. I have had no better classmates for the sheer joy they directed to learning, and most of all, laughing.

Finally, thank you, the reader, for choosing to pick up this book and read it. I hope, like a match, it had moments of joy, horror, agony and ecstasy before concluding at the finish. All the emotional tumult is what makes sport so addictive.